Studies in American Jewish Literature

Studies in American Jewish Literature is the journal of the Society for Study of American Jewish Literature. *SAJL* is published annually by Purdue University Press.

Studies in American Jewish Literature

For subscription information, contact
>
> Subscription Manager, SAJL
> Purdue University Press
> P.O. Box 388
> Ashland, OH 44805
> 1-800-247-6553

SUBMISSIONS

Manuscripts and book reviews must be prepared according to the MLA Style Manual and should contain endnotes rather than footnotes. Please place both endnotes and works cited at the end of the article. Individuals (members/subscribers only) whose works are accepted for publication must supply them in both paper and electronic form (Microsoft Word). Articles should be between 10 and 20 pages in length. Please include a SASE with submission. Address submissions to:

> Daniel Walden, Editor
> *Studies in American Jewish Literature*
> 116 Burrowes Building
> Penn State University
> University Park, PA 16802

To order this publication, please call our toll free number, 1-800-247-6553. *SAJL* is also available online through various databases, including Project MUSE at https://muse.jhu.edu/journals/studies_in_american_jewish_literature/ and Gale/Cengage Learning.

Articles appearing in this journal are abstracted and indexed in Index to Jewish Periodicals.

Volume 29 (2010)
ISSN 0271-9274

Studies in American Jewish Literature
Volume 29, A Special Issue in Honor of Sarah Blacher Cohen

Daniel Walden, Editor

Carole Kessner, Guest Editor

Ann Shapiro, Guest Editor

Contents

Introduction

Carole Kessner and Ann Shapiro

When Sarah Blacher Cohen died in November 2008, a profound sadness went through the community of colleagues and friends who knew and worked with her in the field of Jewish American literature. Despite the crippling effects of Charcot-Marie-Tooth, a degenerative congenital disease that eventually left her confined to a wheelchair and unable to speak above a whisper, Sarah had remained indefatigable. Nothing would ever be quite the same without Sarah, who contributed until the very end as scholar, teacher, playwright, and editor,

all the while supporting each of us in our own academic endeavors.

American Jewish literature as a recognized academic field has been in existence for barely thirty-five years. Sarah Blacher Cohen must be honored as one of its earliest champions. Over the years Sarah contributed to the discipline in a profusion of genres, from scholarly to popular, from essay to drama, and despite the slow progression of her disability, always with wit and comic humor. Sarah wrote or edited seven books of her own, and also wrote and produced several plays with her longtime collaborator, Joanne B. Koch. At her death she was working on a scholarly book on Cynthia Ozick and a personal memoir, tentatively titled "A Memoir of a Junk Dealer's Daughter." Recognized as a major voice in her field, she was awarded the Lifetime Achievement Award from the Muscular Dystrophy Society, served as media consultant to the National Endowment for the Humanities, and worked as a humor consultant for the Library of Congress.

The contributors to this volume all knew Sarah and were eager to honor her.

What better legacy than to continue the work that she valued so passionately. The selections reflect Sarah's wide interests. Most are scholarly essays about American Jewish literature, reflecting her interests as professor at SUNY Albany and editor of the Modern Jewish Literature and Culture series at SUNY Press. But there are also plays, fiction, memoir, and poetry, all of which were of great importance to her. While contributors, with two important exceptions, were not specifically asked to write about Sarah herself, poets Miriyam Glazer and Myra Sklarew were moved to express their memories in poetry. In addition, we asked Rabbi Julie Pelc, Sarah's niece, and also her very close friend, Cynthia Ozick, for their extraordinary tributes, read at Sarah's funeral.

The contributors echo gratitude for her friendship and professional support as well as lasting admiration for her courage. Gila Safran-Naveh poignantly speaks for many of us in recalling Sarah's influence:

> Her humor could literally flow though the phone wires. She was to me a teacher, a role model, a generous friend, an inspired and passionate fighter. Most importantly, she was . . . the quintessential survivor. I shall always cherish Sarah's memory, her gargantuan laughter in the face of adversity, her generous embrace of all people, her fiery tongue, and most of all, her luminous spirit.

Others add their own memories. Myra Sklarew reflects, "I will be grateful to the end of my days for knowing Sarah, who encouraged so many of us. How she had the strength to live her several lives and, at the same time, see to so many others is a great mystery." Elaine Safer remembers Sarah as "the most courageous person I have ever known," who helped her see "the comic aspects of our daily lives." Vicki Aarons explains, "Sarah was tremendously important to me as both a friend and colleague. She read voraciously and was always attuned to new voices in American Jewish literature. . . . She had a sharp eye for subtlety and wit, her own cleverness always a match for any one of the writers she so loved." Norma Rosen remembers that when Norma's book was published by SUNY Press, Sarah made "a wonderful publisher's party at her home, with good guests, good food, and a Russian violinist." Janet Burstein recalls Sarah's "warm, friendly interest" in her work and her importance as a role model: "she shows us what it means to stay engaged, creative—despite everything the aging body will do to suffocate that spirit." Like Gilah, we all ask ourselves, "how it was possible for such awesome power to dwell in such a fragile little body."

Sarah, this special issue of *SAJL* is for you in gratitude from your friends and colleagues, who will continue to be guided by your love of words, your ability to laugh, your courage, and your infectious spirit. We thank Sarah's longtime close friend, Dan Walden, for his assistance as editor of *SAJL* in facilitating this special issue.

Carole Kessner, SUNY Stony Brook
Ann Shapiro, Farmingdale State College, SUNY

"They Find You, Those Sons Of Moses":

Collective Memory And The Disconnected Jew

Ellen Schiff

In a PMLA article entitled "Racial Memory and Literary History," Stephen Greenblatt describes a riveting keynote address he heard at the 1996 International Shakespeare Association meeting. The speaker was actor, director, and civil rights activist Janet Suzman, who told the story of the remarkable production of *Othello* she had directed in her native Johannesburg in the mid-1970s. Because violent anti-apartheid riots were raging in Soweto, the theatrical representation of interracial marriage was a daring act bordering on provocation. To get to rehearsals, John Kani, the black playwright-actor cast in the title role, had to make his way through "a nightmarish landscape of oppression and bloodshed and submit to humiliating questions and searches" (Greenblatt 54). Kani would arrive at the theater so paralyzed with rage that he could not unlock his clenched jaw enough to produce the round, plangent "O's" that punctuate Othello's speeches ("O, Iago, the pity of it, Iago"). Suzman's persistent efforts to coach Kani only made him angrier. Finally she realized he needed to find his voice in an antithetical racial experience. Could he summon from his memories the tranquil safety of starry nights in a rural African village? He could. The strategy worked. Kani's accomplishment is all the more striking given that he is an urbanite; he has always lived in Johannesburg. The memories he accessed did not come from personal experience. They came, rather, from what Suzman and Greenblatt call "racial memory."

Greenblatt met Janet Suzman after her talk and told her how moved he had been by her courage and resourcefulness. At the same time, he confessed skepticism about the invocation of racial memories and discomfort with a term indelibly defiled by history. "Did she think," a somewhat vexed Greenblatt asked, "that I could access racial memories somewhere inside of me of the smoky Lithuanian nights in the *shtetl* near Vilna, the place my grandparents had the wit or good fortune to leave in the 1890s?" "You could," Suzman answered. "If you were an actor . . . you would have to" (55). This exchange, and especially Janet Suzman's assertion—"if you were an actor"—intrigued me. Greenblatt cites the episode in his argument about the misuse of racial memory in constructing teleological studies of a national literary history that prioritize the work of the most recent dominant group. He decides Suzman's notion of racial memory is a "fictive construction," belonging entirely to "theatrical performance." I take Greenblatt at his word. I suspect that, distinguished Shakespeare scholar that he is, he might agree that the theater is, by definition, a "fictive construction." Paradoxically, I read what he intended as a dismissal as an enticement to look for other roles that racial memory might serve in the theater. Is finding inspiration in memories that come from one's people rather than from personal experience just an extension of Method acting? Is translating the personal relevance of racial memories into performance limited to the professional strategies of actors and directors? Their ultimate responsibility, after all, is to the text they are bringing to life. It is hard to imagine that playwrights do not drink at the same source, the more so when their racial memories bubble with appeals to the sensibilities as Kani's do. Like Greenblatt, I wondered immediately about the accessibility of correlative memories for Jews (perhaps that was Suzman's inspiration in the first place). Since my interest lies in plays that represent Jews and Jewish experience, my inquiry came to focus on the ways American Jewish playwrights draw on racial memories, or, more precisely, on how they use the viewpoints and emotions triggered by these memories.

Before I looked for evidence, I needed to define the kind of memory I was looking for and find a more accurate name for it. I share Greenblatt's distaste for the term "racial memory," partly because it is freighted with odious connotations for reasons that are obvious, although hardly irrelevant to the subject of my inquiry. Moreover, the use of the word "racial" is inapt in the study of the artistic portrayal of Jews in a country where Jewish identity is not imposed, as it was in Nazi Europe, but, rather, voluntarily constructed in the crucible of coexisting beliefs, ideologies, loyalties—and memories. In approaching American Jewish plays, their authors, and their characters, I made a wide swath around the enduringly problematic question, "Who is Jewish?" I took as apodictic that, at least in the theater, Jews are those who affirm in some way their own connection with Judaism and the Jewish people, irrespective of declarations of simultaneous allegiances to other identities and heritage. (Indeed, perhaps the single most dominant subject of drama about American Jewish life is the struggle to hyphenate meaningfully.)

As I have demonstrated elsewhere, Jewish playwrights have made it a signature practice to toggle between Jewish and non-Jewish subjects. Whether or not they are writing out of personal memories, they have often mined the dramatic potential of major Jewish practices and rituals. The American stage has been the scene of representations of Bar Mitzvahs (Donald Margulies's *The Loman Family Picnic*), weddings (Joseph Stein, Jerry Bock, and Sheldon Harnick's *Fiddler on the Roof*), funerals (Deborah Zoe Laufer's *The Last Schwartz*), and Seders, (Jennifer Maisel's *The Last Seder*). Shabbat candles are kindled (and blown out) in Wendy Wasserstein's *The*

Sisters Rosensweig. Paddy Chayefsky's *The Tenth Man* incorporates whole sections of the synagogue morning prayers.

Although such public representations of Jewish rites and rituals serve as valid indicators of the working of a people's memory, it is not the memory of religious traditions whose role I sought. Nor is it historical memory. Documented history aims at accuracy and completeness, attributes with which dramatists can play free (Goodrich and Hackett's *The Diary of Anne Frank*, Albert Urhy's portrayal of the Leo Frank affair, *Parade).* A more promising source might be oral history in which memory and the imagination join in the attempt to make sense of history. As Alessandro Portelli, a leading practitioner, argues, oral history contains "errors, inventions and myths that lead us through and beyond facts to their meanings" (2). However, at most, history—documented or oral—provides only one dimension of collective memory.

The phenomenon I am pursuing appears less structured and more intuitive than a body of information consciously acquired. The memories whose use in playwriting I have been seeking are not always even conscious. In *The Glass Menagerie,* Tennessee Williams writes that memory is seated primarily in the heart. I have not discovered where collective memories are stored, but I think I have learned what they are made of. Their substance is "la matière juive"—all the things that have happened to Jews or that Jews have made happen because they are Jewish. They are the legacy of Jews, irrespective of how uneducated or indifferent to Jewish religion, history, ethics, practices, languages, and literature they may be. Jung describes such ancestral property as part of the "collective unconscious," which "does not owe its existence to personal experience and consequently is not a personal acquisition" ("The Concept of the Collective Unconscious").

Perhaps the most accurate term for the entity whose function in playwriting I am chasing down is the one used by sociologist Maurice Halbwachs: collective memory. Halbwachs defines the phenomenon as "a reconstruction of the past in the light of the present" (34). He distinguishes collective memory from autobiographical or historical memory by observing that the collective is socially constructed and socially triggered: "It is, of course, individuals who remember, not groups or institutions, but . . . individuals, being located in a specific group context, draw on that setting to remember or recreate the past" (22). What is particularly useful to theater scholarship are the three contexts that the French sociologist identified as the milieus where collective memory is preserved and activated: social class, religion, and family.

While those turn out to be the operative settings for the plays that I am going to discuss, they may require amplification in ongoing studies. Halbwachs did not live to continue his work in radically restructured postwar societies (he died in Buchenwald in 1945). He did, however recognize the living, organic nature, and the role of the present in contributing to collective memory. It would be appropriate for future studies of collective memory in drama about American Jewish life after World War II to admit what Halbwachs called "recent psychological and social data" into the working definitions of the three contexts that serve as both the origins of and the repositories for collective memory (119). Hence, recollections preserved in what the sociologist called social class are today often inseparable from those of professional life. Memories of religious life are screened through expanded notions of denominations, observances, and gender roles in Judaism. Even the oldest social unit, Halbwachs' third category, family, has not escaped contemporary redefinitions. Moreover, the new fields of cognitive behavior and cognitive cultural studies contribute significant insights into the relationships of cognition and memory and the relevance of cognition to communication and the arts.[1]

The challenge for theater artists is to translate texts built from collective memories into terms that audiences understand and to which they respond. The success of a theatrical work may be largely the result of how effectively it finds and exploits those resonances. Hence, the associations and emotions triggered by collective memories on both sides of the stage can be more important and more powerful than the memories, as Kani presumably called on the reassuring calm of the starry nights rather than the nights themselves.

It would be presumptuous to attempt to establish the source of dramatists' inspirations or to account for the attitudes and emotions memories reveal in their work. Perhaps they themselves cannot. I do not think Harold Pinter was being coy when he said, in a different context, that his characters tell him just so much and no more. My purpose here is not to explain how, why, or what actual or fictional people remember. It is, rather, to demonstrate the role assigned to collective memory in the formal elements of three Jewish plays.

In David Mamet's work, memory is triggered when a man returns to what remains of the society where he grew up. Ira Levin's play involves a character who finds himself responding to the imperatives of a Jewish heritage he did not even know he had. Two of Herb Gardner's protagonists wrestle with the familial demands memory makes on them.

David Mamet wrote his mischievously-titled one-act, *The Disappearance of the Jews*, in 1983. This play takes place in the anonymity of a hotel room, the setting reinforcing the trilogy's ironic title. Fourteen years later, *Disappearance* became the first part of his trilogy, *The Old Neighborhood* (1997), a memory play composed of three scenes that depict the return of forty-something Bobby Gould to the Chicago neighborhood where he had grown up.

Bobby is reunited with his boyhood best friend, Joey Lewis, whose opening line, "What I remember . . ." (3), launches the stream of reminiscences and regrets on which the play is built. The men's recollections are stained with recognition of bad decisions and the sourness of disappointments.

Joey and Bobby grew up in a predominantly Jewish milieu with little meaningful appreciation of their own Jewishness or anybody else's. They are, for instance, amazed to learn that Mr. White, the "goy" from whom they bought their shoes, had been the *shammes* at Temple Zion for thirty years. They gloat in recalling the Greenberg kid they tormented at camp, the interchangeable Debbies they dated, and their macho prowling (Joey teases Bobby that he used to say, "Let's find some Jew broads and discuss the Talmud" [12]).

Jewishness in adulthood has been not only less carefree, but the source of anxiety and guilt. Mamet's two have stumbled into middle age without a moral compass, an ethical guidebook, or even a destination. Bobby ruefully admits that he made no response to his gentile wife's observation that Jews must deserve their long history of oppression. He is perplexed at her asking him, "What are you going to tell the kids?" For Bobby, there is no question that his son is a Jew. When Joey points out that "the law" (of matrilineage) is clear, Bobby grows defiant—"Fuck the law"—but he is whistling in the dark and he knows it. Whatever the security of the lives they have lived, it fails to ease innate Jewish vulnerability, like Bobby's, "they start knocking heads in the schoolyard looking for Jews, you fuckin' think they aren't going to take my kid?" (14). Joey has a ready explanation of anti-Semitism: "the reason the goyim hate us is . . . we don't descend to their level . . . we have our mind on higher things" (16). His swagger, like Bobby's, is unconvincing. He used to dismiss as foolish his father's predictions that anti-Semitic persecution would recur. "But," he adds, "I know he was right" (17).

Vulnerability and fears of oppression are not all that has survived of Jewish memory for Joey and Bobby. They longingly conjure up the more authentic and purposeful Jewish life they might have led in experiences they patch together from Jewish collective memory. It is in this part of the play that they grow most animated. Joey, who prides himself on his physical strength, claims he would have been "a great man in Europe," glorying in manual labor outdoors in winter. "We should be farming somewhere," he tells Bobby, "Building things, carrying things" (19). Intelligence is misdirected in their time. The scholars, lawyers, and teachers who complain of anomie ought to be studying Talmud. "[W]e should be able to come to them and to say, 'What is the truth . . ?' And they should tell us. What the talmud [sic] says, what this one said, what Hillel said" (19).

Joey's sense of entitlement to the strength of Samson and the wisdom of Solomon does not palliate his personal regret for "the life we were supposed to live." However, Bobby takes strong exception to Joey's longing to have lived in Europe, reminding him that it was "no picnic there." This time, the bravado is Joey's: "Fuck the Nazis, Bob. I'm saying, give a guy a chance to stand up . . . .Give 'im something to stand for" (20). He might, he thinks, have realized his potential as an immigrant in America: "Many times I wished to go back . . . to when my folks came here . . . to Orchard Street . . . to pushcarts" (25). Bobby fantasizes a more romantic era: "I would have loved to go, in the twenties, to be in Hollywood . . . . I know they had a good time there . . . five smart Jew boys from Russia" (25).

It is striking that as these middle-aged adolescents wallow in the colorful and the grim, they never ponder what might have sustained the Jews who may actually have had the experiences they envy, or what they may have "stood for," or what united them in a communal life that eludes them. "Everything is so far from us today. And we have no connection," complains Joey, yearning for the joy of a life "where questions are answered by ritual . . . . that you didn't make up, but existed" (33-34). He "invents ceremonies,"—like prayer—but cannot keep them up. He and his wife do try to visit the cemetery regularly, and they have recently joined a synagogue, though he does not appear to derive from it the affirmation of identity that collective memories offer. Even finding continuity with the Jews they actually remember does not come easily. Joey's mention of cemetery visits prompts Bobby to suggest, perhaps somewhat guiltily, that they go the next day, but their plans sound more dutiful than heartfelt.

> Bobby: Would you like to go out?
> Joey: We could go. Yes.
> . . . .
> Bobby: I'll pick you up.
> Joey: All right.
> Bobby: We're really going to go.
> Joey: All right (17-18).

The sad irony is that little in their own lives as Jews confers the dignity, self-worth, and communal pride they easily locate in recollections of Jewish martyrdom, persecution, and insecurity, as well as of strength, wisdom, and faith. Like children exploring a trunk of heirloom clothes, they try on costumes fashioned from collective memory in which they fail to recognize themselves because the clothes do not fit. Jewish lives uninformed by genuine knowledge and appreciation of heritage have since become a recurring theme for Mamet. Rarely has he treated it with more ironic wit than in *The Disappearance of the Jews*.[2]

The Chicago hotel room where Bobby and Joey rendezvous is far removed from the apartment on Manhattan's Lower East Side recently purchased by Warren Ives, a commodities trader, and his girlfriend, Lesley Rosen, a publicist, in Ira Levin's *Cantorial* (1988). The space had earlier been a synagogue; an elaborate entertainment center has been installed in a niche that once housed the ark. Lesley speculates with delight that her great-grandparents might well have been congregants. Warren's only exposure to a synagogue, he says, was when his politician father took him along on campaign tours: "I felt their main reason for adopting me, his anyway, was to have a kid to show to the voters" (10).

So nothing prepares the new homeowners for the beautiful tenor voice that comes out of nowhere, singing, "B'nay base-choh k'vot chee-lohhhh" (23). They first assume that the previous owners had rigged up a practical joke with a tape recorder on a timer. When that theory explodes, the mystery deepens: the singing ceases entirely when there are no Jews in the apartment, but grows louder and more insistent during the visits of Lesley's family or eighty-year-old Morris Lipkind of the neighborhood deli, who befriends them. Lipkind explains that the *chazzan* is chanting a verse from the holiday Musaf service. He translates it: "Build your house the way it was."

Lesley: "He wants us—to make it a synagogue again . . .!"
Warren (emphatically): "Sorry! No way!" (24).

Morris, who is drawn to the couple and their unusual lodger, offers to contact the few survivors of what had been Congregation Ahavat Zedek. That is how he learns that the extraordinary trained voice could only be that of Isaac Schlansky, the original cantor. Schlansky was something of an eccentric, a man known not just for his musical talent, but for his meticulousness in observing religious law and in practicing woodcraft. He made all the woodwork in the synagogue.

As determined as Lesley and Warren are to assert their proprietorship, Warren is intrigued by the account of the legendary cantor-carpentry artist. But mostly, he is preoccupied with his own receptivity to the voice. The depth of his otherwise inexplicable response to hearing Kol Nidre leads Warren to conclude that his biological parents must have been Jewish. "It would explain why I—*feel* him . . . And it would explain why he thought we might do it in the first place" (47). Recalling the carved posts and railings he had cleaned out of the cellar thinking them useless, Warren taps the recess that holds the entertainment center. To Lesley's consternation, he pulls down the entire wall, revealing a dusty carved mahogany interior—and unleashing cultural memories that exercise their imperative on him. Taking a three month leave from his lucrative stockbroker's job (Levin wrote the play in 1988), he devotes himself entirely to restoring the synagogue. Lesley, unsympathetic to what she sees as his obsession with proving an improbable ancestry, summons Warren's father who assures Warren that *he* is certainly not Jewish, nor was Warren's mother, a secretary in his firm that did not hire Jews.

Warren is unconvinced and undeterred. Nothing can dissuade him from what he finds "the most fulfilling thing I've ever done" (64). He is motivated to do what Mamet's Joey feels he ought to be doing, "Working with my hands this way, making something" (64). Levin's script makes clear that what drives Warren is more than a yuppie's elaborate self-indulgence in an ambitious architectural project. Once the restoration of Ahavat Zedak is complete, Warren is determined that it will again function as a synagogue. Under Morris' amazed tutelage, he tracks down the purchasers of its eternal light and persuades them to donate it back. He sells the last of his IBM stock to purchase a Torah. He convinces Morris to lead the High Holiday services. And, as Lesley, the publicist, realizes, once the restored synagogue story becomes public knowledge, there will be no problem attracting donations and members. She even overcomes her own skepticism. At the young couple's realization that the mysterious cantor is no longer singing to them, she says, "He knew he had accomplished what he hung around for" (98).

Levin's play demonstrates the force of collective memory without accounting for its source. Perhaps, as Lesley speculates, Warren's mother's mother could have been Jewish (98). What trumps all speculation is the play's confidence that the house where Jews worship will be rebuilt. That conviction too may come from collective memory.

By contrast with Ira Levin's young professionals, who are learning to make Jewishness part of their lives, and Mamet's middle-aged kvetches, who wish they already had, the central character of Herb Gardner's autobiographical *Conversations With My Father* cannot leave it far enough behind. It is 1936 and Eddie Ross, having emigrated from his native Odessa, wants passionately to be 100% American. In the determined pursuit of the American dream, Eddie, né Itzik Goldberg, changes his own and his family's names, in addition to the names and decor of his Canal Street tavern. Eddie is equally passionate about who he does *not* want to be: an East European Jew. He has escaped Eastern Europe; the Jewish part is harder.

The problem is, Eddie does not know how to be Jewish and American. He bitterly cites the terrible fate of his own orthodox father, also a tavern keeper, who met a terrible end during Prohibition when his allegiance to God and the law were no protection against bootleggers. Although Eddie scoffs, "He had his head in the Talmud, his foot in the grave," he cannot get the paternal voice out of his head (436).[3] He lays the blame on the annual postcard he gets from the Sons of Moses, reminding him of his father's Yarzheit. "Wherever you go, they find you, those Sons of Moses," he fumes (438).

Eddie has not renounced Judaism; he has just made his own "deal with God," doing the minimum observance to keep Him "calm and on his good side." That sends mixed messages to his two sons. He insists that Charlie attend Hebrew school until his Bar Mitzvah, "Because all God's gotta do is come through *once* to make Him worth your time….just when you die so you ain't scared shitless" (474). But when Charlie leaves the house wearing his *kippah*, Eddie explodes, "How many times I gotta tell ya, kid—that is *not* an outdoor garment. That is an indoor garment *only*" (444). The older son, Joey, having absorbed his father's principles and ethnic pride, enlists in the Navy the morning after he sees the vandalism on the sign over the *Jewish Daily Forward* to make it read, "*Jew is for war*" (483). "Show 'em kid," cheers the proud Eddie, "*show* 'em how a Jew fights" (484). But when Joey is killed, having refused to leave his battle station, Eddie is mad with grief and rage: " . . . *tonight* I go to *Beth El*, I go to the *East Window* because this is where God's supposed t'hear ya better—and I tell 'im . . . get *this*, God. I ain't a *Jew* no more! *Over*, pal! Fifty years of bein' a Jew Loser . . . *Take* 'em, take the *resta* them, they're *yours*—*you* chose 'em, *you* got 'em" (493).

Twenty years later, the adult Charlie confronts Eddie with the consequences of his upbringing. One of the happier ones is the critical and financial success Charlie, a writer, has had with his novels about a feisty immigrant bartender and his two sons. Eddie stubbornly withholds recognition of Charlie's accomplishments. He dismisses Charlie's Izzie character as unbelievable: "What kind of Jew is that?" he demands. Charlie retorts: "He's your Jew, Pop, you made him up. He's your Jew and so am I; no history, no memory, the only thing I'm linked to is a chain of bookstores" (499).

That, of course, is not true. Although Charlie will obey Eddie's dying wish to be buried in "an aggressively non-sectarian joint," he lights a Yahrzeit candle for him and recites Kaddish. Besides, he cannot forget; he gets an annual postcard from the Sons of Moses. "They *find* me," he says, defeated by his own emotion, "those Sons of Moses" (504).

The last conversations between fathers and sons—Eddie and Charlie, Charlie with his own son, Josh—drive home Gardner's play's argument for the impossibility (and, finally, the undesirability) of escaping parental heritage and the collective memories it preserves.

However, there is another heritage and other memories central to *Conversations With My Father* that transcend its plot and elicit strong feelings on both sides of the stage. The play effectively appropriates a collective memory cherished by many descendants of East European Jewry. Yiddish may have become largely an academic specialty in the United States, but it has retained its power to stir even otherwise disaffected Jews whose command of Yiddish is limited to words that have passed into standard English usage. As in so many cases (including that of Mamet's pair), it is not the phenomenon that is remembered—here, the language—it is the associations that attach to it.

However alienated Charlie claims to be, he betrays himself early in the play. We have barely met the present-day Charlie when he steps out of character to address the audience. He launches into what can only be described as a paean to Yiddish, praising its superiority to convey meaning, nuance, and attitude: "Why go into battle with a punch, a jab, a sock and a swing when you could be armed with a klop, a frosk, a zetz and a chamalia?[4] Can poor undernourished English turn an answer into a question, a proposition into a conclusion, a sigh into an opera?" (428). As Charlie's mother, Gusta, puts it, ignoring Eddie's command for "English, English," "English just don't do the job."

Dramaturgically, Charlie's praise of Yiddish does not move the play anywhere. In fact, the demonstration of the linguistic and affective superiority of Yiddish interrupts the forward action and all but subverts the validity of English, the language of the play. Moreover, the affection in Charlie's praise contradicts the negativity he will reveal about his confused Jewish upbringing. (Conflicting feelings about being Jewish may well be another ingredient of collective memory in Gardner's autobiographical play.)

Nor is Charlie's long speech the only time the work relies on powerful emotional memories evoked by Yiddish. As the lights go down and even before the curtain rises, the auditorium is filled with "the zesty, full spirited voice of Aaron Lebedeff, backed by a wailing Klezmer Band, singing the beginning of an old Yiddish Musical Hall song called 'Rumania, Rumania'. . . .The song speaks of Rumania but it could be telling us about Odessa, Budapest, Warsaw, . . .the places of an older and better world *that may never have existed but certainly should have*" [emphasis added] (422). Joey and Bobby would agree.

It is not just a lump in the throat that that Yiddish is meant to evoke. At the climax of the scene in which Eddie faces down two toughs who visit to sell him "protection," he puts a slug in the jukebox to play the Lebedeff record. "I got a need to hear one o' those Hollering Hebes," he says, defiantly (457). (I think of John

Kani's finding the freedom from threat in his collective memories to pronounce those Shakespearean O's.)

Although Eddie Ross is a formidable fighter, there are antagonists he cannot best. One of them is Yiddish and the world it makes resonate. Eddie's dogged pursuit of iconic American themes as decor for his tavern never succeeds. It is patrimony and authenticity that finally triumph. Renamed the Homeland Tavern, it becomes the "in spot" for the changing population of its Canal Street neighborhood. The main attraction is Gusta's brisket *tsimmes* and *lokshen kugel*, which went nowhere as Mulligan stew and hot apple pie. Eddie muses about his clientele: "They come in strangers, they go out grandchildren" (497).

There is nothing original about plays that demonstrate that, as Sholom Aleichem had it, it is hard to be a Jew. These three make the case that it is hard to stop being Jewish, even when, as Mamet demonstrates, you have strayed blindly, or, as in *Cantorial*, you cannot explain its claim on you, or, like Gardner's Eddie Ross, you have resigned. Wherever you are, they find you, those Sons of Moses.

The pull of collective memory is irresistible.

Notes

1.	I am grateful to Professor Dorothy Chansky who called my attention to these studies.

2.	In work subsequent to *The Disappearance of the Jews*, Mamet deepens and sharpens his assessment of questionable Jewish attitudes toward religion, identity, tradition, and culture. He is especially critical of pride more readily expressed for achievements in the larger society than for the specifically Jewish. See, for example, the one act *Goldberg Street* (1985, *Fruitful and Multiplying: Nine Contemporary Plays from the American Jewish Repertoire*, Ellen Schiff, ed. New York: Penguin/Mentor, 1996, 183-88); "The Decoration of Jewish Houses" and other essays in *Some Freaks* (New York: Viking, 1989); the 1991 film *Homicide*; and *The Wicked Son: Anti-Semitism, Self-Hatred and the Jews* (New York: Shocken/Nextbook, 1996).

3.	Julius Novick discusses and demonstrates this struggle in *Beyond the Golden Door: Jewish-American Drama and Jewish-American Experience* (New York: Palgrave Macmillan, 2008.)

4.	Gardner's text does not italicize the Yiddish.

Works Cited

Gardner, Herb. *Conversations With My Father*. Ed. Ellen Schiff. *Awake and Singing: Six Great American Jewish Plays*. New York: Applause, 2004: 419-506. Print.

Greenblatt, Stephen. "Racial Memory and Literary History," *PMLA* 116: 1 (200l): 48-63. Print.

Halbwachs, Maurice. *On Collective Memory*. Trans. and ed. Lewis A. Coser. Chicago: Chicago UP, 1992. Print.

Jung, C. G. "The Concept of the Collective Unconscious." "The Jung Page: Reflections on Psychology, Culture and Life." Web. http://www.cgjungpage.org/index.php?option=com.

Levin, Ira. *Cantorial*. New York: Samuel French, 1990. Print.

Mamet, David. *The Disappearance of the Jews*. *The Old Neighborhood*. New York: Random House/Vintage, 1998: 1-40. Print.

Portelli, Alessandro. *The Death of Luigi Trastulli and Other Stories: Form and Meaning in Oral History.* Albany: SUNY UP, 1991. Print.

Stille, Alexander. "Prospecting for Truth Amid the Distortions of Oral History." Web. http;//www.racemattersw.org/distortionsoforalhistory.htm.

Ellen Schiff, Massachusetts College of Liberal Arts

A Kaddish for History:

Holocaust Memory in Ehud Havazelet's Bearing the Body

Victoria Aarons

When Sol Mirsky, Holocaust survivor and bereft father, in Ehud Havazelet's novel *Bearing the Body*, wonders "what world is this?," readers are made painfully aware of the collapse of time that prevents a stable demarcation between then and now, between a pre- and post-Holocaust universe (108). Instead, the past collides with the present, moving it aside for the real time of memory, which takes hold in dizzying moments of disorientation and spatial confusion, inchoate fragments of despair, what Havazelet calls "shards refracting no more than their miserable incompleteness" (133). Sol Mirsky, shattered by his past, no longer recognizable even to himself, in his attempts to navigate an uneasily positioned post-Holocaust world, finds himself not so much thrust back in time but contained there, frozen in time, enshrouded in a past that blurs not only the temporality of the present, but the linearity of narrative as well. If history is narrative, then the Holocaust breaks the sequential unfolding of time and space, leaping generations, returning reiteratively to the point of traumatic, arresting origin. As Sol's oldest son Daniel sorely acknowledges, for his parents, Holocaust survivors, time is not a story with a conveniently reassuring procession of beginnings and endings. Theirs does not take on a "story's consoling shape," but consists rather of a succession of chronic, unremitting fragments of memory, shards of time, the sharp edges of narrative and broken ends of history: "a night, a year, a terrible mistaken instant, never ending, its term never elapsed—and they, trapped inside like insects in amber" (132). Theirs is a life narrated in fragments, but fragments of narrative made into a life, a grave bequest to the next generation, a behest from the grave "to take memory in the body and carry it, forever" (242).

For surely we have learned in the disposition of time since the Holocaust that the irreversible memory of events is not contained in the individual histories of those who survived the atrocities. Rather, the memories of the Holocaust—the intractable fact of the Holocaust—are carried over, witnessed anew, by subsequent generations, generations for whom the Holocaust, despite the elliptically cryptic silence that often surrounds it, has, from the very beginning, indelibly formed and informed the lives of the second- and third-generation, a past that, as one of Havazelet's characters in the short story "To Live in Tiflis in the Springtime" puts it, "seeped across the walls and floor. It was no longer something to be recalled from a distance—it was there in front of him, to walk into if he dared" (239). These are generations who must bear the weight of history, generations for whom consciousness of the Holocaust has been entrusted, if reluctantly and despairingly so—even in the ellipses of silence. As a kind of cautionary *midrash*, Havazelet's *Bearing the Body* unsparingly exposes the conditions by which children of Holocaust survivors attempt to redeem the suffering of their parents, a shared grief that, as Daniel Mirsky laments, "wasn't supposed to be ours" (48). And even though Daniel wants to convince himself that one "can't lose what you never had," for the children of survivors, the weight of the Holocaust becomes by necessity and inevitability a shared loss (132). For Havazelet's characters, moving through a post-Holocaust world is a matter of pushing aside the seemingly endless detritus of history in order to give meaning, not only to their parents' lives, but to their own fragmented lives, too, in the ongoing rupture of the past.

In *Bearing the Body*, to give meaning to the Holocaust is to create, in its absence, a *midrashic* narrative told posthumously, that is, a narrative that evokes the voices of the dead as well as the singed voices of memory. Throughout the novel, the Holocaust essentially is conveyed by its absence, in the spaces and pauses that break the ongoing narrative of the present. But these fissures are openings for *midrashic* moments of continuity and extension, an invitation to carry the weight of memory into the present. As Jonathan Safran Foer observes in the novel *Everything is Illuminated*, "the origin of a story is always an absence," one that in a long tradition of Jewish storytelling carries with it the obligation to be filled, to bear witness to the particulars of Jewish history and survival (230). But sometimes such telling, "before you lose the chance," as Sol Mirsky comes belatedly to recognize, requires a hiatus, a silence in which one might reconstruct the fragments of memory into something larger than the fleeting descent of traumatic recall (254). For, as Sol's son Nathan, confronted by broken extracts of narratives, cautions, "each bit of information seemed isolated, from a different story, a piece to a different puzzle" (186). As one of Grace Paley's narrators, in the short story "Debts," insists, "there is a long time in me between knowing and telling," between, that is, identifying the unconscious threads of memory and locating and articulating the language of loss (*Enormous Changes* 9).

Making a story out of absence, out of the caesura born of rupture and loss, is all the more imperative and precarious when the narrative hopes to transmit the experiences of the Holocaust—imperative because the increasing distance from the events imperils memory, dangerous because bearing witness to the Holocaust exposes what one does not, cannot know. Here, absences are openings, moments of extensional disclosures, at the heart of which is the core of character, of the impulse for evasion constrained by an ethic of bearing witness to a narrative of trauma. And although the Holocaust survivor in Sol Mirsky would like to delude himself into believing that memory "was contained, bounded by event...recollection...a matter of choice," it is his memory that betrays him ironically by being faithful to his own painfully traumatic history, a narrative willfully projecting itself onto the specious advent of time (70). As Sol's son Daniel cruelly concedes in a grim appropriation of Horace, "Quam minimum credula postero," place no trust in tomorrow, that is, in the unconscious projection of a future divorced from the ambushes of the past (132).

Bearing the Body tells the story of two sons, Nathan and Daniel Mirsky, who come of age in America during the turbulent period of the 1960s, and of their father, Sol Mirsky, a survivor of the Holocaust, who devotes his life to collecting and archiving names and photographs of those who perished at the hands of the Nazis, those all but lost to history. In attempting to locate and record the dates of departure, transport number, and place of incarceration of the victims and so provide their surviving families with some, if scarce, knowledge of their horrifying fate, Sol attempts to find a metaphorical burial ground for those whose deaths otherwise would remain unchronicled, eclipsed by history. Sol's solitary vigilance—an isolated vigil—becomes a kind of self-imposed penance. After working all day in the shoe factory, his nights are spent isolated with the dead, "night after sleepless night in his dusty, half-lit cave, buried in paper, charts, letters, photographs, his private inviolable domain," a space uninfringeable, not to be disturbed by his sons (95). Nathan, recalling an early foray into his father's private world, "sneaking...when his father wasn't around, just to look. He remembered thinking, So this is where he lives. Once...he'd taken a thick file from the shelves. What he found inside was incomprehensible—timetables, lists of names and numbers, foreign place names so full of consonants they hurt the eyes" (95). Startled in his trespass by his father, "Nathan had no idea what to do; the urge to run, so common in him, rose. Inside, the familiar queasy moil of feelings he had whenever his father looked at him—regret, a spreading shame....Nathan...heard himself thinking. Other kids play catch. Other fathers speak. Sol's immobile face unwatchable, severe, and hardest of all to see, a little wild in the eyes, as if with fright. What could Nathan have possibly found out? Nobody said a word" (95-6). The fraught sense of shame is rooted for father and son in an impossibly articulated, unconscious fear of trespass and culpability, in having exposed something reprehensibly secretive in the other and in having done so, uncovered an ignoble weakness in oneself. They are tied together by something primal in their silence, an instinctive response to fear and exhibition. While Nathan's silence is aggrieved, Sol's is cynically defensive.

Sol, living in the shattered past, trying to piece together that which has been irretrievably broken, cuts loose his sons, willfully, if ineffectually, preventing their entry into a world from which he wishes to protect them. "'What was a man to tell his children,'" Sol wonders. "'Everything? And what could he say?... Once I had a family, like this one....Once, once, once—what was the point? What could be gained?...

Once there was a pond so full of human ash it was muddy gray and the wind was full of it like snow. Once people died around me every day.…This? This to small boys?" (279). The elliptical mantra "once, once, once"—blessing and curse—both arrests time and evokes a timeless condition of despair and raw desire. It is in the ellipsis, the trope of omission, that Sol's silence is both an act of defiance and shame—a provocative, incendiary silence bequeathed to his sons. Sol Mirsky is a man who erroneously has forced himself to believe, after his incarceration in the concentration camps, that "nothing…would touch him ever again" (76). It will take his sons' seemingly irreverent denial of their father's history and, ultimately, the tragic death of his oldest son Daniel to prove Sol irrevocably wrong.

Set primarily in San Francisco in the mid-1990s, the novel moves back and forth in time and place, traversing an American landscape from the 1960s into the 1990s, a period piece of distinct moments of social and political unrest amidst the confusions and seductions of autonomous self-determinism and self-destructive obliviousness. The novel opens in 1968. America is at war with its own, and the Mirsky family's dinner is upended by the unexpected sight of their brilliant oldest son, Daniel, a student at Columbia, sitting on the ledge of a campus building in the midst of a political demonstration, smiling directly at the camera as he is dragged off by the police. This is an important opening scene for it reveals paradoxically the isolation of the family in the very heart of family life. The presumed ordinariness and routinized comfort evoked by the portrait of a family at dinner suggests here its menacing opposite and ominous other. Indeed, the contrived simulacrum of family—Nathan, his father, and mother—makes all the more apparent their anxious separation from each other. Having learned well, as Nathan puts it, "the art of segregating himself," he and his parents apprehensively are brought together in the charged electric air of the Mirsky household only by the image of Daniel Mirsky on the television set—Daniel, whose defiant bravado in the face of his family's stunned silence, from the novel's beginning, sets the stage for the unresolved tensions that animate a history unwound and reimagined (4). Although miles away, Daniel's presence looms large, his transmogrification conjuring him up anew, eerily sucking all the air out of the room. His name alone, a solitary incantation uttered by his mother as Daniel's image fills the screen, brings into sharp focus the uncontrollable accidents of occasion and character, a compression of time and history. For the novel quickly shifts to the year 1995 and the notice by letter of Daniel's drug-related murder in San Francisco. With the letter comes the insufferable knowledge that Nathan Mirsky, Daniel's self-loathing, phobically reluctant younger brother, must embark on a journey with his intractable and unreachable father to take possession of the ashes of their dead brother and son, ashes contained in a box not unlike the pictures of the dead so reverently preserved in shoe boxes stored on the shelves of Sol's sequestered room.

Bearing the Body, with cunning elasticity, also moves back in time to the Holocaust, the catastrophic events of which are pieced together in retrospect, painfully brought to the surface by Sol Mirsky's treacherous memory, a memory reawakened by the tragic death of his long estranged son, Daniel. It is Daniel's death that brings Sol and Nathan together as they travel to San Francisco to claim Daniel's ashes. And thus Sol must bear the body of his son just as he bears the bodies of the victims who died in the Holocaust and whose deaths, like Daniel's, haunt him still. In bearing the weight of Daniel's body, both literally and figuratively, Sol and Nathan Mirsky, unwitting companions in grief, bear the weight of history, of histories colliding and colluding.

Bearing the Body covers perilous and unstable terrain: the vulnerability of family; the destabilizing political and social upheaval of the 1960s; the drug-infected violence of urban America; the isolation and fragmentation of contemporary life; the incapacitating memory of the Holocaust; the alienation wrought by trauma; and the recurring ambushes of history, both global and personal. It is at the intersection of these narratives that the magnitude of loss and grief is so palpably felt. And through a complex web of narrative layering, moderated by memory both lapsed and elongated, the Holocaust surfaces in Havazelet's novel as the ultimate measure of all psychic and cultural estrangement, the final marker of personhood for the entire Mirsky family. Havazelet's novel is a searing portrait of loss and fragmentation, a story of a singular family's anguish and betrayal in the face of a history that would consume them. This is a story of the dissolution of a family and the disastrous consequences left in its wake, an ancient and contemporary story of biblical proportions set against the specter of the Holocaust, whose tentacles reach far into the next generation, a generation that bears the weight of a history both of its own and not of its own making.

Indeed, for Sol's son Daniel, a generation removed from the events of the Holocaust, "another history, not his, not one he'd ever know, sifted its weight over him like ash," like the ashes of the dead, a precursor to his own premature, violent death (133). Here the Holocaust is the measure of history, where all tracks lead—personal and political—the window through which everything is witnessed and interpreted, a narrative "overheard" by the children of survivors, exhumed by memory. And despite Sol's bargain with his wife not to impose their past trauma upon their sons—a history never to "be shared, could never be (were it even possible), with the boys. Let them look forward; wasn't this what a parent gave a child, a ground from which to look out at life…Wasn't that love?" (248)—they, too, are haunted by a history inadvertently bequeathed to them, a history that follows them persistently, resistant to the insistent demands of the present.

Bearing the Body calls into sharp question our limited ability to make sense of time and history in the wake of the Holocaust. Surely for Sol and his wife Freda, survivors of the atrocities, the linearity of time is thrown off, arrested by their past experiences, never again to be steered sequentially, "making all that came after a lie" (132). So, too, their pre-Holocaust lives seemingly have been erased by all that came after, never to be reclaimed. But the memory of the Holocaust is not generationally contained; rather, it becomes the filter through which all motives and actions are measured, all found to be wanting, distorted, magnified, and diminished. Daniel,

American-born, a child of seemingly free passage into an age of autonomous self-expression, believes his life to be eclipsed by the horrors of his father's past. Daniel, sounding not unlike his disenchanted and disenfranchised father, wonders, too, at the shape and scope of the psychic landscape in which he is forced to negotiate: "Where was the world he had brought me into, taught me to live in?...Where the violence, the betrayal? Where was God, cynical, patient, holding all the cards, with eternity to watch our failures unfold? This world, his world, suddenly gone" (50-1). And Daniel's anxious brother Nathan also feels the destabilizing weight of the past, "the world around him…a complicated balance miraculously poised against chaos. One wrong move and he would topple, taking it all with him" (232). It is as if the Mirsky family holds its collective breath; the only sure thing for them is impending disaster. And while Daniel insists that "what everyone does, what you figure's coming to you, is your own story, your life. It's your own history you're trying to make," his life and his brother's are tied inseparably to Sol's (288).

It is no surprise that the center of tension locates itself among father and sons, Freda, wife and mother, long since dead and unable to mediate the fear and anger that both tears her husband and sons apart and binds them irretrievably together. It is not Sol's fate alone "to take memory in the body and carry it, forever" (242). For Nathan and Daniel are held hostage by the ever-remote yet palpably visualized dead, their lives determined by the inheritance of history. Within this moral calculus, everyone fails everyone else and predictably so. Havazelet throughout the novel makes clear in his characters' myopic defensiveness and displaced fear the desperate impossibilities we expect from others. Nathan refuses Daniel's desperate overtures, believing that he has long since discharged his obligations to his drug-addled brother, convincing himself that Daniel's self-destruction was a form of betrayal, seeing in Daniel's ruin and defection from the family his own abandonment: "He left. He disappeared. He lied to me about what the world was" (189). And even though Nathan justifies his own defection from his brother as an act of helplessness—"to see him fall apart so thoroughly so miserably. I couldn't do it. I couldn't stop it and I couldn't stand anymore to help it happen" (188)—his renunciation is nonetheless a desertion for which he will pay dearly. And even Freda unintentionally, but no less markedly, betrays her sons by failing to protect them from their father's uncontainable wrath and accusatory silence, ultimately failing them all by dying.

The most crushing failure, of course, is Sol's, who believes himself to have failed everyone, "the truth being there was no one is his long life he had not betrayed" (254). Perhaps the most egregious failure, however, is that of the covenant. For Sol, no longer a believer, "the only prayers he knew, didn't know really, just the sound of the words, their cadence, carrying absolutely no meaning to him," the belief in something larger than himself became simply the recognition that there are no limits to what one man will inflict on another (171). In the articulation of such knowledge, the covenant, utterly bankrupt and impotent, lays fallow. The failure of the covenant is here the failure of conscience, for Sol the whole human enterprise no more than a cosmic joke. Railing against a blackness that would have obliterated him were it not for chance or fate or uncertain luck, Sol, "wav[ing] his fists at the empty sky," nonetheless indicts a God he no longer believes exists: "This, you sonofabitch. This" (280). And even for Sol's brother Chaim, who perished in the Holocaust, and who, despite all evidence to the contrary, "despite the daily weight of evidence, believed in the Jewish God, a deity of provenance and mercy and alert resourceful care," the covenant cannot withstand the weight of ultimate human failure. So even God— the Holocaust as proof—fails, the covenant discharged.

Sol's history is an unwelcome but no less defining legacy crushingly carried on by his sons. For Daniel, in particular, who all his life has attempted to refigure himself as distinct from his distant, reproachful father, the events of the Holocaust, like the pictures archived in his father's deathly collection, are indelibly etched on his consciousness: "the pictures of the roundups disturb most…Jews gathering in Amsterdam for the trains—little boy in shorts and black shoes. Sol somewhere, not much older. In the barracks, horror…startling in their familiarity" (288). And while he would like to think of those whose lives were destroyed as "removed, artifacts of a different world," he knows them to be an ineffaceable part of his own life (288). Daniel comes to recognize that, like it or not, neither he nor his brother can sepa- rate himself from the dead who precede them. Both brothers, like their remote and disparaging father, are beholden to and defined by the same shape of history that, as Daniel puts it in a note written before his death, "you never chose. But here it is. And soon enough it is yours. Soon enough you come to see it always was" (288).

But such knowledge comes too late. The sense of betrayal and failure that motivate the dynamics among Sol and his two sons is so immense that neither son can forgive his father for being the man he haphazardly became, a man not of his own design, but shaped by the duplicitous indifference of a history that defrauded him. Silently keening for the lost man he might once have been, Sol bitterly admits: "I saw things I can't explain, even tell. I got changed…. Parts of me killed off—how do I know they weren't the best parts?" (279). But, if Nathan and Daniel cannot forgive their father, neither can Sol forgive his sons for what he believes to be their intolerable betrayal in willfully turning from this history. In a single moment of exposure, but a scene the novel has been hurtling toward all along, time becomes frozen and the vast differences in experience and character bring into sharp focus the incalculable loss. During a labor strike at Sol's shoe factory in the late 1960s, "the union breaking in, workers looking at him suddenly like he was a jailer, a *Kommandant*," his employees, waiting at the loading docks, systematically tear open box after box of shoes, throwing them into a pile "as high as the loading plat- form, hundreds of Well-Built shoes, glistening new with polish, some still trailing blue tissue paper; shoes for people to wear, now a pile of garbage. It made him sick, physically sick, to watch….It was all he could do now not to fall to his knees and heave the bile that swam in his mouth" (249-50). Arrested by the sight of the shoes thrown so carelessly in such heedless, wanton abandon, shoes heaped higher and higher, Sol is dragged back to another time and place, the piles of shoes taken from the dead, his world before he deceptively thought he could exchange it, start anew without the cunning intervention of the past, all chicanery, a trick of the imagination, since "for Sol…there was no past, no present, one eternal Now erasing all that came before [the Holocaust], making all that came after a lie" (132). Characteristic of second-generation writing, such categories as past and present fail to represent the extent of the distortion of time and place engendered by the defining rupture of the Holocaust. The past and present collapse, as if the very air is sucked out of possibility, the future a chimera.

As Sol, stunned and reeling from the sight of the mounds of shoes piled higher and higher, as if without end, a metonymic extension of the swells of dead bodies that follow him, Sol spies on the other side of the chain link fence his two sons, standing in bemused satisfaction, insouciantly laughing, the protest to them nothing but sport. For this, for their willful absence of conscience and memory, for their careless denial of their own history, Sol cannot bring himself to forgive them. Indeed, for Sol, blinded and blindsided, the world becomes reduced only to this: "the factory…shoes glinting, small popping sounds as new ones hit, rolled, his own yard a mound of corpses, and beyond it, his own sons in a casual embrace, laughing" (253). Outraged, ambushed by this indefensible act of filial betrayal, Sol believes his sons to have made a mockery, not only of his own life—"all we went through, and this, so they can make a joke, a parade" (261)—but of history, of the vast, collective expression of suffering. Sol's worst fears transpire anew: that the past will have no meaning and that his experience is no more than an accident of history. Of course, in his act of treachery, Daniel figuratively slays the father and in doing so, ultimately, replaces the father, his own death sadly the embodiment of the death that would have been Sol's, the death that was designed for him but that he fortuitously eluded. But in this primal scene, Sol can only see his sons aligned with an arbitrary and faithless universe, "laughing at my life, my memory, all I ever had." And so, in an unretractable moment Sol beseechingly, "prayed to the god I knew wasn't there to blast us all dead on the spot (279). And here it is, not surprisingly, to Daniel, his oldest son, that Sol directs his greatest fury: "To me you're dead" (261). Denying Daniel's existence is, inexorably, a death sentence just as sure as if Sol took aim and fired. Sol casts out Daniel as he himself was "cast out" of the stream of normal life. And the loss, for both father and son, is irrevocable, Sol's words, like blessings and curses, never to be recanted. As Sol crushingly laments, "once you are cast out there is no getting back in" (280). For as the prophetic voice of the biblical Israel makes painfully clear, "If I am bereaved of my children, I am bereaved," thus dramatizing the failure of the covenant (Genesis 43:14).

Both Sol's and Daniel's acutely felt sense of betrayal is transformative, securing the antagonisms and resentments that have been in the background of their relationship all along, widening the gap between father and son until neither can be reached, despite the truth, as Sol's wife in the face of her husband's unutterable decree and her sons' unthinking folly knows to be certain, that "the only sins you will never be forgiven are the ones you commit against yourself" (262). In Daniel's dismissal and, by default, Nathan's dubious ascendancy, we are reminded here, in some ways, of the anxiously figured story of Jacob and Esau, two brothers vying for the father's blessing, purloined by the younger brother through stealth and deceit. Yet in this instance, neither son receives the blessing of the father, who is so transformed by the Holocaust that he can only see in his sons a distorted reflection of his own suffering and failure. And Daniel, in a desperate attempt to run from his father's past and the immensity of his own sense of failure and betrayal, opts out of this precarious world for the dangerously false panacea of a drug-induced oblivion, a chemical eradication of all that he cannot face about himself. In attempting to escape from the pain and the gnawing awareness of the enormity of the past, Daniel "had made his choice. He would, at last, choose the present, no past insistently hovering, no future holding out its spurious soft lies" (130). However, the present here is indelibly mortgaged to the past, so much so that even one's immediate failures are not entirely one's own. As Havazelet makes tragically clear, the present age can only be seen in relation to a past that is at once impossibly unspoken and unspeakably possible.

As the narrative events move back and forth in time, Daniel's voice emerges in flashbacks, ultimately taking over the narrative, and readers come to know him in death as well as those characters whose lives become increasingly intertwined as the novel progresses. It is Daniel whose voice resurfaces in shards, in fragments, slivers of erratic, disconnected thoughts written on scraps of paper, words from a dead man, found by Nathan in the flat in San Francisco that Daniel shared with his lover Abby and her young son Ben. It is Ben, the fatherless boy who, with Daniel, constructs a world on paper, and for whom Daniel briefly stands in as father. Daniel thus unconsciously attempting to assuage his own father's guilt and redeem himself, but he ultimately fails Ben, too. As Daniel tries to write his way back into life through fractured notes written to a brother who will only see them when it is too late, the found fragments of dissonant, aborted chords, thoughts cut off, elliptical, are unmailed but ultimately not unspoken by Daniel's weighted, posthumous voice. Daniel's voice has been waiting in the wings, only to emerge as the central dramatic force in the novel's final pages. Thus in giving voice to Daniel long after his death, Havazelet brings him back to life. That is, through prosopopoeia, the rhetorical trope in which the voices of the dead are summoned and thus reanimated, Havazelet exposes the extent of Daniel's suffering and redeems him. So, too, Sol Mirsky, on a mission to wrest meaning from the ruins of the Holocaust and lessen his fear that his experiences and those of others who suffered are more than a mere accident of history, evokes the presence of the dead in his tireless search for the missing. Taking on the burden of attempting to locate and uncover the fate of those who were deported, sent to concentration camps, and lost to their surviving families, Sol brings them back from the dead if only for a moment of acknowledged recognition. Prosopopoeia may be seen as a fractional, fleeting antidote to the absence that is the Holocaust. Giving a presence to obscurity, a weight to absence, through the figure of prosopopoeia, allows the dead to speak, unmediated, without intercession from the tempering distortions of time or memory. In writing about Holocaust poetry,

Susan Gubar suggests that "prosopopoeia allows the authors who manipulate it to summon the posthumous voice...and thereby to suggest that the anguish of the Shoah does not, and will not, dissipate" (192). Prosopopoeia is not so much a matter of speaking for the dead as much as it is a trope that fills an absence with the voiced presence of the dead, thus locating, as Gubar poses, "a language for the staggering horror" (191). In this regard, Daniel's death—a dying that takes place not in the concentration camps, but against the charred landscape of urban America—evokes the death of those murdered before him. As Havazelet suggests, the Holocaust cannot be made a figure of representation; one can only represent the impossibility of doing so. Daniel, so indifferently gunned down in a naïve attempt to confront the sale of drugs to school children, embodies, in his dying, an expression of the absolute disregard for life, a moral failure of human conscience and design. It is thus that Daniel Mirsky's found voice reaches his brother Nathan only after his death, his voice found on scraps of paper, fragmented notes, and letters unsent but kept by Daniel's lover and handed over to Nathan as an offering, as embodied story.

The story of the Mirsky brothers is also a version of Cain and Abel set against the isolation of contemporary America, in which Nathan Mirsky deeply resents the obligatory imposition of his magnetic older brother, Daniel, the "Aquarian golden boy" (130), from whom Nathan has tried to extricate himself and toward whom he mistakenly "consoled himself with visions of his bright future and with the thought he's finally outgrown his older brother...free to be his own man" (181). His early adolescent infatuation with his brother eroded, Nathan has long since dissociated himself from his demanding, drug-hazed brother, the weight of his obligation to Daniel far too much for him to bear, Daniel's words falling on deaf ears, like "hundreds of phones ringing in empty rooms where no one lived anymore and where no one would be hurrying back to pick them up and say, Hello, sorry, are you still there?" (228-9). Nathan, falsely believing that his obligation to his brother was long ago spent, in refusing to respond to Daniel's erratic letters, cuts his brother loose, so that for Daniel "writing his brother [was] like flinging a lifeline three thousand miles out to sea and never feeling it land" (130). Nathan, willfully, self-destructively turning his back on his brother's precarious condition and obvious weakness, does everything he can to cause others to hate him as much as he loathes himself. Unable to sustain a relationship, Nathan chooses rather to look from a safe distance through the shuttered windows of other people's lives. If Daniel responds to his father by anesthetizing himself in drugs, then Nathan does so by inuring himself to the burden of intimacy, seeking, rather, the numbing sedative of self-containment and hardened inaccessibility in the face of an "emotional mayhem that left him wanting, more than anything, to run" (35).

What Nathan tragically comes to find in the course of the novel is that his willful abdication of his responsibility toward his brother has sentenced him, like Cain, to uneasy wandering, cut off from the consoling community of others. It is through Nathan's inadvertent connection with Abby and Ben that Nathan is finally able to do belatedly for his brother what he could never bring himself to do during

Daniel's impulsive and misspent life. It is only through the accidental interruption of strangers—Abby and Ben—that he can at least partially atone for his failures. It is only, in fact, through his chance encounter with Abby and her young son Ben, whose pure, unadulterated love for Daniel and in whom Nathan must see something of his younger self, that Nathan, finally, can bear the burden of the heartbreakingly intimate enmeshment of family, coming finally to realize that he "loved his brother. And the loss, the misery suffered mostly alone…settled over Nathan as a new weight, different, not entirely unwelcome. Nathan loved his brother, and how hard it would be now, knowing he'd never be able to tell him so" (269).

At the same time, Sol, the wandering Jew, roaming the foreign streets of San Francisco, displaced as he once had been as a newly disembarked immigrant, felt "like he had again just arrived from Europe, foolish, agape, incongruous in his heavy winter coat and cap, watching a spectacle he had no hope of understanding or making his way into" (39). This time, however, Sol carries with him the ashes of his son, "the box in his hands, spattered with sweat and streaked gray…hauling him downward, heavier every step.…This is not what a father should do. A father shouldn't be carrying his dead son deeper and deeper into a place he didn't know, all that was left of him in a plastic box. Surely, if there was any reason, an order to anything at all, this was wrong. Daniel, he found himself saying.…He clutched the box to him one last time and turned up another hill" (280). Sol will not, cannot, relinquish the box of ashes, for, as his son Nathan learned long ago, "you don't fill an absence by taking more away" (23). Sol carries the ashes as a totem to memory, and so the remains of his son become the metonymically irreducible mark of a life historicized by the six million murdered.

Bearing the Body is among a new generation of Holocaust novels, ones that carry the originating loss into the twenty-first century, ongoing narratives in which memory is carried in much the same way that Sol carries the ashes of his dead son: like an offering borne before him to be transmitted with care to the next generation. So, too, the young child Ben, his drugged mother unconscious in their flat, walks the streets with an old cigar box containing the broken remains of a toy dog, "number 36," destroyed in his grief and rage when Daniel, his last hope for permanence and security, by his dying betrays him too. As Jewish legend would have it, there are thirty-six *tzaddikim* in the world, thirty-six *lamed vov*, righteous, just men, upon whom the world depends. The *lamed vov* are indistinguishable from other people and are unaware of their appointed role, but, through acts of compassion, they bear the suffering of the Jewish people. Such messengers appear in the least predictable forms when one least anticipates them, emerging, for Havazelet, in those most vulnerable: the young, abandoned child, Ben; the tenuously anchored Daniel; the homeless veteran whose barely coherent ramblings about angels and heralds are prayers for the most vulnerable among us, all products of our age and history and anxieties about the past and the future. As one *lamed vov* leaves this earth, another takes his place in order to redeem the world from suffering. But if *Bearing the Body* is a novel of loss, it is also a novel of redemption—of redemption failed by lassitude, by arrogance, by weakness, and by fear, but also of redemption carried out, as often as not by fortuitous encounters, by the expression of *rachmones*, compassion for others born from shared suffering. For it is finally in the collective expression of shared suffering that one might begin to redeem the suffering of others.

As Sol carries the box of ashes through the labyrinthine streets of San Francisco, he comes to bear the fragile weight of his son's body and his own. He, like both his sons, bears that which is also borne upon him. For to bear the weight of the body is to take it on, to acknowledge responsibility for it, to accept it, as one accepts defeat, or love. All Havazelet's characters come to bear the weight of history—a history both proximate and distant: the weight of family, the weight of addiction, the weight of loss, the weight of regret, the weight of the past, the weight of the dead, the weight of memory, the weight of their times. At the novel's close, the characters, previously lost, scattered, isolated in their grief and confusion, come together at the Pacific's edge to scatter Daniel's ashes, and in their momentary stay against the debilitating weight of their fear, they find the possibility for what it means to bear witness to this life. Here they find redemption in memory through the symbolic reenactment of the ritual of *tashlich*, the casting off of one's sins in the water, and here too, the sins of history. And so, to Havazelet's question, "How do you miss a ghost?" the only answer is: carefully, so that its memory does not dissolve in the corrosiveness of time. Thus *Bearing the Body*, finally, is a kind of kaddish, a prayer for the dead, not only for Daniel, and for those who perished in the Holocaust, but also for the unending ravages of post-Holocaust history and memory unburied.

Works Cited

Foer, Jonathan Safran. *Everything Is Illuminated*. New York: Houghton Mifflin, 2002. Print.

Gubar, Susan. "Prosopopoeia and Holocaust Poetry in English: Sylvia Plath and Her Contemporaries," *The Yale Journal of Criticism* 14:1 (2001): 191-215. Print.

Havazelet, Ehud. *Bearing the Body*. New York: Farrar, Straus and Giroux, 2007. Print.

———. "To Live in Tiflis in the Springtime," *Like Never Before*. New York: Farrar, Straus and Giroux, 1998. Print.

Paley, Grace. "Debts," in *Enormous Changes At the Last Minute*. 1960. Reprint, New York: Farrar, Straus and Giroux, 1983. Print.

Victoria Aarons, Trinity University

Through an American Lens:

Dreaming Utopia in Early Israeli Cinema

Janet Burstein

> Every age has its official preachers and prophets who castigate its vices and
> call to a better life. Yet it is not by them that its deepest malaise is revealed,
> but in the artists and thinkers dedicated to the more painful and difficult
> task of creating, description and analysis—it is they, the poets, the novel-
> ists, the critics, who live through the moral agony of their society in their
> own personal experience; and it is they, their victories and their defeats,
> that affect the fate of their generation and leave the most authentic testi-
> mony of the battle itself for the benefit of interested posterity.
>
> Isaiah Berlin
>
> Russian Thinkers

Alive with messages for Americans, Otto Preminger's 1960 film, *Exodus*, identified Jewish Palestine with the drama of "rescue." Preminger embedded this drama
within a context that embraced ancient as well as recent Jewish suffering, naming
the film—like the novel on which it was based—for both the biblical rescue of the
Jewish people from its slavery in Egypt, and the battered ship that carries Holocaust
survivors in the film to Palestine.[1] Opening credits appear against a night sky in
which, as in the biblical wilderness, a single pillar of fire gleams—like a beacon. But
just before the story begins, this flame multiplies and fills the screen: it is not a beacon any longer, but a holocaust. Like the title, the image links the rescued remnant
of European Jewry to the ancient rescue and liberation of an enslaved people.

As this visual link becomes thematically important, it strengthens the film's
appeal to an audience that remembered America's role in the liberation of occupied
Europe and the concentration camps. The film, which locates familiar American
virtues within gallant Palestinian Jews, became extraordinarily appealing.[2] Neatly
dividing humanity into good guys and bad guys, *Exodus* transplanted the heroic
possibilities of G. I. Joe and the American cowboy to a land as photogenic as Mon-

tana—but saturated with a biblical past. To American Jews, given the long shudder induced by the suffering and extermination of European Jewry in the camps and ovens of a darkened Europe, the sunlight of Palestine, the toughness, strength, and resourcefulness of Jews born in that land were irresistible. To at least one Israeli critic, *Exodus* looked like a "conscious cinematic attempt to turn history into a contemporary Zionist myth" (Loshitzky 2). But to Americans, the film offered a mythic figuration of cherished American virtues emerging within the cultural history of Palestine/Israel.[3]

In the popular American imagination the promise that these virtues were not only attractive but also transformative was concentrated in one Palestinian phenomenon in particular: the collective agricultural settlement called "kibbutz." Recognized even today as "one of the grand social experiments of our lifetime," (Mort and Brenner x), the kibbutz in the early decades of the century seemed to be a powerful primary agent of rescue and redemptive transformation. It appeared to be capable of healing and redeeming into new life a people oppressed by long exile and by recent victimization by the Nazis; a barren, neglected land; and the very nature of the Jew. In what contemporary researchers see now as a "romantic vision," observers saw then "the only example of pure voluntary communism in the twentieth century" (Mort and Brenner x). That vision became, in time, darker and more complex. Israeli cinematic treatment of the kibbutz between 1935 and 1967 constructs its initially "romantic" image and then slowly explores its subtext, revealing the conflicts beneath its shining surface.

American Jews, of course, knew the virtues of the kibbutz well before *Exodus*. As early as 1852,[4] American Jewish newspapers carried sympathetic reports of agricultural enterprise in Palestine. By the 1930s newspapers like the *Jewish Exponent* were associating the pioneers who settled in the early kibbutzim with heroic virtues that appear also in films made both in Palestine and America in that decade.[5] American Jews understood that the people who settled in the earliest communities of what became the kibbutz movement were driven in part by the need to escape pogroms in East Europe that drove thousands of other Jews westward, many to America. But settlers of the early waves of immigration (*aliyot*) to Israel were also moving toward a utopian vision. They saw Palestine as a refuge. Nevertheless, animated in part by the political and ideological movement called "Zionism," the pioneers wanted to become farmers instead of city dwellers; they wanted to share property, work, and profits instead of competing for them.[6] They believed, one historian suggests, that "their actions in settling Palestine were the beginning of a new era in Jewish life. Culturally and morally, they intended to become the focus of a Jewish revival…" (Near 10).These settlers carried into the early efforts to create small, socialist groups in Palestine the entwined utopian ideas of rescue and transformation. They believed they would redeem into new fruitfulness a supposedly neglected land. And in the process they intended to change themselves from small business people into farmers; from urban into rural dwellers; from dependent into self-sufficient citizens.

These entwined expectations cling to the image of the kibbutz that appears everywhere in the earliest films made in Palestine in the thirties. Always there is the assumption that the land had suffered and become desolate in the absence of its Jews. And that returning Jews would rescue it from its desolation. Judah Leman's *Land of Promise* (1934), Helmar Lerski's *Avodah* (1934), Baruch Agadati's *This is the Land* (1935), for example, all insist on the barrenness of the land to which the European *halutzim* (pioneers) come. We see in these films the primitive agricultural practices and simple handcrafts of indigenous Palestinians juxtaposed with images of the massive road building, stone quarrying, mechanized well-digging of the pioneers who seem to restore the land as they build cities on sandy wastes, who cultivate art and industry now that they are in communion again with their homeland.

In this cavalcade of enterprise and productivity, "The kibbutz environment is singled out for particular attention" (Tryster 12). We see groups of people, always groups: building, plowing, harvesting, making bricks, drilling for the water needed to redeem the land. Agadati's *This is the Land* notices also the physical cost to the *halutzim* of their labor to redeem the land. A close-up of a glass pitcher being filled with foul water, thick with mosquito larvae, precedes a sequence in which a man staggers and falls to the earth behind his plough, is carried from the field, and dies of malaria as his wife weeps. But this film also praises work on the land, contrasting it with the easier life of the city. "The city is rotten," two kibbutzniks insist; "leave cities; go to the fields; remember, comrades, why did we come here if not for the revival of the nation?" After 1948 this emphasis on the sterility of urban life will complicate Israeli perception of Americans who stayed in their cities, continuing to resist the invitation to "come" to the homeland. But as the camera dwells in 1935 on fields, flowers, and trees of the kibbutzim, as we see men, women, and children at work and play—we notice mainly that the land recovers, and that the humans who struggle on it are themselves renewed. The agricultural kibbutz appears both the site and the agency of this rescue and transformation.

The first films produced near the end of the forties intensify the appeal of the agricultural collective by muting socialist and economic issues and emphasizing the healing power of work and the redemptive virtue of comrades—especially for survivors of the Holocaust. *My Father's House* (1947), for example, embodies what it calls "enduring…truths" in the life of one child, brought barefoot in the dark from Europe to Palestine. While other refugees are fed, clothed, and welcomed by soldiers and kibbutzniks, this child spends most of the film searching for his father, lost in the Holocaust. In the end he will be "mothered" by another refugee and taken with her to a new settlement—where a kibbutznik turns up from the earth an old stone with the child's family name, "Ha Levi," inscribed on it. Thus he is rescued into collective history and living community.

In America, to a nation of immigrants only a generation removed from Europe, the power of the kibbutz to draw in the homeless, the wounded, the lost; to revitalize them by connecting them to a collective past; to give them comrades who could work with them to restore a collective homeland: this power seemed, as Bosley

Crowther observed, "irresistible."[7] Another film of the same period (*Tomorrow's a Wonderful Day* [1949]) tracks another child, rescued by Hadassah's "youth aliyah" program, similarly nurtured and absorbed by a children's village. An historical introduction to the film furnishes the data for these similar narratives of rescue and transformation. By 1947, 35,000 children had already been "brought home," and Hadassah was working to rescue the 60,000 "who have yet to come." In film, such data become part of a heroic myth whose significant features recur, entering collective memory like elements of a familiar ritual, to remind us, as Susan Sontag pointed out, "that *this* is important, and this is the story about how it happened, with the pictures that lock the story in our minds" (86). Saturated with emotion, like myths, these films offer again and again the crucial promise of the kibbutz: that people and their land can be renewed by work and comradeship.[8]

Even before the state was declared, the kibbutzim—which seemed to embody the primary virtues of the Jewish homeland—were associated with an agenda that became important, and that was also familiar, to Americans. Allon Gal, a historian, calls this agenda "survivalist" because it identified the homeland with the need to rescue European Jewry—a need that was implicit in the earliest settlements and became more crucial during the Nazi period. But Gal points out that American Jews also saw another, more "universalistic" agenda in the image of the homeland; they saw it as "an instrument for the absorption and refinement of American goals" (15). For example, by 1918 the ZOA expected that the new culture being constructed in Palestine would satisfy expectations developed during the exilic past: for "political and civil equality irrespective of race, sex, or faith of all the inhabitants of the land." Other American Jewish organizations expected after 1948 that Israel would pursue "a compassionate foreign policy…combining…the Jewish prophetic heritage with the best of the American liberal tradition" (27). According to Jonathan Sarna, "the Israel of American Jews was for centuries a mythic Zion, a Zion that reveals more about American Jewish ideals than about the realities of *eretz israel*….the brawny Jewish farmer [appeared to be]…the answer…to those who claimed that Jews were mere parasites, radically incapable of 'productive labor…'" (41). Thus the redemptive work of the kibbutz could be symbolically stretched to improve even the self-image of American Jews.

In the years after the war, however, the reluctance of American Jews to become kibbutzniks qualified, to some extent, the mythic image of what Aryeh Goren calls "Zionism's most exalted achievement" (83). An important wrinkle in the fabric of American expectations of Israel enfolded a disjunction between American and Israeli ideas about the future of the Diaspora. Refusing to accept the European—and later the Israeli—belief in the "negation of the exile" or *shelilat ha-golah*,[9] American Jews stressed instead the continuity of Jewish history, insisting upon the continuing vitality and value of the American Jewish Diaspora.[10] To a very large extent, this disjunction between Americans Jews' and Israelis' sense of what "renewal" meant, this American rejection of the absolute priority—assigned first by European Zionists and later by Israelis—of settlement in the homeland explains the relatively modest number of Americans who actually joined the kibbutz movement.

Of course, the birth of Israel in what Gal calls a "bloody and heroic defensive war (1947-1949)" (24) and its reception of many thousands of survivors and later refugees from Africa and Arab lands intensified the importance to Americans of "survival" in the image of Israel in general and the kibbutz in particular as a "haven-fortress." But the refusal of capitalistic, individualistic Americans to affirm the old Zionist belief in the "negation of the Diaspora," and the wishful insistence on Israel as a fulfillment of American democratic ideals, continued to complicate American Jewry's image of the emergent state.

One needs, then, to recognize a mixture of ingredients in the American vision of Israel and the kibbutz as its most characteristic and laudable accomplishment. From the 1920s on, Aryeh Goren observes, "the communal settlements...were Zionism's most exalted achievement....a singular example of a democratic, egalitarian, and just society-in-the-making." The kibbutzim offered "evidence...that the return to Zion, inspired by the universal prophetic ethic, transcended narrow nationalism" (92). But some American critics began early to comment on the "ideological rigidity of the kibbutz and the deleterious effect of collectivism on the individual"; others became uncertain about "problems of sexual promiscuity...open irreligiosity and militant secularism of the kibbutz" (Goren 92); one even observed "a contamination of our life by the supineness, the mass-life, the morbid and dangerous submersion of personality" (Ludwig Lewisohn, qtd. in Goren 94). Despite the powerful appeal of the kibbutz, American individualists recoiled from certain facets of kibbutz life. However, committed absolutely to the right of the Jewish people to exist in this new state as a goal unto itself, American Jews also continued to project onto Israel their own sense of American virtues and their own desire that the new state fulfill prophetic ideals.

Perhaps because one's critical lens is ground by such complex cultural givens, American viewers may see more readily than Israelis the ways in which Israeli films made even during the so-called "heroic nationalist" period between the War of Independence and the Six Day War begin to develop a critical subtext within the image of the kibbutz. In these years the agricultural settlements make significant contributions[11] to the development of the new state, but—as Isaiah Berlin predicted—filmmakers, like writers, also begin to explore the "malaise" that they sensed within the lived experience of the kibbutz.

Three films of this period speak to a disturbing mixture of—not always compatible—visions of Israel and of the kibbutz as primary carrier of the new state's virtues. *Out of Evil* (1950), for example, insists on persistent conflicts that work against collective ideals that remain, nevertheless, precious. Associated in earlier films with heroic commitment and idealistic self-sacrifice, the kibbutz becomes in this film a place of contentious and stubborn willfulness. The narrator, Josef, recalls the kibbutz first as a place of obstruction: to protect their fields the pioneers have placed a barbed wire fence across the track of an ancient caravan route to Damascus. One camel, leading a caravan, stumbles into this fence; we see his soft nose pressing against the barbed wire. We recognize the dismay of the Arab traders, suddenly denied their accustomed path. We sense the conflicting needs of two cultures in one land.

The Arab trader, invited for coffee with the kibbutzniks, apprehends their sense of collective identity, but warns them that individual needs will persist, will flourish, will demand satisfaction despite commitment to the collective: "you will be destroyed…by that man and woman….what happens if they fall in love? will everyone share in the delight?" he asks. To an American critic, predisposed by nature and nurture to applaud the struggle of individual need against collective authority, this conflict becomes central to this complicated film. Kibbutz members fear that romantic love and the family that springs from it will be a "selfishness," and the lovers, distressed, leave the kibbutz for Europe—where they will be murdered by the Nazis. Their child will return, as a young man, to the kibbutz where he was born—now on the eve of the 1948 war; the timing reinforces this film's emphasis upon conflict that persists: between individuals and the group, and between groups.

The particular struggle between satisfaction of individual need and commitment to collective good emerges clearly again in Baruch Dienar's 1961 film *They Were Ten*. The kibbutz here is a place of striking hardship: the land given to ten young pioneers from Odessa is barren and malarial; they find on it only a derelict stone shelter: dirt floor, missing walls, one large room in which nine men and one woman will need to cook, sleep, and care for one another. We watch these pioneers experience the first backache; the first blister; the first opening their shovels make in the earth. As the sun sets, we see them lying, exhausted, on the earth they have tried to dig. When they limp back to their shelter, there is light within the cleaned up place; the group is singing a Russian song; there is laughter and then dancing, and food. But when they lie down to sleep on the floor, we see the tension between the husband and wife—wanting one another, but unable to satisfy desire in a room crowded with other men.

There are other tensions as well. Like the initial uneasy encounter between Arab traders and kibbutzniks in *Out of Evil*, this film complicates the pioneer experience in communal settlements by recognizing the uneasiness of the kibbutz's Arab neighbors, who teach the Jews how to use their ancient plough, but withhold water from the shared well; who offer charcoal in a bitter winter, but steal a horse. The debates inspired among the settlers by these uncertainties reveal yet another layer of unresolved struggle within the Jewish collective: between the desire to leave and the will to stay, between the commitment to avoid violence, and the determination to take by force what is withheld: "they'll understand only force," one settler insists.[12]

What seems important here is the perceptual shift that makes visible an insight into the changing image of kibbutz: what had been in earlier films primarily an agent of rescue and a site of transformation becomes in these post-World War II films a place where struggle predominates, not just the healing struggle of human beings to renew themselves, to restore fertility to the land and to build communities upon it, but the ongoing, erosive struggle to resolve political, social, economic, and psychological conflicts within the structure of a collective community.

In *He Walked Through the Fields* (1967, Yosef Millo), the erosive effects of communal life become even more apparent. Although this film is widely praised by Israeli critics for its representation of heroic self-sacrifice and the ongoing life of fallen heroes in the life of their children and the nation, its subtext reveals—to an American critic, at least—significant damage to the quality of individual relationships in a collective community. When the young protagonist, Uri, returns in 1946 to his kibbutz from an agricultural school that also trains men as Palmach warriors, he does not experience the general, enthusiastic welcome that greeted either Josef in *Out of Evil* or the young Jewish Brigade soldier on leave in *Tomorrow's a Wonderful Day*. Uri is the kibbutz's firstborn. But when he returns from school, he has to "look for someone to say hello" to him. In the shower house he is greeted coolly by other men. On his way to the shower he sees his mother caressing a man who is not his father. He learns from a kibbutznik that his father is about to travel again, on another rescue mission to Europe, against the wishes of the kibbutz. And he sees that his father has become intimate with a woman who is not his mother.[13]

These changes in personal connections among comrades and lovers, the instability of his parents' union, trouble and enrage him. The climate of the kibbutz as a whole is different from the sunny, welcoming, harmonious ambiance of earlier kibbutzim in Israeli cinema. We hear kibbutzniks complain about the scarcity of material comforts, about the quality of work contributed by children recently rescued from Teheran. We see the carelessness of these young immigrants in a faucet left open, wasting precious water in a barren field; in the bullying of one young harvester by another over a full basket of grapes; in the slacking off of two boys who play cards when they should be working. The redemptive value of work—for the land and for the worker—has disappeared from among the primary attributes of the cinematic kibbutz of earlier films.

And the deep, enduring values that hold together people who commit themselves to one another within the collective seem also to have eroded. Unlike the debates about principle in *They Were Ten*, arguments about whether or not Uri's girlfriend is suitable for him, about whether or not his father, Willy, will be allowed to go back to Europe, about whether or not Uri will be permitted to join his group in the Palmach, predominate here. Feelings have gone underground: neither of Uri's parents can speak to him of what has happened to their union; Uri himself describes a wall that has grown up around his heart; his girlfriend cannot tell him that she is pregnant with his child. And in part, although both Uri and his father serve the needs of the collective—one by rescuing survivors and one by fighting the British to bring survivors illegally into Palestine—the devotion of both men to their duty seems to serve as well a private purpose.[14] Willy's absence insulates him from his wife's absorption in a new relationship, and Uri's military service distances him from the conflicting claims of his affair with the young immigrant, Mika. "In my position," he tells her, "a mother, a father, relatives are all fine as long as they don't get in the way." "Don't worry," she responds, "I won't get in your way." She refuses to speak to him of her pregnancy and decides to abort their baby.

Although the kibbutz has denied him permission, for "family reasons," to serve in the Palmach, and although a friend of Mika's does tell him she is pregnant, Uri volunteers for a dangerous assignment and is killed. Mika decides not to abort their child. This child will carry his fallen father's memory into the next generation of soldiers who serve the needs of the larger collective, the state. Here the "myth of the fallen," that promises the continuation of individual life in the life of the collective for which it was sacrificed, is writ large. But the film also writes large the wider effects of collective life and the sacrifices it demands of the living: in terms of the erosion of personal relationships and the underlying fabric of collective moral commitment upon which the kibbutz as a place of rescue and transformation was originally grounded. When illegal immigrants are brought to the kibbutz we see them feeding hungrily, served by kibbutzniks. This function of the kibbutz has remained intact, rooted in historical necessity. But we have seen as well the effect of these newcomers on the utopian assumptions that brought the kibbutz into being.

It is useful to remember that films of the period from 1948 through the 1960s, the third period of "Zionist realism" in Israeli cinema, are understood by Israeli critics to belong to what they call "the heroic-nationalist genre" in which Zionist ideology and "heroic stories of the national revival"[15] occupy the foreground. To be sure, *Out of Evil, They Were Ten,* and *He Walked Through the Fields* do feature the nationalistic emphasis on the building and defense of a Jewish state as well as the heroic ordeals of individuals who serve the needs of the Jewish collective. But the changing image of the kibbutz in these three films suggests that filmmakers are beginning—earlier than one would expect—to clarify problematic cultural issues connected with the Zionist project. [16]

"Beginning" is an important word here. Unlike what Nurith Gertz calls "mainstream fiction of the sixties" in Israel, which simply denied that collective and personal values could become "harmonious," these films raise doubts that coexist, unresolved—side by side with older beliefs. For example, Yosef in *They Were Ten* wants, at one point, to leave the kibbutz, but he stays; and although the group adopts strategies that seem, for the moment, successful, principled questions about ways to deal with Arab hostility are never resolved. In *Out of Evil,* the protagonist called from his studies to defend the homeland from which his parents fled recalls—even as he levels his gun at attackers—that the most persistently destructive threats to the life of this people come from within. And in *He Walked in the Fields,* Uri's rage and disappointment at the failure of his parents' commitment to one another coexist in tension with his own inability to hear the secret of his unborn child or to honor his commitment to the child's mother: his love for her does not even prevent his flirtation with another woman while he serves in the Palmach. The failures of human connection in this film write large the cost of commitment to the collective that had been embodied, since the 1930s, in Israeli cinema's image of the kibbutz.[17]

One Israeli critic has seen a failure of "coherence" in this film's inability to either reject the collective values of heroic-nationalist films, or to integrate them with the values of later, "personal" films that emphasize individual rather than collective experience. But perhaps neither "integration" nor clear choice among values is possible during a profound cultural shift that is still in process. Like uncertainties of weather that alternately chill and warm the days of early spring, the confusions and vacillations of protagonists in these films offer poignant images of what it feels like to live through a time when values and expectations are changing. By the early 1980s, when the kibbutz becomes again a prominent subject for Israeli films, the arc of cultural change is clearer in the more resolute behavior of cinematic protagonists. But films about the kibbutz made between 1950—two years after the founding of the state—and 1967—the year of its greatest military achievement—seem to insist on complexity, on uncertainty rather than clarity.

Within this complexity several Israeli critics see an important cultural transition from what Judd Ne'eman calls a "defensive...to an offensive ethos" (5). Ne'eman and others attribute this transition to the founding of the state. Anita Shapira argues that a military ethos crystallizes at the end of the 1930s for Palestinian Jewish youths who assumed the role of warrior to defend the "soil of the homeland," which they worked as pioneers (qtd. in Ne'eman 6). In *They Were Ten* and *Out of Evil* "the pioneer guard stands with gun in hand ready to defend the collective. The small pioneering group, not the Yishuv [pre-state Jewish community in Palestine] as a whole, is what gives the individual a sense of belonging and common purpose.... [I]t gave the individual strong personal ties that connected him with other young men and women who together formed a group maintaining emotional solidarity" (qtd. in Ne'eman 7). But after World War II, Ne'eman explains, the role of agricultural laborer becomes secondary to the role of warrior. In *He Walked in the Fields*, set in the moments just before the declaration of the state, Ne'eman points out, Uri's commander tells him, "If there won't be a Palmach, there won't be a kibbutz." But, like men in other films after the Six Day War when this film was actually made, the young warrior will recognize himself as belonging to the Palmach first, the kibbutz and his incipient family only second: "Thirty men are waiting for me in the wadi," Uri tells his lover as she struggles to reveal the secret of her pregnancy; "they are more important than me and you combined" (21).

For American viewers, this shift in priorities and in the warrior's sense of himself seems to respond to the hostility and belligerence directed against Israel by its neighbors. The power of the kibbutz to produce exceptional warriors has long been a source of pride to Americans. And a profile of American awareness of the kibbutz between the 1950s and the Six Day War, reflected in a sampling of press clippings, reveals the emphasis on hostility from without that validates the militant components of the kibbutz's image in these years. Reports of assaults on kibbutzim, of terrorist infiltrators and bombs laid in kibbutz football fields, of shelling from gun positions in the Syrian Golan, of children sleeping in shelters, and farmers carrying guns as they work the land, continue even after the 1967 victory to nurture awareness of extraordinary provocations against the communal settlements.[18]

But Israeli critics look from a different perspective into reasons why the warrior figure undergoes a metamorphosis in post-World War II films. They see what gets lost when militaristic commitment increases. And they discern—within their own culture—salient forces that partly account for such change. They explain that "with the establishment of the state a new worldview was born—statism. The state replaced the collective group, and from then on the state represented the collective whole" (Ne'eman 9).[19] This new sense of what "collective" meant generated other changes as well: in the years after 1948, Israelis became "a nation in uniform," and militarism was transformed "from an ideology maintained by small elite groups"— like the guards [*shomrim*], one of whom protects and advises members of the early kibbutz in *They Were Ten*, who speaks Arabic and befriends the neighboring Arab sheik—"into a project meant for the whole of Jewish society" (Ben Eliezer qtd. in Ne'eman 10). After the War of Independence, then, "the complex elitist code of identification of the Yishuv" that had been associated primarily with the kibbutz and "that was based on Socialism and Humanism was replaced by a more restrictive code of identification that was based on patriotism. This more restrictive, or 'statist' code was based on national values, the state, and security" (Ne'eman 11). Early films show settlers thrashing out the socialist, humanist issues that punctuated kibbutz discourse: how can we share; how can we use weapons against neighbors. But by 1968, as we have seen in *He Walked in the Fields*, discourse—like the nature of the warrior and the quality of "personal ties"—has radically changed.

Americans tend to understand the disjunction between their own and Israeli critics' readings of such changes in terms of "left" and "right," "hawk" and "dove." But binary judgments rarely honor the complexity of human transactions. It may be that hostility and misunderstanding—political and military as well as personal— need to be seen from several points of view, taking into account forces that act from within as well as from outside. In any case, the films offer no formula for restoring luster to the early vision of harmonious pioneer life in agricultural collectives. Instead, in the changes they portray, in their use of multiple cinematic forms and multiple time periods, in the confusions of their protagonists who cannot resolve inner conflicts—after the earlier insistence of Israeli films on the heroic commitment of the pioneers to a single purpose—post-World War II films offer what Homi Bhabha called the "perplexity of the living in the midst of pedagogical representations of the fullness of life" (Babha 307). When all the explicit messages abroad in a culture celebrate a unified pattern of ideals and expectations, people struggle to accommodate awarenesses that simply do not match the pattern.[20] That struggle, as Isaiah Berlin understood, enters into what gets written and filmed. In such works, the cultural struggle becomes visible but is not resolved.

Thus, while the earliest films represent the kibbutz as a celebratory symbol of settlement and development of a homeland, later films begin to record uncertainty: they probe and interrogate prevailing representations, complicating the image of the Jewish state's most promising experiment in collective living. In Israeli cinema, the kibbutz, a social construct intended to rescue and redeem, becomes a site of deeply mixed blessings. And Americans who screen these films see the changes and begin their own cultural struggle: to cherish the early promise even as they absorb the disjunction between it and the critical insights that develop as Israeli cinema matures. I have heard Americans, troubled by these films, rise to the defense of the kibbutz, insisting that the films misrepresent it. But I suspect that the pain Americans feel only mirrors the discomfort of the filmmakers themselves, struggling to clarify and to record traces of cultural malaise within the iconic, utopian dream of the Israeli kibbutz.

Notes

1.   The historic ship of that name suffered a very different fate: see Yosefa Loshitzky, 3-4.

2.   *Variety* (14 Dec. 1960) reported a "record advance sale of $1,000,000.00 for the film whose earnings in the first year totaled $8,332,000.00." Though *The New Republic* liked the film, *Newsweek's* critic complained about the film's four hour length and dullness (19 Dec. 1960) 87-88; the *New Yorker's* critic complained that Preminger permitted "nearly everyone in his large cast to state his ideological and political convictions before and after each new turn of events, and the result is an awesome talkfest" (17 Dec. 1960); *Film Quarterly's* critic complained about the film's "distortions" (14:3, Spring 1961) 56-59; and the *New York Times's* Bosley Crowther called it both a "massive, overlong, episodic, involved and generally inconclusive 'cinerama'" and a "dazzling, eye-filling, nerve-tingling...reflection of experience that rips the heart" (16 Dec. 1960) 44.

3.   Compare Stephen J. Whitfield's "Israel as Reel" 293-318. Whitfield argues that the film succeeds mainly in changing (i.e., improving) the way people see Jews by creating sympathy for Jews as "the Good Guys" (302) and by creating "empathy" for Israelis who cannot "be differentiated from Americans" (303).

4.   See Jonathan Sarna, "News of the agricultural colonization of Jews in Palestine first reached the American Jewish community through its newspapers...Isaac Leeser ...editor of... *The Occident*...spoke out in favor of Jewish agriculture in Palestine as early as 1852" (49 in Gal's *Envisioning Israel*).

5.   See, for example, Felix Warburg's "'Palestine Day' In the Nation's Capital: Why American Jews Should Support the Movement" in *The Jewish Exponent* (16 Jan. 1935) 8: "...the homeless among the Jewish people have been engaged in an unprecedented effort to reestablish their existence on soil hallowed to them by tradition and sentiment. They have not been conquerors but colonizers, imbued with a spirit of social idealism that traces its ancestry to the prophets who once preached in the land."

6.   This theme was especially attractive to Dalton Trumbo, screenwriter of *Exodus,* who had been blacklisted for refusing to cooperate with Joseph McCarthy's Committee on Un-American Activities—and who had belonged at an earlier time to the Communist Party.

7.   "It is a poignant yet thoroughly heartening story," he wrote ("Palestinian film in Premiere here: 'My Father's House,' Based on Meyer Levin's Novel, Opens at Ambassador Theater" (*New York Times* 26 Sept. 1947: 28).

8.   Joseph Leytes' *The Great Promise* (1947) tells a similar story.

9.   A major source for this belief is Ahad ha Am, whose "The Negation of the Diaspora" (1909) explained that "isolated groups of Jews wandering about the world here, there, and everywhere can be nothing more than a sort of formless raw material until they are provided with a single permanent center, which can exert a 'pull' on all of them, and so transform the scattered atoms into a single entity with a definite and self subsistent character of its own" (276). "In exile," he believed, "Judaism cannot...develop its individuality in its own way"

("The Jewish State and the Jewish Problem [1897] in Arthur Hertzberg, ed. *The Zionist Idea.* NY: Atheneum, 1977: 267).

10. Eliezer Livneh, sent by Ben Gurion in 1950 to study American Jewry—whose support was so vital to the new state—was handicapped in his assessment, Ganin believes, by his own acceptance of the "traditional Zionist premise of the centrality of the Jewish national home, and his definition of Zionism...still rooted in the principle of the negation of exile. 'Zionism,' he remarked in the report, 'means the Jew's resistance to his own exile,' an implied definition of America as exile vehemently opposed not only by the non-Zionists of the American Jewish Committee, but by the American Zionists themselves" (Zvi Ganin, *An Uneasy Relationship: American Jewish Leadership and Israel 1948-1957.* Syracuse: Syracuse UP, 2005: 66-67).

11. Collective agricultural settlements served as training grounds, one remembers, for young members of the Palmach—the earliest incarnation of the Israel Defense Force. And the kibbutz became a model of the kind of settlement constructed on land newly vacated after the war of independence. Anne O'Hare McCormick described "plans for establishing fifty-one settlements of the 'Kibbutz' or communal type" on land "left behind by fleeing Arabs" in "Israel Speeds Resettlement of Areas Left by the Arabs" (*New York Times* 18 January 1949: 1).

12. Yehuda Judd Ne'eman's "Tragic Sense of Zionism: Shadow Cinema and the Holocaust" in *Shofar* 24:1 (2005) argues that the internal debate about the use of force reflects the "displaced consciousness of the oppressed," the awareness of Jewish helplessness in Europe that "informs the Jewish pioneers' consciousness in their new country" even though the conflict over land and water rights in Palestine is so different from European anti-Semitism (24-25).

13. In a short play that preceded this film by nearly a decade, based on an even earlier novel by Moshe Shamir (1947), this erosion of bonds within the collective is even more explicit. "Mom's not here," Uri Explains, "she has her own affairs to worry about." And Ruthke, his mother, confirms this observation: "Everyone is for himself. Everyone has his own troubles." ("He Walked Through the Fields," trans. Aubrey Hodes. Jerusalem: World Zionist Organization, Department for Education and Culture in the Diaspora, 1959).

14. But cf. Nurith Gertz's "The Book and the Film: A Case Study of 'He Walked Through the Fields'" in *Modern Hebrew Literature* (Fall/Winter 1995) 22-26.

15. Judd Ne'eman's "The sinking in of new Atlantis in early Zionist cinema" (unpublished, 4); see also his "The Death Mask of the Moderns: A Genealogy of *New Sensibility* Cinema in Israel" (*Israel Studies* 4:1 [1999] 100-27), for example, in which Ne'eman describes *He Walked Through the Fields* and *They Were Ten* as retaining "the essentials of the Zionist master-narrative" (107). Ella Shoat in *Israeli Cinema: East/West and the Politics of Representation* (Austen: U of Texas P, 1989) draws attention to the heroic protagonist of *He Walked Through the Fields,* noting that the Hebrew words *gibor* (hero), *gever* (man), *gvura* (bravery), *ligbor* (to conquer, to overpower), and *ligbor al* (to win) all derive from the same etymological root (GBR), reflecting concepts of mastery, masculinity, and bravery as closely linked—all interwoven with the Palmach-generation literature and its cinematic analogue, the heroic-nationalist films" (93).

16. But Judd Ne'eman argues in "'A Curse Into a Blessing': A Film From Palestine—the Land of Israel" originally published in *50 to 48: Fifty Years to Forty-Eight, a special volume of the journal Teoriah Vebikoret* (1999), that beneath the propaganda value of the film *Out of Evil*, there is "another layer...principally around [the character of] Balaam's wife, that disavows... the ethos of the fallen soldiers that crystallized during the Independence War.....Balaam's wife symbolizes a first cinematic step towards non-Zionist thought about Zionism" (2).

17. Nurith Gertz's "The Book and the Film: A Case Study of *He Walked Through the Fields*" in *Modern Hebrew Literature* 15 (1995) 22-26, attributes this sense of unresolved conflict within the film to the relative youthfulness of the industry, to its reliance on Hollywood westerns on one hand, Soviet realism on the other, and—in the next decades—to the emergence of "personal cinema" modeled on films from France.

18. See, for example, *The New York Times* pieces on 2/4/53 (Dana Adams Schmidt: "Israel Says Arabs Derailed Freight..."); 6/14/53 (Dana Adams Schmidt "Israel's 'Little War' of the Borders"); 6/20/54 ("3 Israelis Killed in Clash on Border"); 8/28/55 (Kenneth Love: "...Nahal Oz...works armed"); 4/8/56 (Homer Bigart: "Arab Squads Raid Israel from Gaza"); 1/25/59 (Gertrude Samuels: "First Line of Defense for Israel: Along its borders, pioneers of the kibbutzim...guard the nation from hostile neighbors while working the land to enrich the Israeli economy."); 8/23/62 ("Syrians Accuse Israelis of Incursion by Bulldozer"); 5/2/65 (Drew Middleton: "Israeli Settlers Defy Nearby Foe"); 9/30/65 (James Feron: "Israel concerned by border infiltrations from Jordan"); 10/10/66 (James Feron: "Four Israelis killed by border mine: second incident in 2 days laid to Syrians"); 1/21/67 ("Israelis Find Mine Near Syrian Border"); 2/15/56 ("Israeli shot in second day of fire on Syrian line"); 4/11/67 (James Feron: "Israelis again work fields after Syrian Attack"); 5/7/67 (James Feron: "Israel charges shelling from Lebanon....200 led in Israel to shelter"); 6/3/67 ("Israel-Syria fray at border kills three"); 6/11/67 (James Feron: "19 year siege ends in border kibbutz"); 9/16/67 ("Arab raiders kill first Israeli since end of war; boy, 3, is victim as farm home is dynamited").

19. This disjunction between American and Israeli perspective continues. In his *Jerusalem Post* essay on 2 Sept. 2009, an American-born writer, Daniel Gordis who lives in Israel, attributes the decades-long Israeli occupation of the West Bank to "a defensive war that it did not seek." But the Israeli professor who has aroused Gordis's interest and many Americans' fury by asking for an international boycott to "save Israel from itself" is looking inward, into his own culture, to identify sources of continuing distress.

20. Judd Ne'eman, following Jacques Rancier and Kaja Silverman, calls such patterns "dominant fictions."

Works cited

Avodah. Dir. Helmar Lerski. 1935. Film.

Bhaba, Homi K. "DissemiNation" in *Nation and Narration*. Ed. Homi K. Bhaba. London, NY: Routledge, 1990. Print.

Exodus. Dir. Otto Preminger. United Artists, 1960. Film.

Gal, Allon, ed. *Envisioning Israel: The Changing Ideals and Images of North American Jews.* Jerusalem: Magnes Press; Detroit: State University Press, 1996. Print.

———. "Overview." *Envisioning Israel*. 13-40.

Goren, Arthur Aryeh. "'Anu banu artza' in America: The Americanization of the *halutz* Ideal." Gal. *Envisioning Israel*. 81-116.

He Walked Through the Fields/Hu Halach Be'Sadot. Dir. Yoseph Millo. 1967. Film.

Land of Promise/Lechayim Hadashim. Dir. Judah Leman. 1934. Film.

Loshitzky, Yosefa. *Identity Politics on the Israeli Screen.* Austin: Texas UP, 2001. Print.

Mort, Jo-Ann and Gary Brenner. *Our Hearts Invented a Place: Can Kibbutzim Survive in To-day's Israel?* Ithaca and London: Cornell UP, 2003. Print.

My Father's House/Beit Avi. Dir. Herbert Kline. 1947. Film.

Near, Henry. *The Kibbutz Movement: A History.* Vol. 1. Oxford: Oxford University Press, 1992. Print.

Ne'eman, Judd. "The Fields of Dominant Fiction." *Sadan—Studies in Hebrew Literature—Battle Cry and the Morning After*. Eds. Hannah Naveh and Menda-Levy Oded. Vol 5. Tel Aviv University, 2002. 401-415 (Hebrew), from author's copy, in English translation. Print.

Out of Evil/Mi Klalah Le Brachah. Dir. Joseph Krumgold. 1950. Film.

Sarna, Jonathan D. "A Projection of America as it Ought to Be: Zion in the Mind's Eye of American Jews." Gal. *Envisioning Israel*. 41-59. Print.

Sontag, Susan. *Regarding the Pain of Others*. NY: Farrar, Straus and Giroux, 2003. Print.

They Were Ten/Hem Hayu Asarah. Dir. Baruch Dienar. 1960. Film.

This is the Land/Zot Hi Ha'Aretz. Dir. Baruch Agadati. 1935. Film.

Tomorrow's a Wonderful Day. Dir. Dr. Siegfried Lehmann. 1949. Film.

Tryster, Hillel. "The Land of Promise: A Case Study in Zionist Film Propaganda—1935," *Historical Journal of Film, Radio and Television* 15:2 (June 1995): 187-217. Print.

Whitfield, Stephen J. "Israel as Reel: The Depiction of Israel in Mainstream American Films." Gal. *Envisioning Israel*. 293-318.

Janet Burstein, Drew University

Shall Japheth Dwell in the Tents of Shem?:

Hellenisms and Hebraisms in Selected American Jewish Literature

Lew Fried

I

There is an often emotionally charged movement in the American Jewish novel: an enduring recoil from the worship and making of literal and metaphorical idols— whether of gods, or ideologies, or cultures. Such a response illuminates either the protagonist's or writer's comportment with Judaism, certainly with its foundational texts and commentary, such as Torah and Talmud. Often, when these seminal works are mostly forgotten by Jews, an aversion to idols remains.

I propose that we look at *rejections* of *idolatries* and examine their presence in several seminal works that span some 125 years: Emma Lazarus's "Venus of the Louvre" (1884); Milton Steinberg's *As a Driven Leaf* (1939); and Philip Roth's *The Human Stain* (2000). I shall focus specifically on their presentation of the conflicts between Jerusalem and Athens: the former, a metaphor for the keeping of the Law; the latter, a metonym for the often described idolizing and idolatrous free-spirited psyche of Greece and Rome. Foundational Judaic texts such as the Mishnah's *Avodah Zarah* (the worship of idols, approx. 200 CE), Matthew Arnold's "Hebraism and Hellenism" in his *Culture and Anarchy* (1869), and Heinrich Heine's understanding of the "matter of Greece" in his reflections as well as "The Gods of Greece" (1826) provide an indispensable background.

Each of the above mentioned works by Lazarus, Steinberg, and Roth offers readers a different perspective on Hellas and Hebraism as well as dissimilar paganisms and Judaisms, suggesting the flexibility of the terms and their strategic uses. Theologically, these "cities" of Jerusalem and Athens are as distant as Scripture from sculpture; historically, they frame, for example, the Talmudic dialogue of the imagined Jew with the scoffing Hellene; aesthetically, they convey the pull of Hellenism on the Jewish protagonist (or narrator). Nevertheless, for all of the Hebraic proscriptions against the primacy and worship of other gods, and for all of the Enlightenment's fury against superstition, and for all the secularization wrought by the culture of industrialization, the spirit of Hellas and the God of Jerusalem are strikingly alive, still commanding us.

Hebraism and Hellas have always had a homeland and a habitation (both material and spiritual): witness the politics of return to a homeland on the part of Zionists and the attractiveness of a sweet Diaspora for those who have chosen to live "outside the land" of Israel in what Orthodox rabbis would see as a Hellenic culture. Although these opposing positions are large and simplified, they give American Jewish literature its paradoxically variable character and strength in exploring the nature of freedom and the Jewish self.

Nevertheless, writing *between* Athens and Jerusalem is not the same as writing against Jerusalem or accepting Athens. In fact, this "middle distance" characterizes the classic challenges to faith. One can enjoy both a willing suspension of disbelief and of belief. In fact, one often holds in mind multiple interpretations and perspectives, including Socratic irony as well as Talmudic disputation. For with the abandonment of Jewish foundational texts and what can be called their coherent, binding discourse that identified the Jewish community of faith as characteristically an historical people, the American Jewish writer has been immersed in literatures that seem to have erased the presence of Hebrew Scriptures and Talmud. However, the aversion to idolatry is an identifiable response; it is there; we often *are* averse; we have possibly forgotten our traditions.

As a result, in order to understand part of American Jewish literary history and culture, in other words, ourselves, it is worth looking at the above mentioned works by Lazarus, Steinberg, and Roth to see how American Jewish writers define and redefine the varying attitudes toward Athens and Jerusalem. For have we ever stopped asking who we and our communities are? As a textual community so variously creative, what is our foundational culture?

II

Tanach (Hebrew Scriptures) is stringent in its prohibition of idolatry, but we should also pay attention both to the debates in *Avodah Zarah* about one's comportment with forms of idolatry as well as Rabbi Akiva's pronouncement in the Jerusalem Talmud's *Sanhedrin* (approx. sixth century CE). How should one read non-canonical works? Akiva argues that reading Homer is like reading a letter. Perhaps, we can conjecture, as a harmless pleasure; perhaps as an act in which no financial benefit is derived; certainly as an engagement with a text in which idolatry is not effaced, but our faith is not diminished, as stated in *Sanhedrin*, chapter 11, 90a.

Yet where are boundaries drawn? In Kehati's edition of *Avodah Zarah*, chapter 3, *Mishnah* 4 speaks, for example, about the fine lines between worship of images and the recognition of them. In the tract, Rabbi Gamliel, asked by Proclus why he was bathing in the bathhouse of Aphrodite, replies that he did not come into her place; she came into his. Of course, going to idols is one thing; finding them in the environment (natural or political) is another (39).

III

Matthew Arnold's "Hebraism and Hellenism" presents *the* Athens and Jerusalem engraved in modern letters. His categories are less poetic than therapeutic. Arnold hoped to tie a perfection of self to a perfection of culture in an industrialized, psychologically disabling society. He posed the issue in broad, dramatic strokes. Western civilization had been marked by the contributions of Hebraism and Hellenism. Arnold presented them—at least on the surface—as responses to authority and experience. Human nature expressed both, and the two had the realization of personality as either perfection or righteousness as their goal. Yet could human nature move beyond the barriers of Hebraism and Hellenism? "The uppermost idea with Hellenism," Arnold wrote, "is to see things as they really are; the uppermost idea with Hebraism is conduct and obedience." In one of the most memorable lines in *Culture and Anarchy* Arnold declared, "The governing idea of Hellenism is spontaneity of consciousness; that of Hebraism, strictness of conscience" (132).

Arnold's tropes of conscience and consciousness are categories of being. Hebraism and Hellenism characterize the frailties of a modern culture that looks either to Athens *or* to Jerusalem for a flourishing life; in other words, to metaphorical places that were homelands themselves of the displaced spirit. For Arnold, Hebraism and Hellenism, again metonyms for a culture unable to complete itself, *are* the point. Judaism opposed, as much as did Hellas, the completion of human nature.[1]

IV

Heine enters modern American Jewish letters through Emma Lazarus's translation of his poems and ballads, and it is because of him that Lazarus's "Venus of the Louvre" becomes yet more poignant. Lazarus's relationship to Heine was manifold. Aside from her translations of his work, her "Venus of the Louvre" served as the epigraph to her essay "Heine, the Poet" in *Century Magazine*, December, 1884. By virtue of influence and inspiration, Heine and Lazarus constitute a fairly modern tradition dealing with the poet who felt anguish that one had to choose giving homage to the gods or to God or to humankind. The works of both Lazarus and Heine raise the question of alliance, whether to the spirit of Hebraism or to Hellenism. Could the modern Jewish poet forsake the enchanting gods of Greece without a wistful gaze? Or, as Lazarus put it, by doing so, could the Jewish poet not suffer "Hebraic pain"?

In "Heine, the Poet," Lazarus made use of Arnold's distinction between Hebraism and Hellenism. Lazarus termed Heine "a Jew, with the mind and eyes of a Greek." The Greek Heine, "a creature of laughter and sunshine," was in "perpetual conflict" with "the somber Hebrew." She quoted Heine's apologia: "I see now that the Greeks were only beautiful youths, whilst the Jews were always men, and powerful, indomitable...even today" (210).

Revering Heine, Lazarus visited the "Venus of the Louvre" at whose pedestal Heine had fallen. Heine explained:

> It was in May, 1848, the last day I went out, that I took leave of my lovely idols whom I had worshipped in the time of my happiness. I crawled painfully as far as the Louvre, and I almost fainted away when I entered the lofty hall, where the ever-blessed Goddess of Beauty, our beloved Lady of Milo, stands upon her pedestal. I lay for a long time at her feet, and I wept so bitterly that even a stone would have pitied me. And indeed the goddess looked down upon me compassionately, yet at the same time so disconsolately, as if she would say: "Do you not see that I have no arms, and that I cannot help you." (qtd. in Lazarus, "Heine" 211)

Heine confronted Hellas in his remarkable poem, "The Gods of Greece," found in the second cycle of his "The North Sea Poems." The poem is worth looking at in relation to "Venus of the Louvre" because it informs both its sensibility and content. In Lazarus's moving translation, we have a "Full-blooming moon" providing a "daylight clearness, yet twilight enchantment." The moonlight illuminates clouds appearing as the deities of Greece, who once ruled the world with joy, but are now "supplanted and dead." Looking upon this pantheon in the heavens, the poet's gaze falls on one god and goddess after another. Aphrodite, once golden, is now silver. Appropriately, as Venus, she seems a "goddess-corpse / Venus Libitina!" the Venus of funerals and death. "For to me," Heine writes, "are the Greeks antipathetic, / And even the Romans are hateful" (266–68).

Heine's narrator is nonetheless deeply moved, and foreshadowing Nietzsche's condemnation of Christianity, he finds the Greek deities "supplanted" by "new, reigning, dolorous gods, / Mischief-plotters in the sheep's clothing of humility." Wishing to struggle for Greek gods "to shatter the new Temples," Heine also wants to sink to his knees, to supplicate them. Knowing that these ancient divinities looked with approval on those who prevail, yet were less generous than humans, Heine casts his lot with those who fail. Man "now takes the part / Of the gods who have been vanquished." In a quick turn, the gods disappear; the moon is concealed by "dark, advancing clouds." Yet the poet remains, hearing the cry of the sea and looking at the triumphantly appearing eternal stars (268-69).

Heine's "The Gods of Greece" invokes a culture equal to the poet's sensibility. The clustered themes—the transfiguring poetic imagination, the opposition between the old and the new gods, the poet's identification with the Greek gods, who are supplanted, as well as with those who affirm them—reveal a willfulness of the poetic imagination. Nevertheless, the gods of Hellas transfix Heine's imagination; they offer a vocabulary of the profane; they push the God of Hebrew Scripture out of the text. In fact, out of consideration.

There are few poems that so clearly repudiate the temptation to idolize art, to make it direct if not absorb one's life, than Lazarus's "Venus of the Louvre." This poem presents the Jewish writer's relationship to both a tradition and an individual talent. It is in part homage to Hellenism and to a torn Jewish consciousness. Heine is the mournful presence in Lazarus's "Venus of the Louvre." In Lazarus's eyes, Heine is both a poet, no longer sustained by the gods of Greece, and a Jew, who is enchanted by the radiance of an idol. Although the rabbis of the Talmud debated in *Avodah Zarah* whether one might enjoy looking at a statue or idol, in "Venus of the Louvre," Heine prostrates himself before the goddess. Lazarus writes that "I saw not her alone…But at her feet a pale, death-stricken Jew, / Her life adorer…" Unwilling to separate herself from Heine, Lazarus transforms a singular gaze to a communal one. This, she argues, is how Venus must be seen by the Jewish poet: in the company of one who has lived within the nations (*Poems* 210).

Venus, the "foam-born mother of Love," maimed by time, glistening "like a star," dazzles the narrator. Although "transfixed to stone, / Yet none the less immortal," Venus brings Heine before Lazarus's eyes. "Here *Heine* wept!" Lazarus writes, italicizing the poet's name, suggesting that it confers importance beyond that of Venus herself. "Here still he weeps anew," casting a shadow that shall neither lift nor move, "While mourns one ardent heart, one poet-brain, / For vanished Hellas and Hebraic pain." Is Lazarus talking about Heine or herself at this point, the ambiguous "one ardent heart"? Or is she collapsing her own and Heine's poetic sensibilities? Nevertheless, the narrator is no longer looking at Venus but at the weeping Heine (*Poems* 210).

In Lazarus's poem, the attraction of the forbidden reminds readers of the injunction against worshipping other gods. Yet both Lazarus and Heine found that the gods of Greece and the representations of Greek culture were essential to their imaginations, and essential again in terms of their opposition to "Hebraic" suffering. Is this the pain of the incomplete? The pain of legitimate denial? The suffering brought about by understanding the poet's submission to a poetic culture and its ancestry? Heine's "The Gods of Greece" is resignation to the thematic periodization of history: the God of Hebrew Scripture, the gods of Greece, of Rome, of Christianity—all mark an age and vie for one's allegiance and imagination. At yet another point in time, they contested each other, forming one of the tensions of present myth. One could not turn away. Nevertheless, Hellas could not only be abandoned, it could lose its enchantment. In Lazarus's "August Moon," Ralph, the "artist," in lines reminiscent of Heine's "The Gods of Greece," declaims that he sees "in place/ of Astarte's silver face,/ Or veiled Isis' radiant robe/Nothing but a rugged globe/ Seamed with awful rents and scars" (*Poems* 51).

If we turn to Steinberg's *As a Driven Leaf*, the confrontation between Athens and Jerusalem is literally a battle of the books: the Torah versus Euclid's *Geometry*. The novel presents faith and the assumptions of logic as warring texts and seemingly incompatible casts of mind. Both in the novel and in his essays, especially in his *Anatomy of Faith* (1960), Steinberg explored the conflict between faith and science. Induction as well as deduction depended upon accepting assumptions and hypotheses that, in the last analysis, could be challenged. Unsurprisingly, the quest for certainty, as Steinberg presents it, demands asking not only how one can see life steadily and completely, but also how one must adjust to the impossibility of achieving certainty. Ethical conceptions—for example the dignity of humanity—are not self-evident, but are connected to faith in God. The answer in his essays and his novel is that one can have "firmness of opinion." Elisha, the protagonist of *As a Driven Leaf*, is given a correlate: firmness of doubt (Steinberg 103).

In reimagining Elisha ben Abuyah, a rabbi portrayed in Jewish tradition as a harmful, tragic apostate, Steinberg also creates the typologies of Hellas and Jerusalem. Yet in *As a Driven Leaf*, it is not so much the spontaneity of consciousness that makes the spirit of Hellas what *it* is, but rather the nature of its wisdom. It is not so much love of God, but serene resignation to the Law, protecting the believing self, that makes the spirit of Jerusalem what *it* is. Steinberg writes of the dialogue between logician and believer. Rabbi Johanan ben Zaccai [sic] describes the closed circle that Elisha will dedicate his life to opening: "There is no Truth without Faith. There is no Truth unless first there be a Faith upon which it is based" (13).

Tracing Elisha's loyalties to Hellenic culture and to that of the sages, Steinberg gauges the pressure that Rome and Jerusalem exert upon Elisha's psyche and travels. The novel opens with Rabbi Gamliel addressing the members of the large Sanhedrin and asking if a faithful Jew might learn "the tongue of the Greeks?" (11). The debate moves back and forth between the claims of reason and faith. Can a rational worldview be established without faith, without faith in something?

Excommunicated because of his denial of God (in reality, the proof of God and His justice) and a world explainable by Judaism, Elisha travels to Antioch, the cosmopolis of the novel. A polyglot city of glittering prizes, Antioch drives Elisha deeper into the attractions of Hellas. Yet Elisha is exposed to its underside: disbelief and irony violate his spirit. He is repulsed by the cruelty of the stadium, its bloodlust, and its loss of psychological boundaries making for dignity. Plato had argued that the good man only dreams of what the evil man does. Steinberg retorts with a grand, Tolstoyan question, marking Elisha's own perplexities: how can people do these things? Although his almost repressed character is seduced by pleasure, his temperament is driven paradoxically to ground belief in doubt. In the large company of skeptics, cynics, Stoics, and more, Elisha discovers that Hellas offers no more certainty than does Jerusalem. It provides him with more boundaries to be crossed. His choices seem to make him less than he originally was, but it is his struggle that makes him a type.

One can argue that the novel has as its armature Socrates's chariot of the psyche, but just as importantly, the book conveys the struggle between the impulse for good and the impulse for evil. In fact, the love for Hebraic tradition and human security shines through while Steinberg dramatizes the Talmudic love of argument and of matching assertion against prooftext. Elisha, who is so intent upon discovering a foundation for truth, extends that faith to the possibility of an answer, not understanding that the rational universe may collapse under the need for certainty. Although this too is not merely a Jewish problem, Steinberg reminds readers of its difference from Arnold's Hebraism and Hellenism. When their assumptions are revealed, each indicates the questionable importance of the other as the model for human nature and conduct.

The novel concludes that we have to accept indeterminacy, a willingness to believe in some assumptions in order to live and to mature. Steinberg's essays suggest the hard-won conciliation between description and interpretation, between the laws of nature and the claims of ethics—if we wish to conduct our lives with some measure of security. Elisha denies himself this recognition. Whereas Lazarus's persona in "Venus of the Louvre" could look upon the consummate embodiment of the Hellenic imagination, she does cast her lot with "Hebraic pain." For Elisha, neither Hellas nor Jerusalem is satisfactory, but the novel suggests that it is Elisha who cannot reconcile himself to the human condition. Hellas is the assumption upon which logic rests; Jerusalem, the assumptions of faith and ethics. Hellas is not the worship of statues, but the beckoning of "Greek" science; Jerusalem, the commitment to one's national culture and faith: in this case, freedom, love, and respect.

In yet another version of Athens and Jerusalem, *The Human Stain* offers readers a notion of Jerusalem and Hellas that owes much to Jewish commentary and classical Greek literature. The narrator, Nathan Zuckerman, is now in retreat, living in a cabin in the Berkshires, enduring the calamities of aging. His wife's death, his prostate cancer, his incontinence, and his weariness with the world lead to his willing exile. In the Berkshires, he is now near the center of a self-proclaimed American Greece, Athena College.

At Athena readers meet Coleman Silk, an African-American posing as a Jew, whose intellectual life is the teaching of the classics. Pushed out of Athena, Coleman, a former dean, is livid. Yet, there is more: he, too, suffers from the ruination of age. His wife is dead; he is estranged from his children. He is in love with the spirit of Greece, sensual—enraged—and erotic Faunia Farley. Called Voluptas and Helen of Troy by Coleman, Nathan describes her "like Coleman's Greeks. Like their gods" who rage and murder and hate" (Roth 242).

Nathan's allusions to the wrath of Achilles, the rage of Philoctetes, Coleman's hubris and fury, all are situated within the very structure of Greek epic. Nathan writes that Mark Silk, Coleman's "angry" son, after saying kaddish for his father, cannot believe that his father is not alive to hate yet again, as though the drama of Coleman's life were to be performed on the "southern hillside of the Athenian acropolis," in a theater dedicated to Dionysus, the dramatic unities being observed and a catharsis produced (Roth 314).

We can think of the arguments so lovingly put in the Mishna's *Pirkei Avot* (the *Ethics of the Fathers*) that one of the pillars of the world is the study of Torah, and that one must not separate one's self from the community. Judaism transforms Greek and Roman heroics: piety preserves community. For Roth and for Nathan Zuckerman, the narrator, one chooses Yavneh, the center granted by the Romans to Johanan ben Zakkai, who began the arduous practice of preserving Judaism outside Jerusalem, and not the justifiable, military resistance of either Bar Kochba or the Maccabees. Rejected, most importantly for the novel, is the brutality marking Hellenic culture.

Although the *The Human Stain* reflects Hellas's spirit of anger, eros, and pacification of the gods, the book is *aggadah* in the subjunctive: a Jewish homily upon Greek ferocity, expounding the hope that justice *might* prevail, that righteousness *could* be pursued—in spite of Hellenic culture. For all of this, the novel becomes Nathan's exercise in holding both Athens and Jerusalem in his mind, as if these were ironies believed in but to which one was not committed without agony.

For Nathan battles to recount, if not imagine, Silk's naiveté: he was charged as a racist after using the word "spooks" to refer to absent students, who, it turns out, are black. He means ghosts. He cannot reveal his innocence in using the term without belittling his strenuously created identity. As if to compound the situation, he has locked horns with Delphine, a spouter of French post-modernist jargon. What comic humans live in Roth's house? Coleman, a former boxer, now pretending to be Jewish, and expounding the classics? Faunia, who poses as an illiterate? Nathan, living in the fantasy of the pastoral, far away from the urban life that created his recognition of representative American frailties and dreams?

Nathan's sensibilities are his strength: he bears witness, recounting moral betrayal. His task is to mourn as well as to judge by virtue of his powerlessness. Readers ought to look at him as the waning Jewish conscience, someone rootless, living a would-be pastoral life yet searching for an authoritative frame of reference that his novel cannot provide. He is, sadly, a Jewish man of letters whose potency is so much on the wane that readers find it both poignant and comic when Coleman turns him into a dancing partner. Yet his novel, his story, is his judgment.

V

By recreating the Hellenic temper, or rather, the spirit of Hellas, American Jewish literature lays bare the conundrum of its authors—trembling before the holy but also before the vocation of being human, of being, as one says, a *mensch*. Since when is being human not the Law? And since when is the Law not without the agony of faith? Are these questions not found resonating in Abraham's "*Hineni*"? Do these questions form an overwhelming paradox for American Jewish writers who often admit that they write inside a Hellenism—outside Judaism's theology—but yet evoke praise for their enduring, renascent Jewish imagination?

Notes

1.   My discussion of Arnold has been published in a fuller variation as "Creating Hebraism, Confronting Hellenism." *The American Jewish Archives Journal* LII, 1 & 2 (2001): 147-74.

Works Cited

Avodah Zarah . Ed. and trans. Pinhas Kehati. Jerusalem: Department for Torah Education and Culture in the Diaspora of the World Zionist Organization, 1987. Print.

Arnold, Matthew. *Culture and Anarchy*, Ed. J. Dover Wilson. Cambridge: Cambridge University Press,1966. Print.

Heine, Heinrich. *Poems & Ballad*. Ed. and trans. Emma Lazarus. New York: Permagiants, 1950. Print.

Lazarus, Emma. *Emma Lazarus, Selected Poems*. Ed. John Hollander. N.p: Library of America, 2005. Print.

———. "The Poet, Heine," *Century Magazine*. 29 (Dec. 1884): 210-17. Print.

Roth, Philip. *The Human Stain*. New York: Vintage, 2001. Print.

"Sanhedrin." Jerusalem Talmud quoted in "Sanhedrin" of Babylonian Talmud. Ed. and trans. H. Freedman. London: Soncino Press, 1969. Print.

Steinberg, Milton. *Anatomy of Faith*. New York: Harcourt, Brace, 1960.

———. *As a Driven Leaf*. New York: Behrman House, 1996. Print.

Lew Fried, Kent State University

Kaddish—

The Final Frontier

Sara R. Horowitz

The depiction of Jewish ritual on American television stands out from ordinary TV fare. Not surprisingly, since its early popularization the culture of television in America has been vaguely Christian. Vaguely, because television programs depict a fairly secularized culture, with religion often left unstated and unobtrusive; Christian, because the dominant culture in America is Christian, and thus need not be specified. Religious markers, when they appear in the course of regular television series, are Christian, and their use implies the presumption of an audience that grasps the set of meanings associated with them—for example, the Christmas tree and carols linked with peace, love, and coming together. Jewish ritual, when it appears, puts into relief the Christianness of TV-land. Jewish difference makes apparent the unstated but presumed Christianity, and at the same time, it highlights the general absence of the Other. Infrequent enough to warrant attention, these televised moments of Judaism and Jewishness raise complex questions about the nature of the American multiculture, and the negotiation of ethnic, national, and religious identities, through the prism of Jewish exclusion and belonging.

The last two decades of the twentieth century brought greater diversity to the screen and an increased number of identifiably Jewish characters as regulars on television series.[1] While situation-comedies play on popular stereotypes (such as the Jewish princess, the Jewish mother, the effeminate Jewish man), television dramas examine a set of issues relating to Jewish identity through the portrayal of the enactment of Jewish ritual. As presented on American television, these rituals mix the familiar with the alien, the ordinary with the exotic. Rare but never entirely absent, the function of televised Jewish ritual—particularly life cycle ritual—has shifted over time. Life cycle ritual—marking such events as birth, puberty, marriage, and death—couples the emotional charge universally inherent to those events with particular cultural signifiers that are also emotionally charged. Part of the impact of these events obtains from the momentous life-changes that such rituals mark. Each life-cycle ritual represents a transition from one phase to another, symbolically resolving a liminal state. Birth is, after all, not only the beginning of the independent life of the infant, but also the beginning of a new phase for the adult who becomes a parent, shifting from man to father or woman to mother. Marriage similarly connotes the passage from single life to couplehood, and the transition from man to husband, or woman to wife. Death, the end of life, is, for mourners, the termination of a particular relationship with the deceased, and the concomitant change in self definition—for example, from the child of a parent to an orphan, or from a wife to a widow. Rituals focalize, carry, and discharge emotional excess. Their public nature is essential. Whether love, loss, grief, or some combination, the presence of community makes public a private state.

There is, of course, an element of artifice enfolded into life cycle events, in that ritual poses as a moment of clear transition, a resolution of liminality, a sharp division of phases whose boundaries in actuality are fuzzy. For example, even before birth, during pregnancy, parents already engage in the functions of parenthood—protection, nurturance, even education; a pregnant woman might refrain from alcoholic beverages, take special care with nutrition, play specially chosen music in proximity to the fetus. Once born, a child is still not fully "cooked," cannot be sustained without a committed caregiving adult. Parental identity, moreover, happens over time. Similarly, the loss of a parent often happens over time, the process beginning well before death and continuing long after; the relationship with an aging parent may become inverted, with the child "parenting" the parent, and the dynamics of that relationship may be ongoing and concurrent with bereavement. Thus, the emotional charge of rituals that mark such events emerges not so much because of some sense of their "importance," but because of the complexity of these transitions and their lack of clear resolution. This enduring liminality points to an instability of identity. Thus, Jewish tradition, like other cultures, has viewed life cycle events not only as celebratory, but also as dangerous. Custom and folktales mandate that special care be taken to safeguard the person at point of passage—whether the neonate from Lilith or the bride from demons or the unburied dead from evil spirits. Because dramatized ritual negotiates not merely life events, but also Jewish American identity, the element of danger associated with rites of passage relates also to the instability of Jewish identity in America. While life cycle events correspond to the human in general terms, the rituals that mark them are culturally specific, particularistic, and enmeshed with a wider set of cultural values. The scripted choice to enact them, refuse them, change them, or deny them works with or against cultural expectations, and results in visual images laden with implications.

In the earlier decades of television, Jewish ritual, on the infrequent occasions when it was dramatized, often functioned didactically. Showing viewers how Jews mourn, marry, or mark the birth of a child, these televised enactments of ritual both illustrated Jewish difference from the dominant culture, and at the same time, erased that difference by showing that, at heart, all Americans are alike. Moved by the same human events and emotions, "all of us" celebrate or lament in our own particular way, but the values that underlie the rituals are shared ones. Scenes of Jewish ritual opened a window onto what for many viewers was the unknown. In so doing, they served to demystify, domesticate, and absorb Jewish practice into the American continuum, neutralizing the danger posed by an alien Other. They served up a taste of the exotic that ended up diffusing the exoticism.

If dramatized Jewish ritual in an earlier era of television created "teachable moments" designed to bring to a wide audience information about what Jews do, the past twenty-five years used ritual to engage vexed issues of identity. Television programming of earlier decades presented Jews enacting Jewish practices; by the 1990s, programs present the ambivalence of modern Jews struggling with the place of Jewish ritual in their lives as well as their own place in America. Whereas once, the fact that life cycle events are both American and Jewish negated the otherness of the Jews, in more contemporary shows the possibility for ritual performance presents choices that throw identity into crisis. Televised ritual becomes something other than a display that affirms Jewish belonging to the American mainstream. Jewish characters must decide between specifically Jewish or more generically American ways of being. As major characters of television dramas, Jews in the last quarter century of programming have been defined largely secularly, ethnically, by origin rather than by practice. They reflect, in fact, the broad and shifting demographics of an acculturated, Americanized Jewish population that no longer lives in Jewish neighborhoods, no longer selects primarily Jewish friends, lovers, or spouses. Thus, it may be both expected and yet not a foregone conclusion that life events will be commemorated Jewishly. One might say, as well, that the need to mark life events effectively outs Jews who had been passing.

In analyzing the significance of liminality in religious ritual, Victor Turner observes an intensification of identity performances at times of cultural crisis or re-integration. In times of intense or rapid social change, people become more aware of the instability of identity and of communal boundaries. "Ritual and drama involves selves, not self," Turner notes (25). Examining the ways in which performance, and in particular, the performance of ritual, operates on the "threshold," he points to the role of ritual in enacting and then resolving liminality, or in-betweenness. In their introduction to *Insider/Outsider: American Jews and Multiculturalism*, David Biale, Michael Galchinsky, and Susannah Heschel refer to an enduring self-perception of American Jews that they occupy fundamentally a "liminal zone," an "anomalous status: insiders who are outsiders and outsiders who are insiders ... a boundary case whose very lack of belonging to a recognizable category creates a sense of unease" (5). Vincent Brook points to the "constructed and highly contested nature of Jewish identity" as crucial in explaining the proliferation of Jewish characters on televisions sitcoms beginning in the late 1980s (1). Linking this development with "a complex negotiation of assimilationist and multiculturalist pressures specific to the American Jewish experience, Brooks observes that although it appears to be "a breakthrough in Jewish representation," it also signals "a renewed crisis in Jewish identity formation." The tension between assimilation into the dominant American culture, on the one hand, and maintaining Jewish distinction, on the other, disrupts the "delicate balance between the senses of 'sameness' and of 'otherness'" inherent to construction of Jewish American identity (2). The dynamics that Brooks identifies in television sitcoms work themselves through TV drama, as well. Turner makes clear the potential of ritual not only to anchor but also to destabilize, and thus to make visible the dynamic aspect of culture. Performances challenge what have been perceived as fixed norms, destabilizing the boundaries between insider and outsider, belonging and exclusion. At some level, these dynamics denaturalize the sense of both communal and individual identity, revealing complicated sets of interactions between individuals and their chosen communities. Even at it asserts a claim of cultural stability, ritual performance at such liminal moments as life cycle events also reveals the provisional nature of inside and outside, challenging these binary categories. In the dramatized enactment of ritual on television, the liminality at the heart of life event rituals is layered onto the inbetweenness of cultural identity and communal belonging, becoming both a metaphor for and an instance of the negotiation of multiple, hybrid, and conflicting identities.

All life cycle rituals have the potential to engage this nexus of issues relating to identity and community. Indeed, the choices of intermarriage and of circumcision have functioned as the crux of story arcs on a range of TV dramas. But mourning rituals—the shiva, Kaddish, and related rites—are a particularly fruitful focus of exploration. Rituals to mourn the dead mark a connection to the ancestral past, on both an individual and a communal level, linking an inherited tradition with the bereaved and with oneself. But unlike a birth ritual—a circumcision or naming ritual that initiates an infant into the community of Israel—mourning rituals make no promise to the Jewish future. They may assert a continued identification with Jewishness or Judaism, or they may simply function as a coda to the past.

The motif of Kaddish has a strong presence in Jewish American literature. Hana Wirth-Nesher has observed the ways in which "Jewish American fiction has tended to treat the Kaddish as a signifier of the 'essence' of Judaism or Jewishness, as a ritual untouched by the process of assimilation or accommodation" (Magnified 122). An ancient liturgical formula that praises and glorifies God and prays for the reestablishment of God's kingdom on earth, whose public recitation is noted in the Talmud, the Kaddish is in Aramaic, an ancient Semitic tongue central to rabbinic discourse. A particular version of the Kaddish, which came to be termed Mourner's Kaddish, or *Kaddish yatom* (literally: orphan's Kaddish), first came into use during the thirteenth century as a prayer to be recited by close relatives of someone who has died, particularly (although not exclusively) by children of the departed.[2] Even—or perhaps especially—in secularized and assimilated contexts, Wirth-Nesher notes that the recitation of Kaddish functions as "a recurrent sign of collective memory and Jewish identity, a religious text turned marker of ethnic origin" (Magnified 123). The dramatized mourning rituals of recent television programming locates itself within the context of this literary history and gestures toward antecedents in Jewish American literature.

Moreover, unlike other life cycle rituals, recitation of the Kaddish necessitates community; *halakha* (Jewish law) requires that it be recited in the presence of a quorum of ten Jews. Thus the mourners needs an actual Jewish community, which may or may not overlap with, but is rarely identical with, the community in which they live, socialize, and work. In televised story arcs relating to the Kaddish and other mourning rituals, the death of relatives catch characters where they live, literally and symbolically. In order to enact the ritual, the bereaved are forced to examine who they are, where they live, what they identify with or against. The mourners of television dramas often live far from synagogues or are at odds with them, and are sometimes geographically far from other Jews. In that sense, Kaddish is a final frontier, final in its association with death, but also as ultimate arena of identity.

The irony of a mourning ritual serving as an emblem of cultural continuity is not lost on cultural critics. Wirth-Nesher, for example, points out that "It is ironic that the generation writing under the sign of cultural difference and aiming to renew its Jewish identity has focused so heavily on a prayer that marks death" (Language 222). The tenacity of the Kaddish, and particularly its hold on Jews distanced from religious practice, community, and knowledge, can be attributed to the elemental ties between parents and children, to the folk belief that its recitation can redeem a parent's soul, to its assertion of the glory of God and creation even at moments of despair. As depicted on television, the pull of Jewish bereavement rituals is motivated, as well, by contemporary ideas of relationships and mourning, such as making peace with a complicated and troubled bond, fulfilling obligations to other mourners or to the dead, or acknowledging and coping with the randomness of death. Tropes of forgiveness, reconciliation, and redemption frequently are invoked. Ritual performances, like theater, entail release, catharsis, letting go of repressed emotions.

Three episodes from television dramas of the late 1980s and 1990s can serve to illustrate the dynamic of mourning in its encounter with Jewish identity and acculturation in the American multiculture. The episodes are drawn from *Thirtysomething, Northern Exposure, and Babylon 5*, and each episode turns on the enactment of a Jewish mourning ritual. Each of these three series might be said to explore a new frontier.

Thirtysomething, which ran on ABC between 1987 and 1991, combined social realism and innovative style in a way that was new to television, examining the everyday life, relationships, ideals, failures, and disappointments of a group of introspective young professionals in their thirties living in Philadelphia. *Northern Exposure*, which ran on CBS from 1990 to 1995, followed the exploits of a Jewish doctor from New York compelled to practice in a remote village in Alaska. *Babylon 5*, which ran on TNT,[3] after its 1993 pilot, from 1994 to 1998, is a science fiction drama set in a space station between the years 2257 and 2262. Each of the three series contains an episode in which a Jewish character confronts the desire or obligation to enact a Jewish mourning ritual in a situation where doing so presents difficulties that are both pragmatic and psychological. In each episode, the resolution of these difficulties offers a renegotiation of identity as Jews and Americans. Rather than the clear "sign of ... Jewish identity" that Wirth-Nesher observes in Jewish American fiction, Kaddish and Jewish mourning in these television dramas break down polarities between Jewish and Gentile, belonging and exclusion, insider and outsider. Boundaries flex, identities are revealed as fluid and multiple. In mapping Jewish bereavement, these episodes show the anxieties of earlier generations giving way to new possibilities. What might it mean, they ask, to be Jewish in America in the last two decades of the twentieth century?

In "The Mike Van Dyke Show" episode, which ran in the second season of *Thirtysomething*, and originally aired just before Christmas, Michael Steadman, a Jewish advertisement copywriter, struggles with whether and how an intermarried, assimilated, secular Jew should ritually mark the unveiling of his father's gravestone. One of the series' principal characters, Steadman was the first Jewish regular major character on an American television drama series (Zurawik 105). *Thirtysomething* follows Steadman, his family, and network of friends, a group of young Philadelphians, as they contend with careers and relationships, using both the details of everyday life and the push of intermittent catastrophes, to explore issues of meaningfulness for the generation coming of age in late twentieth century America. Steadman is married to Hope Murdoch, a Protestant, and the couple has a daughter, Janey. The "Mike Van Dyke" episode negotiates the question of Jewish identity for Steadman through his grappling with two sets of religious rituals, one connected with Christmas and the other with properly (that is to say, Jewishly) mourning his father. Will the Steadman home have a Christmas tree, and will Steadman recite the Kaddish in his father's memory? In what is presented as an ongoing annual debate in the Steadman household, Hope wants a Christmas tree in their home, and Michael vetoes it. The tree represents a point of pressure that throws into crisis the cultural balance of their marital economy. Intermarriage and dual-heritage children destabilize boundaries. As the show presents it, two people may maintain individual religious identities even in marriage. At the same time, the Christmas tree dilemma suggests that in a shared household, one religion must dominate: there either will or will not be a tree. The Christmas tree debate coincides with the unveiling of Steadman's father's gravestone, and the family expectation that he will recite the Jewish prayer. Yet, he wonders, as an assimilated nonbeliever, how can he do so with integrity? Does not the very fact of his marriage to Hope disqualify him? In other words, in collision with another religion, Steadman's Jewishness comes into relief and demands a presence. He wishes to assert and protect his Jewish identity, his otherness in a dominant culture that is Christian. In dialogue with itself, however, Steadman's Jewishness falters on the question of belief in Judaism, adherence to its practices, and membership in its community. Has he, in effect, walked out of his Jewish identity, sloughed it off, left it behind?

While the fact of the Steadman-Murdoch intermarriage casts Michael as assimilated, Americanized, and removed from Judaism except as a place origin, Christmas brings the two distinct religious traditions into apparent conflict. In the episode's opening scene, Michael and Hope exchange pointed comments on what each considers the absurdities of the other's religion—he the miracle of the Nativity and the virgin birth, she the miracle of Chanukah and the drop of oil that burns for eight days. The Steadman household is placed in a sort of religious limbo, at the same time that the inconsistencies of Michael's Jewish identity come to the forefront. One function of religious ritual, as Turner observes, is precisely to address such liminality, to solidify and stabilize identity and belonging.

A twist of the plot seemingly unrelated to either point of conflict brings both issues to resolution. Hope and Janey go missing for several hours. Eventually Steadman learns that they have been involved in an auto accident, and that Hope may be gravely ill. Given the situation, Steadman decides to cancel his flight to his father's unveiling. It turns out that both wife and daughter are safe, and, in fact, Hope is pregnant. But as Steadman's anxieties mount awaiting word of them, he fantasizes that he is the lead character on "The Mike Van Dyke Show," based on the 1960s situation comedy *The Dick Van Dyke Show*, and his fears play themselves out through that medium. Moreover, without the graveside ritual giving a context that might make the recitation of the Kaddish acceptable to Steadman, he is left only with the possibility of reciting it at a nearby synagogue. Far from the cemetery, the engagement with Jewish liturgy seems more connected to religious faith and communal identity than with individualized bonds of kinship. In the end, the possibility that Steadman might lose his family suddenly and catastrophically resolves both issues that have been central to the episode. Steadman realizes that he loves Hope intensely and wants to make her happy—and so will allow the disputed Christmas tree—and also that he believes in the existence of God, and so feels comfortable reciting the Kaddish.

"The Mike Van Dyke Show" episode takes the question of Jewish American identity in an interesting direction. That this issue is at the crux of both the Christmas tree and the Kaddish dilemmas is clear. Steadman's resolution of the tree debate seems unsatisfactory. One might argue that just as Michael concludes that making his wife happy trumps barring the tree, Hope might just as well conclude that making her husband happy should trump having a tree, leaving them in the same situation in which they began, an updated and multicultural version of O. Henry's famous Christmas story, "The Gift of the Magi." But it is Jewish American identity, and not Protestant identity, that has been put to crisis. Michael, and not Hope, worries about belonging to the multiple groups that constitute the hyphenated or hybrid sense of who he is and where he belongs. For American Jews, setting up a Christmas tree has long been a potent symbol of Jewish acculturation or assimilation. The absence of a tree is often perceived as a token of Jewish resistance to the dominant culture. On the other hand, the Christmas tree has also been viewed as a neutral or secular emblem of a seasonal holiday removed from its religious origins, linked with gifts and family, but not with crucifixion or resurrection, different from a crèche.[4] In buying a Christmas tree, Steadman allows that a home may have both a tree and a Chanukah menorah, that there is space for the religions or cultures of both partners. This suggests a realization that the presence of a Christian emblem, and marriage to a Christian wife, have no bearing on how one thinks of oneself. At the same time, acquiring a Christmas tree pushes Michael to acknowledge his difficulties with the place of Jewishness in his life. It is after purchasing the tree with his cousin Melissa that, while not denying his origins, he admits that Jewishness has long stopped figuring in any meaningful way in his sense of who he is. He muses, "What does it have to do with Little League, and the Beatles and getting girls to go to second? I don't know. It's more than that. It just stopped making sense." Michael reasons that precisely this dissociation made possible his marriage to Hope. If so, then the presence of a Christmas tree in his home symbolizes not so much the possibility for difference, but the reality of indifference.

It is this very indifference that creates an obstacle to mourning his father through Jewish ritual. Aside from his father's funeral, Steadman notes that he has not been in a synagogue since his adolescence. As Ronald Grimes observes, religious rituals are not merely communal and national, they are theological, broadly speaking, connecting participants with some transcendent being responding to human experience (Grimes). Steadman wishes to participate in rituals only if he finds them spiritually meaningful, not simply a link with nation or family or an ancestral but archaic faith. Even his realization, through his fears for Hope's safety, that he believes in God, does not resolve this issue for Steadman, because his belief is in a generalized divinity, not necessarily the God of the Jewish people. He muses to Melissa, "But which God, who God, where God?" For Steadman to attend communal synagogue prayer in order to recite the Kaddish for his father takes supernatural intervention, uncharacteristic of this realistic television drama. He first visits the synagogue at Melissa's urging; she has formed a bond with the young Rabbi Markovitz, and feels that Steadman might connect with him, as well. When Steadman comes to the synagogue, he opens the door of the sanctuary, but decides not to enter and pray. He turns to the rabbi's office, where he finds a Rabbi Markovitz, who is older than he had expected and, moreover, is played by the same actor who played a somewhat ominous Santa Claus in Steadman's Mike Van Dyke fantasy. A bit contentiously, the rabbi challenges Michael's Jewish identity, suggesting that he is an interloper in Jewish sacred space. Later that day, Steadman visits the synagogue once again looking for the rabbi. When a younger man identifies himself as Rabbi Markovitz, Steadman asks for the "other Rabbi Markovitz." But the synagogue has only one rabbi, and no explanation for the mysterious Rabbi/Santa is given. Declining the young rabbi's offer to talk, Steadman opens the door to the sanctuary where a service is being conducted, and enters just as the leader reaches the point where the Mourner's Kaddish is recited. There, for the first time, Steadman says Kaddish for his father.

The circumstances of Steadman's Kaddish affirm his Jewishness, notwithstanding the difficulties of faith and practice raised earlier in the episode. As Michael stands at the sanctuary door, the congregation recites the *Aleinu* prayer in Hebrew. *Aleinu*, like the Kaddish, affirms God's mastery and majesty over all creation. But unlike the Kaddish, *Aleinu* articulates a distinction between Jews and others. Ironically, after overcoming his resistance to acquiring a Christmas tree, Steadman finds himself drawn into a congregation of worshipers whose liturgy affirms the difference between Jewish worship of the true God and the false gods worshiped by the "nations of the lands" (*goyey ha-aratsot*), and the concomitant difference between Jews and the "multitudes" (*hamonam*). Both the aptness of this prayer as a pivot point for Steadman's acknowledgment of his Jewishness, and its irony when juxtaposed with his bicultural household and group of close associates, may well be unintended. Non-Jewish and most Jewish viewers would not likely understand the contents of this prayer. After concluding the *Aleinu*, the leader introduces the Kaddish with the following words: "In solemn testimony to that unbroken faith which links the generations one to another, let those who mourn and those who have *yahrzeit* please rise to magnify the holy name." Not only is the significance of Steadman's participation in the prayer service in memory of his father articulated explicitly, but so are the terms of Steadman's engagement. His doubts notwithstanding, Steadman's Kaddish affirms faith in the Jewish God and an unbroken link with his ancestors.

Taken together, the resolution of the Christmas tree and the Kaddish dilemmas implies that Jewish identity is individual and enduring, related both to faith and family, and that it can not only survive, but thrive in an America of assimilation. While Christmas is represented by a home ritual (the tree and gifts) and Judaism by a communal one (Steadman does not recite the prayer alone), the necessary access to Jewish community for ritual purpose is available no matter what one's actual community of friends and relations. While later episodes of *Thirtysomething* will show Steadman exploring other spiritual possibilities, this early mediation of Jewish identity suggests that Jewish otherness and American likeness can coexist, and that the place of Judaism among the religions of America softens its difference into something parallel, contiguous, and contained.

If in the Mike Van Dyke episode of *Thirtysomething*, recitation of the Kaddish becomes the fulcrum of Steadman's identity as an assimilated and agnostic American Jew, in the "Kaddish, for Uncle Manny" episode of *Northern Exposure* it serves as the vehicle to explore the meaning of community in the mobile American multiculture. Set in the last American frontier, *Northern Exposure* follows the experiences and personal development of Joel Fleischman, a newly minted New York doctor who agrees to serve in Cicely, Alaska in order to repay medical school loans. Jewish and urbanized, he finds life in Cicely culturally alien. As the series progresses, he gets past the culture shock of small town life, its geographic isolation, remoteness from the mainstream, and the diverse and unfamiliar customs of its inhabitants. The unspoiled beauty of Alaska and the longstanding traditions of its native people come to stand for a lost innocence, the vitality and natural ethics of the last American frontier. If Fleischman senses his difference from other Cicely residents, it is a measure of his New Yorkness as much as his Jewishness. While urbanness and

Jewishness are frequently troped together, so much so that they often become synonymous in popular representations, here Fleischman is clearly intended to create a link with viewers. Coming from Queens, rather than "the City," he represents a middle ground between the cultural sophistication of Manhattan and the remoteness of Cicely, one with which geographically diverse viewers might identify.

In fact, the idea of Jewish otherness takes on a different dimension in Cicely, portrayed as a veritable land of otherness, a place where no one is Other because everyone is. As Esther Romeyn and Jack Kugelmass observe in their analysis of the television series, Christianity is not central to *Northern Exposure*'s America. Instead, they note, "different cultural perspectives interpellate each other" and the "acceptance of difference is an underlying ethic of the show" (260). In some measure, this works because there is no dominant culture demanding absorption and exclusive allegiance. In order for Cicely to function as an emblem of the American multiculture, the cultural identity of each of its inhabitants is presented as a given, fixed and stable. Thus, although none of his Cicely friends are Jewish, Fleischman's identity as a Jewish American is never shown to be conflicted. Unlike Steadman in *Thirtysomething*, Fleischman never sets up a Christmas tree in his home, and would not marry a non-Jewish woman. His geographic distance from his family of origin and ethnic neighborhood comes about because of economic pressure and not out of feelings of alienation, rejection, or disconnection.

In the "Kaddish, for Uncle Manny" episode, which ran in the fourth season of *Northern Exposure*, Fleischman has learned of the death of his Uncle Manny, with whom he had a close and loving relationship. Manny had no children of his own, Fleischman explains to his friends, "so he kind of adopted me." Although situated too far to be able to come home for Manny's funeral, in the absence of any children to say Kaddish for his uncle, Fleischman undertakes to do so. The requirement to recite the Kaddish in a minyan, or quorum of ten Jewish men, and the absence of other Jews in Cicely, complicate the idea of multicultural community and its relationship to identity and difference. If *Northern Exposure* presents national, religious, or ethnic identity as an individual matter, with a diverse range of individuals peaceably and respectfully comprising a multicultural society, the obligation of Kaddish threatens to reveal the limitations of this idealized mosaic. "I don't know where I'm gonna find a minyan," Fleischman frets. While the people of Cicely are accustomed to a variety of traditional practices, the need for other Jews to form a minyan forces the question of whether individual Jewish identity is a viable concept outside of Jewish community.

The Kaddish episode provides the opportunity to serve two purposes: to explain a Jewish practice as consonant with American values, and to recalibrate the meaning of community for Jewish Americans. The didactic aim of televised Jewish ritual associated with earlier programming is recapitulated here, as Alaskan friends ask Fleischman, "What's Kaddish?" and "What's a minyan?" Consonant with the validation of native traditions as a source of wisdom and integrity on *Northern Exposure*, the inhabitants of Cicely resolve to help Fleischman fulfill his obligation by finding the necessary Jews to make the minyan. Their comments place the Jewish mourning ritual on the continuum of American practices, domesticating it by providing contemporary explanations—for example, "The minyan thing is so that the mourner doesn't go it alone." The search for Jews within traveling range becomes a means for *Northern Exposure* to take on and then debunk American stereotypes about Jews. After all, the residents of Cecily wonder, how can one tell whether a person is Jewish? Everyone agrees that Jewish people "value family, tradition, education," a philosemitic set of attributes that resonate with the America that *Northern Exposure* imagines, and thereby makes Jews indistinguishable from their neighbors. They note that with circumcision common in America, it no longer serves as a marker for Jewishness. Nor is there a particular Jewish look, they observe, viewing a photograph of a Hassid with earlocks, something confirmed by the parade of Jews they bring in for Fleischman's minyan.

But the didactic thrust of the episode eventually gives way to the more contemporary negotiation of what it means to be a Jewish American. That this second purpose becomes the primary focus of "Kaddish, for Uncle Manny" becomes evident when considering what was left out of the episode. The excision of a long disquisition on the meaning and history of Kaddish, as delivered by two Cecily residents (and available as the outtakes on the season's DVD) undercuts the didactic potential of the episode. Instead, viewers see Fleischman working through the components of his own identity as a Jew. In a scene set in his cabin, Fleischman has taken out an assortment of Jewish paraphernalia that has accompanied him to the last frontier: a tallit, or prayer shawl, a yarmulka from Israel, photographs of his bar mitzvah, "some family stuff I never unpacked," he explains to his friend, pilot Maggie O'Connell, another immigrant from the lower forty-eight. He recollects the many hours spent learning the Torah portion for his bar mitzvah: "I don't remember any of it." The scene and its show-and-tell of Jewish memorabilia puts forth a Jewishness that, while not present in his everyday life, is part of his baggage, as it were. Useful or not, it accompanies him wherever he goes. His relationship with Jewishness is not the struggle with ambivalence that characterizes Michael Steadman in *Thirtysomething*, but a where-one-comes-from that is always quietly part of where and who one is.

The process of examining what it means to be Jewish that Fleischman begins by sorting through these Judaic artifacts triggers a dream sequence that interrogates the notion of community. On a Wild West set, Fleischman encounters a posse riding in on horseback: Jewish cowboys, a Jewish Indian, all wearing six-pointed badges. The dream brings him to a realization. "Why am I praying with these guys?" he wonders. "I don't feel I can say Kaddish with a bunch of hired guns." The community that a minyan constitutes, he decides, is an artificial one, thrown together to meet the technical requirements of Jewish tradition, but without depth or real cohesion. His feeling for his uncle is "a private thing," and he does not want to "open up" to total strangers. His actual community, he realizes, is composed of the people of Cecily; they form the appropriate fellowship in which to fulfill his obligation to his uncle. "I'm no rabbi," he tells his neighbors, "but it seems to me that the purpose of Kaddish is to be with your community. And what I realized this week is that you're my community." Gathering his Cecily neighbors together in the town hall, he enacts a mourning ceremony that both preserves Jewish particularity and opens it up to universal values and emotions. Donning his tallit and yarmulka, which visually mark him as Jewish, he gives a brief eulogy for his uncle, following the Jewish tradition of *hesped* (eulogy). Like the prayer leader in the *Thirtysomething* synagogue, Fleischman says a few words to introduce the mourner's prayer: "Maybe when I say the Kaddish you can think about someone in your own life who you love. And feel free to say a prayer in your own way if you like." While *Thirtysomething* places the prayer in the context of an unbroken Jewish tradition, *Northern Exposure* universalizes it. And, indeed, as he recites the Kaddish in Aramaic, the camera shifts from Fleischman to the others in the room, and viewers see them engrossed in their own prayers, eyes closed, visibly moved.

As *Northern Exposure* presents it, one's identity as a Jew travels wherever one goes, melding into the American landscape while still preserving its distinctiveness. For Jews, for natives, and for others, rituals provide an important connection with the ancestral roots that define who one is, but that do not restrict or encumber one's integration. As a Cecily inhabitant puts it in one of the episode's outtakes, "You do something that you don't understand because your ancestors did it." The challenge of performing a mourning ritual without the presence of other Jews leads to a reconsideration of the idea of community, which emerges not out of the accident of cultural heritage, but out of choice. The episode resonates with *Northern Exposure*'s focus on diversity and difference. The America it presents is a composite of people and peoples who maintain distinctiveness but also comprise a unified community. Jewish American identity does not hinge on Jewish community, but on one's internal relationship to an inherited tradition, and can be lived out anywhere and among anyone in America.

Both Steadman and Fleischman are pulled into the compass of Jewish ritual out of a sense of love and obligation to a father (or surrogate). They seek to do right by the dead in ways that would have been meaningful to him. In that context, it seems appropriate to reach back into a shared past and to affirm generational ties and ancestral traditions. While the impulse to ritually commemorate his father pushes Steadman to probe the implications of his life choices and their impact on his sense of himself as a Jew, Fleischman's redrawing the circle of community leaves his Jewishness intact and unquestioned. In different ways, the two men find that America can contain Jewish practice and that Jewish identity can accommodate itself to hybridization and atomization. In the "TKO" episode of *Babylon 5*, the barrier to ritual mourning is neither the complexity of Jewish identity nor the absence of community, but a strained relationship with the deceased father. Nonetheless, like the episodes of *Thirtysomething* and *Northern Exposure*, "TKO" explores the configuration of Jewish American identity in a society defined by mobility, diversity, and tolerance, where Jewish difference has become diffused.

Set in a remote space station in the twenty-third century, *Babylon 5* is a science fiction dramatic series that follows the adventures, intrigues, and conflicts among an interplanetary and interspecies set of characters brought together as "our last best hope," as the program's tag line phrases it, for peace through diplomacy and economic cooperation, while fighting an inter-galactic war. Although set in the future, like all science fiction *Babylon 5* raises contemporary issues. American ideas about multiculturalism are explored in the context of a space station that brings together not only humans of diverse national, racial, and ethnic origin, but also— and more importantly—a variety of non-human species. The humans are imagined as constituting a post-modern, post-multiculture, post-national society, where various backgrounds add dimension and flavor to characters, and shape their personal and political views, but do not serve as a basis for division or conflicting allegiance. Much as they do on other science fiction television series, humans comprise one people, one race. But the tensions, prejudices, and conflicts of our own era have not disappeared; they have simply been transferred to the arena of interspecies relations. Species comes to connote race and nation, with all that inheres in those terms. The space station and its inhabitants become the plane on which issues of otherness, tolerance, and integration are worked out, brought into the context of what another sci-fi series has termed "the final frontier."

The "TKO" episode, which was initially aired in the first season of *Babylon 5*, utilizes the series' general focus on cultural tolerance and integration to frame questions about Jewish identity in the American multiculture. In the episode, Lieutenant-Commander Susan Ivanova struggles with whether to sit shiva for her father. Ivanova is second in command at the space station. Born in St. Petersburg to a telepathic mother who committed suicide when Ivanova was a child, Ivanova felt isolated as her father withdrew emotionally. Eventually, Ivanova enlisted in the military, against her father's wishes. An earlier episode showed a deathbed conversation between Ivanova and her father, Andrei ("Born to the Purple"), a Russian professor whom she had not seen in years. Made possible by space link technology, the communication allowed the father to apologize for the deep strains in their relationship, and for Ivanova to witness his death and reconcile with him, albeit at a distance. At the time Ivanova chose to tell no one about her father's death or their conversation. "TKO" reveals that Ivanova is not only Russian, but also Jewish. The episode opens with the arrival of a space shuttle, whose passengers include Rabbi Koslov, an old friend of the family, whom Ivanova affectionately calls "Uncle Yossel." Koslov has taken his first space journey, it turns out, to bring to Ivanova—whom he calls Suzishka—a "legacy" from her father, a prized samovar. He quickly establishes that she has not observed the ritual mourning period for her father, that she has not sat shiva. The ensuing plot follows Koslov's attempts to persuade her to do so.

Just as the Kaddish episode presented an opportunity on *Northern Exposure* to explain a Jewish practice in ways attractive to viewers unfamiliar with it, Koslov's desire to engineer a shiva despite Ivanova's resistance enables *Babylon 5* to present Jewish mourning customs in terms consonant with the values of 1990s America.

When Ivanova dismisses the prospect of shiva with the claim that work demands do not allow her time for it, Koslov meets with the commander of Babylon 5 and explains Ivanova's complicated family history and the importance of shiva. He appeals not to the continuity of tradition, but to the psychological needs of the bereaved. Shiva allows "family, friends, members of the Jewish community [to] ... gather at the home of the bereaved to offer comfort and also help fulfill the obligation of prayer for the departed," adding that participating in the ritual would help Ivanova come to terms with her father's death and the complexity of their relationship. The commander agrees to relieve Ivanova of duties so that she can sit shiva. Upset at Koslov's intervention, Ivanova remains firm in her refusal to mourn her father. In her conversation with the rabbi, she makes clear that her reluctance to fulfill the ritual emerges not from a conflict with Judaism—"It's not because I've ceased being a Jew"—but with her father. Notwithstanding the scene of reconciliation several episodes earlier, Ivanova cannot forgive her father for his emotional abandonment. But when she accompanies Koslov to the shuttle to see him off, Ivanova suddenly recollects the deathbed conversation with her father, now shown in flashback. With his final words, "Forgive me, forgive me," she has a sudden change of heart, and calls Koslov back.

In the shiva scene that ensues, Ivanova eulogizes her father in the company of her Babylon 5 friends and colleagues. While the shiva takes place in Ivanova's quarters and not in a synagogue, the ritual observance turns it into Jewish sacred space. A photograph of Andrei stands near a large memorial candle, and what appears to be a tallit bag, or sac to hold a prayer shawl—a blue pouch adorned with a gold, six pointed star of David. Koslov concludes the recitation of the Kaddish in Aramaic, and Ivanova recites another traditional prayer of commemoration, *El Maleh Rahamim*, or God full of Mercy, in English. While the *Thirtysomething* and *Northern Exposure* episodes affirm the meaningfulness of uttering liturgy in its original Jewish language, even as the episodes acknowledge the meaninglessness of its sounds both to the one who recites it and those who listen, *Babylon 5* insists that the meaning of the words is more important than the traditional language. Ivanova prefaces her recitation by noting that although it is customary to recite the mourner's prayer in Hebrew, she has elected to recite it in English "so that my good friend [Babylon 5 Commander] Jeffrey Sinclair may share it with us." Ivanova thus confirms that, unlike *Thirtysomething*'s Steadman and *Northern Exposure*'s Fleischman, she has retained the Jewish teaching of her youth, but also that she claims the freedom to conduct Jewish ritual in the vernacular and inclusively. Shiva is, after all, a home ritual, and the Babylon 5 station is, as the voiceover that introduces each episode declaims, "home away from home." Ivanova's quarters are her personal home, and this serves as Jewish space. But home is also the multicultural space station, which is made both to contain Jewish space and to be brought inside of it.

Just as the shiva is presented simultaneously as Jewish space and multicultural space, the ritual is given both Jewish and universal meaning, placed in a framework both ancient and contemporary. As Fleischman did in Cecily, Koslov and Ivanova observe the tradition of *hesped*, eulogizing the departed. But "TKO" makes clear that mourning rituals are not merely a means to do right by the dead but a path to psychological health for the living, articulated in terms current in the popular culture of 1990s America. As Ivanova recites the prayer, her voice breaks. Her normally cool demeanor cracks, and she cries, at last mourning her father. Thus the performance of ritual allows for catharsis. More importantly, the episode makes clear that ritual facilitates the inner mechanisms of forgiveness, so central to the contemporary American discourse. Earlier, Koslov terms Ivanova's continued and posthumous anger at her father a "tragedy." His concern is not merely with perpetuating the memory of the dead, but with Ivanova's welfare. He tells her, "Without forgiveness you cannot mourn, and without mourning you can never let go of the pain." While the concept of forgiveness has a presence in Jewish thought and practice, Koslov draws on a discourse of forgiveness and an imperative to forgive that is deeply Christian in origin, and by the 1990s had been absorbed into popular psychology. Sitting shiva and reciting a memorial prayer that—unlike the Kaddish—requires that she insert her father's name, function as both the mechanism for and the proof of the Ivanova's forgiving her father. The shiva scene finally shows Ivanova sitting among her friends, warmly reminiscing about her father. Visually, she has changed, indicating that something vital has shifted inside her. Although *Babylon 5* almost always shows Ivanova's hair pulled severely into a tight bun, here she wears her hair loose, and she smiles and laughs. She thanks those present for helping her "find somebody long lost and quite precious to me—the father I loved." Observing the shiva thus has a redemptive function, permitting her to feel her father's love, and because of that, to feel the love of her friends and colleagues on the space station.

The "TKO" episode interweaves Ivanova's struggle with her father's memory and its ritual commemoration with a second story arc, the unlikely comeback of a discredited boxing champion. Barred from boxing because of involvement in a previous scandal, Walker Smith comes to Babylon 5 to redeem his reputation by fighting in the Mutai, a brutal martial arts competition developed by a different humanoid species. The Mutai is a highly regulated alien species' ritual that involves a bloody, no-holds-barred fight to the death. Humans have never before been permitted to participate. Smith pushes against the Mutai establishment and finds a loophole in the regulations that allows him to compete. The Mutai subplot ends with the head of the Mutai declaring that because of Smith's courage and skill, henceforth the Mutai will be open to human challengers. The intertwined stories further the series' multicultural ethics: the Jew who observes Jewish ritual among non-Jewish friends, the human who challenges the no-humans policy among an alien species. Diversity on *Babylon 5* reflects the late twentieth century understanding in America of the inadequacy of the "melting pot" and superiority of the "mosaic" as an ideal for a society of people with diverse origins. By the 1990s, there is general acknowledgment of the critique that the assimilatory project associated with Enlightenment universalism and emblemized by the melting pot does violence to its citizens by homogenizing difference and erasing particularities. A mosaic, by contrast, connotes a society in which there is a shared civic discourse, common values, an inclusive sense of belonging, but that does not erase particularity of divers cultural customs and heritage. Rather than privileging an assimilation that erases cultural difference, one must maintain and respect different traditions. Ivanova mourns her father in a poignant gathering with friends; Smith participates in a contest so violent that the episode was initially banned in Great Britain. Nonetheless, the episode insists that both traditions deserve respect. The two stories acknowledge that cultural rituals should be perpetuated, that they are meaningful, and that they can become inclusive without diminishing their value as cultural folkways.

The paired struggles also comment upon the place of Jewishness in contemporary society. In both story arcs, the notion of redemption is central. Ivanova redeems her relationship with her father, and herself; Smith redeems his shattered reputation and the integrity of the Mutai. Afterward, each goes back to his or her everyday life. Rituals are special events that help to resolve points of pressure. They are invaluable, but also heuristic. Ivanova resumes her duties on the space station, and Smith departs Babylon 5. Just as his rehabilitation does not require Smith to remain and keep fighting in the Mutai, Ivanova's redemption does not require regular participation in Jewish ritual. As it does for Steadman and Fleischman, Jewish practice defines a particular moment but need not make a claim on everyday life. As in *Thirtysomething* and *Northern Exposure*, Jewish identity is individual, a feeling, a claimed heritage, but need not be associated with religious observance, cultural habits, ethnic community. Apart from the occasional ritual, only a declared self-identification distinguishes Ivanova from the other humans on the Babylon 5 station. One might say that Judaism provides a pool of potential rituals, and one selects as one wishes and only if and when one wishes.

Moreover, Jewish observance is protean, accommodating itself to a modernizing society. When Ivanova invites Koslov to dinner and orders a dish made of trill—a food species originating on another planet—the rabbi hesitates, wondering whether the unfamiliar ingredient is kosher, that is, whether it permissible according to religious dietary laws. Ivanova cannot be certain. Then he announces, "I don't recall that trill is mentioned in the Torah, so..." and proceeds to eat it. Thus, trill becomes what Gaye Tuchman and Harry G. Levine, in their discussion of ethnic adaptation, call "safe treyf," a forbidden substance so unrecognizable or unfamiliar that its presence could be ignored. Played by Theodore Bikel, Koslov stands out among the futuristically garbed inhabitants of the space station. In his black suit and tie and yarmulka, he seems to have come not simply from the distant earth, but the distant past, and he speaks English with an accent that is not only Russian, but Jewish. As such, he signifies the "old country" not of earth but of the twentieth century—whether the *zeydes* and *bubbes* of the early half of the century, or the post-Holocaust refugees from a lost world; the Hebrew expressions he tosses off links him also with the American Jewish affiliation with Israel in the last decades of the twentieth century. The rabbi's approval of the alien trill dish presents a modern Judaism that is flexible, integrative, and accepting of other cultures, just as the shiva over which he presides is inclusive rather than exclusionary. The ease of his presence on Babylon 5 suggests that the accommodation of Judaism to a changing world is at once evolving and faithful to the ancestral past.

The juxtaposition of shiva and the Mutai serves another purpose, as well—to provide the opportunity to display a "good" Judaism to a broad-based television audience. When Koslov and Ivanova speak of her father, they call him "a man of God" with strong principles and a deep commitment to peace. Not only was Andrei opposed to Ivanova joining the military, he refused to visit her on Babylon 5, telling her that until peace could be achieved on earth, they had no business in space. Thus, the shiva memorializing Andrei contrasts sharply and favorably with the Mutai, a bloody, battering event. Taken as a whole, Judaism—while distinct from the mainstream—is represented as an evolved, enlightened culture when compared with the other unfamiliar cultures inhabiting Babylon 5. One might say, too, that Ivanova's father is described in Christological terms—a peaceable man of God associated with love, redemption, and forgiveness. Paired together, the Mutai suggests characteristics attributed in Western anti-Semitic discourse to Judaism—primitive, exclusionary, unforgiving, vengeful—leaving a Judaism that is consonant with Christianity. Jewish culture may be distinctive, but it is not alien to the America of the 1990s.

Loss, grief, and bereavement is human and universal, but each of these series presents a character who needs or wishes to mourn liturgically as a Jew. In her astute discussion of the diglossia of Jewish American literature, Wirth-Nesher observes that the recitation of the Kaddish in Aramaic "affirms linguistic otherness as a part of American Jewish identity" (Language 228). She notes that, insofar as many, perhaps most, American Jews find the prayer opaque, it functions only as "a prayer for the dead," its redemptive thrust drowned in a sea of incomprehensibly foreign syllables. Yet, noting the endurance of the Kaddish as the ultimate and irreducible link with Jewishness, she imagines a cadre of readers who—individually and often far from Jewish community—encounter the words of the Kaddish as they appear in the fiction and poems of Jewish American writers. These readers, "in the solitary and quiet act of reading," become the responsive congregation to the writers' Kaddish, thereby continuing Jewish community (Language 228). The Jewish mourning episodes of *Thirtysomething*, *Northern Exposure*, *Babylon 5*, and other television dramas of that era[5] representing a shift in the notion of community, broadening it out so that individual Jewish identity ceases to hinge upon or to reestablish Jewish community.

In his study of ethnicity in America, Werner Sollors distinguishes between groups defined by "descent" and "consent." Groups of descent are characterized by blood ties. They are static and tied to past. Groups of consent, by contrast, are fluid, consciously chosen and constructed; "Descent language emphasizes our positions as heirs, our hereditary qualities, liabilities, and entitlements; consent language stresses our abilities as mature free agents and 'architects of our fates' to choose our spouses, our destinies, and our political systems" (6). The mourner's prayer episodes of *Thirtysomething*, *Northern Exposure*, and *Babylon 5* portray Jewishness as poised between descent and consent. The inconsistencies within each of the episodes suggest that the respective programs would like to have it both ways at once. Steadman's endogamous marriage and deliberations about Kaddish and Jewishness assert his freedom to choose who he is, to invent and reinvent himself. The episode's insistence on a Kaddish recited only in an opaque Aramaic and only in the confines of the synagogue conveys a Jewishness that is unchanging and defined by blood ties. Fleischman's determination to fulfil the obligation of Kaddish in his chosen community places Jewishness in the compass of choice. However, the fixed, and one might say typed, identity not only of the series' Jewish character, but of all its characters situates identity as static and inherited. The post-national society of humans on *Babylon 5* suggests a seamless multiculture that accepts a kind of difference that has shed its divisive, exclusionary characteristics. But the fear, suspicion, and essentialism that vexed late twentieth century discourse have not been resolved. They have been simply transferred to the realm of interplanetary species, who are defined biologically and indelibly.

Thus, the Jewish future resembles the Jewish present, at least as imagined by American television drama. The fluidity, mobility, and choices that begin to characterize American potential not only for Jews but for others in the late twentieth century open up questions about identity, continuity, otherness, and belonging in an evolving multiculture that must play themselves out in the twenty-first. As in the best science fiction, we imagine a future laden with our problems, burdened by our fears, buoyed by our ideals.

Notes

1. See Vincent Brook, *Something Ain't Kosher Here: The Rise of the "Jewish" Sitcom* (New Brunswick, NJ: Rutgers UP, 2003) and David Zurawik, *The Jews of Prime Time* (Hanover: Brandeis UP, 2003). Brooks examines the surgeoncy of Jewish characters in American situation-comedies from 1989 through early 2000, which arises, he notes, "partly as a response to changing industrial conditions in American television, partly as a complex negotiation of assimilationist and multicultural pressures specific to the American Jewish experience" (2). Zurawik observes that there were no clearly identified Jewish leading characters in a weekly network television series from 1954 to 1972, and then again from 1978 to 1987 (9).

2. For discussion of the history and development of the Kaddish, see David de Sola Pool, *The Old Jewish-Aramaic Prayer, the Kaddish* (New York: Bloch Pub. Co., 1909); David Telsner, *The Kaddish: Its History and Significance*, ed. Gabriel A. Sivan (Jerusalem: Tal Orot Institute, 1995); Leon Wieseltier, *Kaddish* (New York: Knopf, 1998).

3. The first few episodes ran on Prime Time Entertainment Network.

4. See, for example, Anne Roiphe. "Christmas Comes to a Jewish Home," *The New York Times* 21 Dec. 1978, C1, and the ensuing letters to the editor.

5. See, for example, the "Kaddish" episodes of NBC's *Homicide: Life on the Streets* (1993-1999) and FOX's *the X-files* (1993-2002).

Works Cited

"Born to the Purple," *Babylon 5*. TNT. Season 1, Episode 3. 9 Feb. 1994. Television; *Babylon 5: The Complete First Season*. Disc 1. Warner Brothers. 2002.

Brook, Vincent. *Something Ain't Kosher Here: The Rise of the "Jewish" Sitcom*. New Brunswick, NJ: Rutgers University Press, 2003. Print.

de Sola Pool, David. *The Old Jewish-Aramaic Prayer, the Kaddish*. New York: Bloch Pub. Co., 1909. Print.

Grimes, Ronald L. *Beginnings in Ritual Studies*. New York: University Press of America, 1982. Print.

"Kaddish for Uncle Manny," *Northern Exposure*. CBS. Season 4, Episode 22. 3 May 1993. Television; *Northern Exposure: The Complete Fourth Season*. Disc 3. Universal. 2006.

Roiphe, Anne. "Christmas Comes To a Jewish Home," *The New York Times* 21 Dec. 1978, C1. Print.

Romeyn, Esther and Jack Kugelmass. "Writing Alaska, Writing the Nation: *Northern Exposure* and the Quest for a New America." *"Writing" Nation and "Writing" Region in America*. Eds. Theo D'hean and Hans Bertens. Amsterdam: VU University Press, 1996: 252–67. Print.

Sollors, Werner. *Beyond Ethnicity: Consent and Descent in American Culture*. New York: Oxford University Press, 1986. Print.

Telsner, David. *The Kaddish: Its History and Significance*. Ed. Gabriel A. Sivan. Jerusalem: Tal Orot Institute, 1995. Print.

"The Mike Van Dyke Show," *Thirtysomething*. ABC. Season 2. Episode 3. 20 Dec. 1988. Television.

"TKO," *Babylon 5*. TNT. Season 1, Episode 14. 25 May 1994. Television; *Babylon 5: The Complete First Season*. Disc 4. Warner Brothers. 2002.

Tuchman, Gaye, and Harry G. Levine. "New York Jews and Chinese Food: The Social Construction of an Ethnic Pattern," *Contemporary Ethnography*. 1992: Vol 22 No. 3. 382-407. Print.

Turner, Victor. *Anthropology of Performance*. New York: PAJ Publications, 1986. Print.

Wieseltier, Leon. *Kaddish*. New York: Knopf, 1998. Print.

Wirth-Nesher. Hana. "Language as Homeland in Jewish-American Literature," *Insider/Outsider: American Jews and Multiculturalism*. Eds. D. Biale, M. Galchinsky, S. Heschel. Berkeley: University of California Press, 1998: 212-30. Print.

———. "Magnified and Sanctified," *Ideology and Jewish Identity in Israeli and American Literature*. Ed. Emily Budick. Albany: SUNY Press, 2001: 115-30. Print.

Zurawik, David. *The Jews of Prime Time*. Hanover: Brandeis University Press, 2003. Print.

Sara R. Horowitz, York University

The Flight of Lilith:

Modern Jewish American Feminist Literature

Ann R. Shapiro

Judaism and Second Wave Feminism: An Overview

Second wave feminism, the movement which began in the 1960s and gained full momentum in the 1970s, reiterated many of the goals of the first wave of the last half of the nineteenth century. While first wave feminists organized around suffrage, the broader goal was equality. The first wave was dominated by educated Protestant women mainly from New York State and New England, but the second wave was remarkably Jewish. Historians often date the beginning of what was then called "women's liberation" to Betty Friedan's *Feminist Mystique* (1963). By 1972 *Ms.: the New Magazine for Women* was launched with an editorial staff that was half Jewish, including Gloria Steinem and Letty Cottin Pogrebin. Historian Gerda Lerner, according to the *New York Times*, is a "godmother of women's history" (Lee B7). Bella Abzug emerged in national politics, while radical feminism was dominated by Robin Morgan, Shulamith Firestone, Andrea Dworkin, and other Jewish women.

Feminist critic Susan Gubar came to acknowledge the significance of her own Jewish origins and those of the leading feminist critics and scholars who emerged in the 1970s in her essay, "Eating the Bread of Affliction" (1994), where she categorically states, "Jewish experience has profoundly shaped the evolution of feminist thinking in our times" (4). The women cited in her essay could be a who's who of feminism: Adrienne Rich, Carolyn Heilbrun, Florence Howe, Annette Kolodny, Alicia Ostriker, Nancy K. Miller, Judith Gardiner, Nina Auerbach, Naomi Weisstein, Lillian Robinson, Elizabeth Abel, Rachel Brownstein, Rachel Adler, Judith Plaskow, Blance Weissen Cook, Natalie Zemon Davis, Estelle Friedman, Linda Gordon, Linda Kerber, Ruth Rosen, Susan Suleiman, and Marianne Hirsch. A notable and probably inadvertent omission is Ellen Moers, whose *Literary Women* (1976) was surely groundbreaking in literary criticism. Indeed it is hard to imagine a feminist movement without the contributions of Jewish American women. Most of these women regarded themselves as secular Jews and initially did not connect their feminism with Judaism.

In an effort to understand the predominance of Jewish feminists, Gubar speculates:

> Clearly those of us who grew up Jewish during the postwar years inherited a distrust of public authority and a reliance on private bonds that anticipate the feminist imperative to integrate (male) institutions and authority and to valorize (feminine) networks of reciprocity. Just as important, we had been served up a monitory lesson about conformity and acquiescence: living through debates over the immorality of "blaming the victim," some of us nevertheless harbored suspicions about a generation of adults blind to the writing on the wall because they had integrated successfully in mainstream European culture. (79)

She adds "devotion to the text and to education" as well as "strong commitment to each individual's social responsibility" as other possible explanations for the preponderance of Jewish feminists (82-3).

Gubar quotes several Jewish feminist literary scholars, who offer their own tentative explanations for the link between Judaism and feminism. Carolyn Heilbrun states, "Having been a Jew had made me an outsider. It had permitted me to be a feminist." Commenting on her suspicions of the world and the academy in particular, Annette Kolodny confesses, "Somewhere lurking in my responses to everyone I meet is the unarticulated question 'Would you hide me?'" Nina Auerbach adds, "the Holocaust and the blacklist were twin specters….official authority has always looked stupid and menacing." Lillian Robinson claims that she came from "a freethinking family" in which she learned "to treat the very idea of a sacred text skeptically, which is a pretty good beginning for someone seeking to expand and enrich the literary canon." Nancy K. Miller concludes somewhat cryptically, "being both Jewish and a feminist is a crucial, even constitutive piece of my self-consciousness as a writer" (82). All of these speculations seem reasonable, none definitive.

Lilith

For Gubar the recognition of Jewish identity evolved. Initially she writes that she had embraced Lilith as prototype, declaring, "Like the rebel Lilith, defiantly inhabiting a liminal zone outside the Jewish community…many schools in the so-called second wave feminism felt themselves embittered, hopeless about receiving spiritual sustenance suited to our desires. . . .[W]e could only forget, deny, distance ourselves from our Jewish backgrounds"(76). She describes the pain of sitting through a *seder* where the *Haggadah* refers to sons, but not daughters, and a male God whose "celebrants in the present function as an exclusive men's club" (71). Until she experienced a second *seder,* which celebrated the four daughters and introduced Miriam, the savior of Moses, Gubar thought of herself as a "Jewish feminist" but not a "feminist Jew" (71).

Gubar sees Lilith as daemonic and therefore "excluded from the human community" (Madwoman 33), but many Jewish feminists have taken a different view, celebrating Lilith as the symbol of the independent woman. While there are multiple sources for the Lilith myth, most contemporary interpretations rely on the first extended representation of Lilith in the medieval text *Alphabet of Ben Sira 23*. There we learn that Lilith was the first wife of Adam, who was created equally with him. When she refused to be submissive and lie beneath him, he attempted to force her compliance, and so she flew away. God instructs Adam to persuade Lilith to return, but Lilith is recalcitrant. Kabbalistic interpretations, written several hundred years later, add that after fleeing the Garden, Lilith kills pregnant women, injures newborns, and excites men in their sleep, taking their semen to manufacture demon children of her own. According to the *Columbia Encyclopedia*, "Lilith is the symbol of sensual lust" (1582). The Web site for *Lilith*, the Jewish feminist magazine founded in 1976, explains the name with a brief quote from the *Alphabet of Ben Sira 23* that states simply, "Lilith said, 'we are equal because we are created from the same earth'" (Lilith.org). The rest of the Lilith story is ignored. Judith Plaskow in a 1972 essay on Lilith wrote a new *midrash*, where she not only eliminated Lilith's daemonic aspects, but reimagined the story so that Eve finally met Lilith on the other side of the garden wall, where they talked and cried "till the bond of sisterhood grew between them" (30). Aviva Cantor laments that the Lilith myth was "contaminated with male bias," and suggests: "What is intrinsic to Lilith, what is the most central aspect of her character is her struggle for independence, her courage in taking risks, her commitment to the equality of woman and man based on their creation as equals by God" (49-50).

The multiple interpretations of Lilith suggest a paradigm, if not a definition, for second wave feminist literature, especially in the 1970s, where Jewish women writers in particular either described the flight from an oppressive patriarchal marriage, where the sensual protagonist expresses her rebellion by taking a real or imagined lover, or a reconciliation and reaffirmation in sisterhood, as suggested in Plaskow's *midrash*. Key examples of these two early Jewish feminist responses, which may be considered prototypical of the Jewish feminist novel, are Erica Jong's *Fear of Flying* (1973) and E. M. Broner's *Weave of Women* (1978).

Fear of Flying

In her new book, *A Jury of Her Peers: American Women Writers from Anne Bradstreet to Annie* Proulx (2009), Elaine Showalter states, "All the feminist critics looking at the 1970s agree that Erica Jong's *Fear of Flying (1973)*, which…defied the restrictions on women's verbal range, sexual candor, and narrative voice, was a key book of the decade" (443-4). The lustful heroine was, of course not unique to Jong. Other Jewish feminists including Alix Kates Shulman in *Memoirs of an Ex-Prom Queen* (1972) and Anne Roiphe in *Up the Sandbox* (1970) also defied expectations for nice Jewish girls by creating protagonists who reveled in sexual adventures, but only *Fear of Flying* sold a reputed 18 million copies and, therefore, both reflected and engaged a generation. One wishes that Showalter would have named some of those feminist critics and detailed what they said and why, but assuming that *Fear of Flying* is a key work of the period, what does it tell us? That it marked a feminist breakthrough, as suggested by Showalter, is undeniable, but I would also argue that it is in several ways a Jewish *bildungsroman* where Isadora Wing not only obsesses about her Jewish identity, but also embodies key aspects of the Lilith prototype, emblematic of the Jewish feminist novel. The novel is not only about Isadora's defiance, metaphorically expressed as flying, but about her fear. In the novel's opening pages, she confesses the panic she experiences in an airplane, but throughout she also expresses her fear of anti-Semitism and her fear of becoming a lonely outcast like Lilith.

Her fear of anti-Semitism surfaces as soon as her plane lands in Vienna, where she is accompanying her psychoanalyst husband to a conference: "Welcome back! Welcome Back! At least those of you who survived Auschwitz, Belsen, the London Blitz and the co-optation of America. *Wilkommen!*" She remembers that Freud fled Vienna because of the Nazi threat and not only had his name been banned but "analysts were expelled (if they were lucky) or gassed (if they were not)" (6). In a chapter recounting her life in Heidelberg, Jong begins with an epigraph by Rudolph Hess acknowledging that people living nearby knew about the exterminations (56). This is followed by a poem, "The 8:29 to Frankfurt," which poignantly sums up her feelings about the train conductor in Germany: "But I am not so dumb/I know where the tracks end/and the train rolls on/into silence. I know the station won't be marked/My hair's as Aryan/as anything/My name is heather. My passport eyes/bluer than Bavarian skies/But he can see the Star of David/in my navel" (57). Isadora White Wing (née Weiss) adds, "I began to feel intensely Jewish and internally paranoid (are they perhaps the same?) the moment I set foot in Germany"(61). Otherwise she insists she was a "pantheist" (67), granddaughter of a Marxist living in an assimilated home, where there were always a Christmas tree and Easter eggs (60). Soon after the publication of *Fear of Flying,* Jong explained to an interviewer, "The German experience was complicated because it made me suddenly realize I was Jewish. I had been raised as an atheist by cosmopolitan parents who didn't care about religion, and living in Germany gave me a sense of being Jewish and being potentially a victim" (Templin 14). Two years later in an interview with *Playboy,* she declared that her goal in *Fear of Flying* was "to be honest about everything" including "being Jewish in Germany" (Templin 41).

Although fear of anti-Semitism is a critical issue in the novel, feminism is its core, and for Jong feminism and Judaism are often related. Reflecting on the issue more than twenty years after she wrote *Fear of Flying,* Jong declared, "The problem of sexism is great for *all* women, but for Jewish women it is perhaps even greater because of that pervasive anti-Semitism that masquerades as class snobbery." Citing as examples, Woody Allen, Philip Roth, Lionel Trilling, and her mother's Russian grandfather, she warns that Jewish men "project all their self-loathing onto Jewish women [because] we remind them of their strong mothers." Of Trilling she adds, "Like my mother's Russian grandfather, Lionel Trilling—then playing God at Columbia—did not pay attention to girls" (*Fear of Fifty* 78-9).

In *Fear of Flying,* Jong's description of the feminist dilemma is not confined to the suffering inflicted upon women by Jewish men, but rather by all men, especially husbands. Isadora's image of "the good woman" is "a kind of Jewish Griselda" who "sits quietly on the upper balcony of the synagogue while the men recite prayers about the inferiority of women" (231). Unwilling to be Griselda, Isadora prefers to be Lilith, the sensuous, bad woman, who takes flight from patriarchal marriage , but in this satiric novel Isadora's flight lasts only two and a half weeks, her lover is impotent most of the time, and she flies back to her husband, albeit unsure of what she will do next, understanding only that she must work, and no man, neither her husband Bennett, nor her lover, Adrian Goodlove, will give her life purpose or solve the infinite mystery of human existence.

Fear of Flying broke new ground in women's fiction in its use of four-letter words and its unabashedly lustful heroine, but its inconclusive final chapter is entitled "A 19th-Century Ending." If, as Elaine Showalter insists, feminist critics agree that it "was a key book of the decade," its feminist appeal is in Isadora's yearning to free herself from conventional expectations for women rather than her success in fulfilling her aspirations. Although much of the book is about Isadora's flight from patriarchal assumptions about women culminating in her fleeing her husband, it is also about her fear of loneliness in an unchartered limbo. Lilith, after all, has been conceived both as liberated woman and ostracized female monster, and Isadora sees herself alternately as one or the other.

Isadora's feminism seems like a primer of second wave feminism. Early in the novel she wonders, "What did it mean to be a woman anyway?" (52-3). She rejects the presumably expert advice of her male psychoanalyst, the choices of her mother and sisters, the lives of women she observes, the institution of marriage, and the images of women in both male and female novels. She decides, "What I really wanted was to give birth to *myself....*" (51). The problem is that there is no precedent—no past to guide her.

Isadora's first flight is from her psychoanalyst, who sees "Women's Lib as a neurotic problem." Before walking out of his office forever, she screams at him, "I also don't think you understand a thing about women....Don't you see that men have *always* defined femininity as a means of keeping women in line?" (20) Her own family provide no better clue to understanding. An aspiring artist, her mother gave up painting when her own father mocked her efforts and painted over her canvasses. Her three sisters, all married with children, are equally distressing role models, who confirm her own hopelessness about marriage. She reflects, "The virtues of marriage were mostly negative virtues. Being unmarried in a man's world was such a hassle that *anything* had to be better" (86). What she wants is "total mutuality," but instead she describes "how men sit there glued to the paper while you clear the table....they pretend to be all thumbs when you ask them to mix the frozen orange juice....they bring friends home and expect you to wait on them and yet feel entitled to sulk and go off into another room if you bring friends home" (87).

Isadora's first marriage ends in divorce when Brian becomes seriously mentally ill. She explains that she married him because she wanted to leave home and did not know what to do after graduating college. He, on the other hand, insisted on marriage because he "wanted to own my soul. He was afraid I'd fly away. So he gave me an ultimatum" (212). When she briefly leaves her second husband for Adrian Goodlove, she announces, "I was flying" (188), but she soon confesses, "I entered a world in which the rules we lived by were his rules—although he pretended there *were* no rules" (193). Even the prospect of motherhood fails to justify marriage because it means "having babies for men. Babies who get *their* names. Babies who lock you by means of love to a man you have to please and serve on pain of abandonment" (52).

Finding no answers to what it means to be a woman in life, Isadora looks to literature, but here too she is frustrated. She laments, "I learned about women from men," and what she learned was her own inferiority (168). Women writers were no help either: "Where was the female Chaucer? One lusty lady who had juice and joy, love and talent too….Almost all women we admire were spinsters and suicides" (109-110). She decides "No lady writers' subjects for me. I was going to have battle and bullfights and jungle safaris" (129), but she confesses that she knows nothing about any of it.

The irony of Isadora's efforts at sexual liberation is that she never feels liberated. She realizes, "What a disproportionate sense of guilt I had over all my petty sexual transgressions. Why had I been cursed with such a hypertrophied superego? Was it being Jewish?" (268). The question bring us full circle.

In the novel, like the Jewish feminist critics, quoted by Gubar, Jong/Isadora explicitly defines her Jewish identity in reaction to anti-Semitism. But I would argue that her rebellion against traditional expectations of women, although not unique to Jewish women, grows in part out of her perception of herself as an outsider. Commenting on the predicament of the Jewish woman writer, Jong states she is "twice marginalized, twice discriminated against. She is discriminated against both as a woman and as a Jew" (*Fear of Fifty* 80).

Jong, like Gubar and others of her generation, eventually found her way back to Judaism by stages. In 1994, in an essay, "How I Got to Be Jewish," Jong reiterates themes already developed in *Fear of Flying,* insisting, "Jews are made by the existence of anti-Semitism…" Always an outsider, the Jew "is a person who is safe *nowhere*" (101). A few years after this in her attempt to define her own Jewish identity, Jong began doing research at YIVO for a new book about Jewish female roots that became *Inventing Memory: A Novel of Mothers and Daughters* (1997). Finally ready to climb over the wall to bond with other women as Plaskow's Lilith did, Jong was no longer obsessed by the Holocaust nor defined by a man, as she attempted to understand herself as a Jewish woman. After leaving her husband, Sara, Jong's new alter ego, secures a job at the Council on Jewish History researching her own Jewish heritage through stories about her female ancestors from 1905 to the present. Near the end of the novel Sara decides that Jews must not allow the Holocaust to define them, complaining, "It's as if we spend all our time arguing with Hitler" (295). Instead she wants to create an exhibition that shows that Jews are not victims but survivors. The family saga that Sara discovers culminates with a letter from her once atheistic mother apologizing for never having had her daughter study to be a bat mitzvah and proclaiming the "great wisdom in our traditions" (247). In the afterword to the novel, Jong ponders the leadership of Jewish women in America and concludes, "It was their Jewishness and femaleness that led them to empathize with the oppressed" (302). There is no trace of the lustful Lilith here. Sara/Jong finds herself by exploring her connection with a century of Jewish women's history.

The Bonding of Lilith and Eve

Other Jewish feminist writers have explored similar terrain in seeking to reconcile Judaism and feminism through fictitious accounts of Jewish women as central participants in the Jewish tradition. If the stories that men told about Jews in the Bible, the *Haggadah*, the *Talmud*, as well as history were about men, women could invent new stories that placed women in the center. After all, storytelling has always been an integral part of Judaism. Therefore E. M. Broner creates new female ritual in *The Weave of Women*; Norma Rosen writes new *midrash* in *Biblical Women Unbound*; Anita Diamant in *The Red Tent* retells the story of Dinah in *Genesis*; Maggie Anton suggests in *Rashi's Daughters* that women were instrumental in writing the Talmud; and Geraldine Brooks uses historical fiction to underscore women's roles in her saga of the Sarajevo *Haggadah*.

Some Jewish feminist writers wrote novels in which heroines escape patriarchal restrictions in imagined female worlds, including Marge Piercy in *Woman at the Edge of Time* and *He, She and It* and Kim Chernin in *The Flame Bearers*. E. M. Broner's *A Weave of Women*, however, provides the most useful prototype of the genre here because it is uniquely Jewish, drawing on Jewish ritual and situated in Jerusalem, the city that embodies Jewish hope for the future.

The idea that women could bond in new communities through shared rituals began for Broner in 1975 in Israel when she and her friend Nomi Nimrod were working on the *Women's Haggadah*, where the patriarchal God became the Shekinah, the four sons, the four daughters and the rabbis "wise women" (*The Telling* 1). In 1976, the first women's *seder* took place in New York, where participants included Phyllis Chesler, Letty Cottin Pogrebin, Gloria Steinem, Aviva Cantor, and Andrea Dworkin. The so-called "Seder Sisters" would eventually also include Bella Abzug and Grace Paley. The feminist *seder* has since, of course, gone through many incarnations as more and more women wrote *haggadot* and came together to celebrate Miriam along with Moses.

A Weave of Women

Broner's community of women in Jerusalem is all-inclusive. The women represent different faiths and different nationalities; they include "wayward girls," an unmarried mother, a woman seeking a divorce, a social worker, a singer, a playwright, a scientist, and an actress. While there are men in their lives, the men are peripheral. The women find comfort with each other and are bound together by the rituals they create to mark the important events in their lives. The women themselves tell their story in their own voices because Broner believes, "There is no chief story teller of women's history—we make history together" ("Of Holy Writing" 269).

While Broner is well versed in Jewish tradition and remains an active participant in a Conservative synagogue, her imagined world is outside the known realms of religion and politics. After the stone house, which is the center of the women's communal life, is destroyed to make way for a male yeshiva, the women establish Havurat Shula, "a women's government in exile" (289) because the laws themselves reject women's needs. Vered's lover, a married man, who finally left Vered and returned to his wife, is a member of the Knesset, who "now upholds the dignity of the family, the honor of womankind, the protection of children and of the innocent...." He takes a position against birth control and abortion; phases out the Home for Wayward Girls; and chairs the Male Gynecological Conference whose motto is "Women, leave your bodies in our hands" (152).

Although Broner uses Jewish tradition as a framework for the lives of the Daughters of Jerusalem, seeking protection in their stone house, there is no more solace in Judaism for women than in politics. After Deedee is stoned for seducing a Talmudic scholar with whom she had consensual sex, "[t]he women pray that they be restored to their own Temple, that they no longer be captive, for there is no God of women...." (258). Without the protection of either the state or any religion, the women have only each other, and in creating a new community they attempt to live and love in a society, which above all protects women from abusive men and draws on Jewish ritual. Where traditional Judaism serves men, the women in the stone house invent new rituals to correct the evils of all patriarchal institutions that define women's lives from birth to death.

At the center of all the rituals is a desire to liberate women from subservient roles, especially in marriage. It is as if the women were still fighting Lilith's battle for equality with Adam—a battle that not only was launched again by Betty Friedan in 1963 at the beginning of the second wave, but was also key to first wave feminism in the nineteenth century.[1] Feminists of each generation understood that traditional marriage had to be redefined if women were to achieve equality.

In Broner's world the unmarried Simha gives birth to her child surrounded by chanting women who braid her hair and bring flowers and herbs in the absence of the kibbutznik father, who marries Simha only at the end of the novel after they have shared suffering. But even after marriage Simha will live only half the year with her husband and the other half with the daughters of Jerusalem in the stone house. The kibbutznik, observing his baby nursing, reflects "There is no need for a father as there was no need for a husband...." (7). The nuclear family is thus displaced.

When the baby girl reaches eight days, she is ready for a ceremony that converts the *brit milah* to a female ceremony called a hymenotomy where her hymen is pierced so that female virginity and the husband's possession of his wife will no longer be presumed. Instead, Dahlia prays, "May she not be delivered intact to her bridegroom or judged by her hymen but by the energies of her life" (25). All of the women are sexually free, asserting ownership of their own bodies. While they seek partners to love, they have little interest in marriage.

In contrast, the married women in the novel suffer abuse from husbands who are protected by Jewish law. Mickey/Mihal's request to the Rabbinical Council for a divorce from her abusive husband is repeatedly denied even though she is brutally beaten each time she returns to him. Eventually she declares a desire for "a new ceremony" where under the bridal *huppah*, the husband will say, "I will never hurt you. I will never punish you. If I shout at you, may my tongue be struck dumb. If I strike at you, may my arms become numb. I will not smash the glass underfoot for fear slivers will enter your heart" (260). The Orthodox husband of Hepzibah is more subtle in his abuse. According to Terry, he terrorizes his wife and daughter in his efforts to control their lives, causing the daughter to become anorexic and attempting to smother his wife's talents as a writer and administrator.

Throughout, expectations of female domesticity are challenged. Terry, for example "found that to love men a lot was to love herself less for they were pleased to let her bathe, comb, wash and feed them. They were pleased to let her shop for them and place their clothes in the cleaners. It gave them pleasure if she typed for them, wrote letters to their mothers and raised their children" (150). When the government threatens to close the Home for Jewish Wayward Girls, the name is briefly changed to the Home for Jewish Future Homemakers, and immediately contributions pour in for stoves, washing machines, and other equipment. "The wayward girls look at the equipment, at the cookbooks, domestic machinery and count the months until they are drafted into the army" (43). Although roles in marriage are never delineated, the underlying idea is that marriage, if chosen, must be egalitarian. In the marriage ceremony at the end of the book, Simha and the kibbutznik each stamp on a glass wrapped in white damask napkins to suggest their equal roles.

Despite her attempts to incorporate Jewish ritual so that women can be full participants, Broner remains at war with the traditional Judaism. The women do not view the ending of the Purim story as happy because even though Haman is defeated Esther remains "a woman sandwiched between two men" [Mordecai and Xerxes[2]], and she is unable to make choices: "They were made for her" (129). Even more troublesome are Orthodox views. When the Daughters of Jerusalem go to the Wall to sing, they are beaten by angry men, who remind them, "It is forbidden for a woman's voice to be raised in song" (64). The wayward girls, Shula and Rina, remember their mothers slapping them at their first menses in keeping with a tradition. They immediately perceive, "No one hit the boys in the family. Slaps, pursuit, curses were for the girls" (199).

Neither Erica Jong nor Esther Broner, in their desires to assert their independence from patriarchal dominance, provides conclusive endings to their novels. The world their characters imagine is still unsafe for women, and the conclusions are simply new versions of the marriage plot. In the final chapter of *Fear of Flying*,

Isadora awaits the return of her husband, while in *A Weave of Women* two of the Daughters of Jerusalem get married. Although Adam had been challenged, he had not been replaced either through individual rebellion or a community of women. It would remain for future generations to seek other ways of reconciling Judaism and feminism.

New Directions

During the 1970s it appeared that God was still on Adam's side. Women were angry, but nothing much had changed. Change, of course, did come with women admitted in equal numbers to the hallowed halls of formerly all male universities and soon moving into all professions and political life. If women were rewriting the *Haggadah* in the 1970s, by the 1980s they were challenging thousands of years of an entire tradition as women in all branches of Judaism except the Orthodox became rabbis and cantors. No longer bobbing their noses or changing their names to become assimilated, many Jews were exploring their roots and returning to Jewish traditions. Jewish identity had become much more than a the reaction to anti-Semitism as once described by Erica Jong and Susan Gubar and her cohorts. A new generation and some older Jewish feminists as well were telling many different stories. Lois Rubin guardedly suggests, "It took many years (and much work in improving women's position in Judaism) until some feminists of Jewish background made peace with Judaism and came to see it as compatible in some respects with feminism" (20-1). Not only Judaism, but feminism was being redefined in an increasingly multiethnic America. Jewish women's literature changed accordingly so that it reflected a feminist Judaism more than a Jewish feminism.

A new generation of writers, including Rebecca Goldstein, Allegra Goodman, and Pearl Abraham were raised in Orthodox homes and are mining that experience in novels. In answer to the question "Where should Jewish American writing move?" Allegra Goodman asserted, "Jewish American writers must recapture the spiritual and the religious dimension of Judaism" (Halio & Siegal 273). Cynthia Ozick, of course, had already been deeply engaged in doing just this, but she continued to protest classification as either a woman writer or a Jewish American writer, though clearly her writing reflects both perspectives.

While the spiritual and religious dimension of Judaism is undeniably significant to many young Jewish women writers, they have been breaking new ground in a variety of ways. The 1990s saw at least two novels that attempted to reclaim a history of the Jewish woman by inventing multi-generational sagas of mothers and daughters, Rebecca Goldstein's *Mazel* (1995) and, as described above, Erica Jong's *Inventing Memory* (1997). While Neil Simon and Woody Allen had explored mainly male Jewish lives in comedy for non-Jewish as well as Jewish audiences, Wendy Wasserstein was the first major American woman playwright to adapt the genre and put the assimilated Jewish woman on stage for a general audience. Moreover, in an increasingly multicultural America, Gish Jen in *Mona in the Promised Land* showed that one does not have to be born Jewish to recreate authentic Jewish cultural experience.

Despite the burgeoning of women in Jewish American literature, however, there is still insufficient recognition of their achievement both past and present. The Norton Anthology, *Jewish American Literature* (2001), lists only twenty-nine selections by women out of a total of 139. Elaine Showalter declared, "when the twentieth century ended for Americans, women's writing as a separate literary tradition, as a definition rather than description, had reached the end of its usefulness." But she added that women are still being omitted from accounts of American literary history and that "no history of American literature that excludes their voices can be complete" (512). The remaining task for Jewish feminists is to make sure that women's literature is included in the Jewish American canon. There must be room for both Lilith and Eve in Adam's world.

Notes

1.   In 1853 Elizabeth Cady Stanton wrote to Susan B. Anthony, "The right idea of marriage is at the foundation of all reforms" (Letter). Suffragist Laura Bullard added, "The solemn and profound question of marriage…is of more vital concern to woman's welfare, reaches down to a deeper depth in woman's heart and more thoroughly constitutes the core of the woman's movement than any such superficial and fragmentary question as woman's suffrage" (*Revolution*). Stanton eventually took the logical next step and advocated "Free Love" (qtd. in Smith 152).

2.   Many modern sources including the *New King James Version* indicate that Esther's husband Ahasuerus and Xerxes the great are one and the same. The name "Xerxes" is used here because Broner identifies Esther's husband as Xerxes.

Works Cited

Broner, E.M. Interview. "Of Holy Writing and Priestly Voices." *Massachusetts Review* 24 (1983): 254-69. Print.

———. *The Telling*. San Francisco: Harper, 1992.

———. *A Weave of Women*. 1978. Bloomington: Indiana UP, 1985.

Bullard, Laura. "What Flag Shall We Fly?" *Revolution*. Oct. 1870: 264. Print.

Cantor Aviva. "The Lilith Question." *Lilith*. Fall, 1976. Rpt. in *On Being a Jewish Feminist: A Reader*. Ed. Susannah Heschel. New York: Schocken, 1983: 40-50. Print.

Gilbert, Sandra, and Susan Gubar. *The Madwoman in the Attic: The Woman Writer and the Nineteenth-Century Literary Imagination*. New Haven: Yale UP, 1979.

Gubar, Susan. "Eating the Bread of Affliction: Judaism and Feminsim," *Tulsa Studies in Women's Literature* 2 (Fall 1994): 293-316. Rpt. in *Critical Condition: Feminism at the Turn of the Century*. Ed. Susan Gabar. New York: Columbia UP, 2000: 69-90. Print.

Goodman, Allegra. "Writing Jewish Fiction In and Out of the Multicultural Context," Halio and Siegel 268-74. Print.

Halio, Jay L., and Ben Siegel, eds. *Daughters of Valor: Contemporary Jewish American Women Writers*. Newark: Delaware UP, 1997. Print.

Jong, Erica. *Fear of Fifty: A Midlife Memoir*. New York: HarperCollins, 1994. Print.

———. *Fear of Flying*. New York: Holt, 1973. Print.

———. "How I Got To Be Jewish." 1994. *Who We Are: On Being (and Not Being) a Jewish American Writer.* Ed. Derek Rubin. New York: Schocken, 2005: 99-113. Print.

———. *Inventing Memory: A Novel of Mothers and Daughters.* 1997. New York: Penguin, 2007.

Lee, Felicia R. "Making History Her Story, Too," *New York Times* 20 July, B7+. Print.

"Lilith,"*The New Columbia Encyclopedia.* 1975. Print.

Lilith. n. p. Web. 5 June 2009.

Plaskow, Judith. "The Coming of Lilith: Toward a Feminist Theology." 1972. Rpt. in *Essays on Feminism, Judaism, and Sexual Ethics 1972-2003.* Ed. Donna Berman and Judith Plaskow. Boston: Beacon, 2005: 223-34. Print.

Rubin, Lois. *Connections and Collisions: Identities in Contemporary Jewish-American Women's Writing.* Ed. Lois Rubin. Newark: Delaware UP, 2005.

Showalter. Elaine. A Jury of Her Peers: American Women Writers from Anne Bradstreet to An-nie Proulx. New York: Knopf, 2009.

Smith, Page. *Daughters of the Promised Land.* Boston: Little, Brown, 1970.

Stanton, Elizabeth Cady. Letter to Susan B. Anthony. 1 March 1853. *The Road to Reno.* Ed. Nelson Manfred Black. New York: Macmillan, 1962: 88. Print.

Templin, Charlotte. "Erica Jong: Becoming a Jewish Writer." Halio and Siegel 126-140.

Ann R. Shapiro, Farmingdale State College, SUNY

Michael Chabon's *The Amazing Adventures of Kavalier & Clay*:

The Return of the Golem*

Alan L. Berger

Michael Chabon's Pulitzer Prize-winning novel, *The Amazing Adventures of Kavalier & Clay*, is marked by intricacy of plot structure and sophisticated use of language. Critics unanimously praised the work: *The New York Times* found the novel to be a "towering achievement," while the *Denver Post* described the author as a "literary Houdini." The novel utilizes different genres of creative writing including that of referencing comics in telling the story of both Prague-born Joseph Kavalier, who escapes from Europe on the eve of the *Shoah*, and his New York cousin Sammy Clay, née Klayman. In the process, Chabon's plot plays out against the background of America's pre-war isolationist policy that advocated an escape from moral responsibility. The novel in fact employs the metaphor of escape as a governing principle. Kavalier studies with an escape artist before escaping his natal city and the *Shoah*; Sammy overcomes or escapes the limitations of his physical handicap; the Holocaust is dealt with only obliquely.

    Kavalier & Clay is comprised of two narratives, a longer and a shorter one. The former story deals with America and the history of the comic book industry and its oppression of creative artists between 1939 and 1955. The latter story treats response to the Holocaust in a distinctive yet problematic manner. Very few critics have, however, analyzed the novel in terms of Holocaust representation in the third, non-witnessing, generation of American-born novelists. Consequently, important issues such as the moral role of fiction, the relationship of imagination to history, and the contemporary use of Jewish myth in representing the *Shoah* have been largely elided.

Third Generation Novelists and the Holocaust

Unlike Lot's wife, the third generation runs the risk of turning into pillars of salt if they do *not* look back. They are the new bearers of *Shoah* representation. But what does it mean to look back from a distance of three score years and ten? How do third generation authors represent the *Shoah* when they lack personal memory of the Jewish catastrophe? In short, third generation works represent the Holocaust through *indirect* means, as Jessica Lang argues in her insightful article "The History of Love, the Contemporary Reader and the Transmission of Holocaust Memory." Lang notes the common thread in the Holocaust writing of authors born in the 1960s or after, whose "fiction regularly refers to and incorporates events from the Holocaust, but it also balances and counters these references with other narrative strategies or counterpoints" (46). Furthermore, third generation authors view the Holocaust "as an indirect part of the narrative, one balanced by other, also important histories" (46). I add that these works tend to be inflected by the use of magical realism and motifs from Jewish myth, folklore, and mysticism.

Chabon's novel is, however, a significant departure from Nicole Kraus's *The History of Love* both in terms of distancing the Holocaust from American concerns and in the way it represents the *Shoah*. His "survivor," Joseph Kavalier, is a refugee who does not have firsthand experience of the camps. Furthermore, unlike Kraus's protagonist, Kavalier does not write a book. Rather, he *draws* over two thousand pages of the adventures of "The Escapist," an action hero based on the golem. Consequently, rather than confronting the horrors of the Holocaust, Chabon's protagonist seeks to escape them. Lee Behlman perceptively writes: "Chabon is most surprising, [in that] his novel guardedly presents the idea that . . . distraction may be itself a valid response. *Kavalier and Clay* is an extended meditation, with comic books as its central subject, on the value of fantasy as a deflective resource rather than a reflective one" (59). Moreover, unlike Art Spiegelman's *Maus* volumes, which use the comic format to bear witness to the real story of his father's Holocaust experience and Art's own traumatic inheritance as a member of the second generation, Chabon's novel avoids encountering the *Shoah*, suggesting instead that escapism is an appropriate response. The novel pivots on Will Eisner's comment, which serves as the book's epigraph: "We have this history of impossible solutions for insoluble problems."

Holocaust Representation in Chabon's Work

Chabon's approach to writing about the Holocaust appears fraught with ambiguity. On the one hand, he told an interviewer that "I think it's obvious from the way I have treated the subject, that I don't think I feel right about approaching it in any but the most indirect way" (qtd. in Maliszewski 6). On the other hand, however, he notes that "The Holocaust itself, in its overall scope and its particulars, just defies credulity, which makes it somewhat fertile territory for deniers" (5). He then provides warrant for his own literary treatment of the *Shoah* by contending: "But I think we expect the incredible from the Holocaust" (5). In addition to *The Amazing Adventures of Kavalier & Clay*, the Holocaust plays a role, although ambiguous and even deceptive, in Chabon's *The Final Solution: A Story of Detection* (2003) and in *The Yiddish Policemen's Union* (2007).

The Final Solution title is a literary tease, a misdirection that suggests one thing—the Holocaust—but provides quite another, a detective story. The work treats a mute German boy who is a Holocaust survivor and a talking parrot who repeats a series of numbers that may be a secret Nazi code. Sherlock Holmes comes out of retirement to solve the mystery of who kills the bird. Muteness means that the reader learns nothing of the *Shoah*. The conceit of *The Yiddish Policemen's Union* is that after the Holocaust, and following the military defeat of the nascent State of Israel by Arab armies, Jews settle in Alaska, becoming "the frozen chosen." The novel includes both implicit and explicit references to Holocaust survivors. Ex-partisans dig tunnels in case they have to fight again. Meyer Landsman, the novel's detective protagonist is the son of a survivor who was a chess master. Landsman's knowledge of the game enables him to solve a bizarre murder. As was the case during the Holocaust, messianic longing both continues and continues to go unfulfilled.

Kavalier & Clay can be read on many levels: it is a *kunstlerroman* and a Jewish-American immigrant novel that contrasts the naïveté and optimism of America with the ominous events in Europe. Furthermore, Chabon's novel explores the role of comics as a serious contribution to American culture and as a means of escaping the grim reality of the Holocaust. The author steadfastly focuses on the major contribution of Jewish artists to comic books. Kavalier and Clay are loosely based on Jerry Siegel and Joe Shuster, the Jewish creators of "Superman." Moreover, as Behlman notes, the novel also is an expression of social realism in describing the unscrupulous ways of corporate culture, in the person of Sheldon Anapol, and his exploitive treatment of Kavalier and Clay (66). Chabon also employs his trademark concern about gay life and homophobia in writing about Sammy's coming out of the closet and his abuse by the police department. There is also a vivid portrayal of Greenwich Village bohemian life in the person of Rosa Luxembourg Sax, who falls in love with Joseph. In addition, Chabon inserts cameo appearances by Salvador Dalí and Orson Welles as well as pivotal references to Harry Houdini.

Following a circuitous route Joseph arrives in America where he joins forces with his cousin Sammy, who fantasizes about writing the great American novel. The cousins produce a series of comic book heroes who vicariously defeat Nazism. Chief among these heroes is the "Escapist," based on the golem, who singlehandedly knocks out Hitler and his armies. Joseph also seeks to rescue his young brother Tommy, who is trapped in Europe. Using the money he has made from his art he charters a ship—*Ark of Miriam*—to bring several hundred children to America. Unlike the biblical Miriam, Moses's sister who watches over him in the bulrushes, thereby ensuring his life and the Jewish people's future, the doomed ship is sunk by a German torpedo. All aboard perish.

The Golem in Jewish Folklore

Chabon is on firm ground in utilizing what he terms the "thinly fictionalized role [the Golem of Prague] plays in . . . *Kavalier & Clay* . . ." (*Maps & Legends* 183). Golem legends abound in the Jewish magical and mystical tradition. Moreover, Gershom Scholem notes, "the special fascination exerted by [the golem], in which so many authors found a symbol of the struggles and conflicts that were nearest their hearts" (158). The best known golem legend is that attributed to the sixteenth century scholar, Rabbi Judah Loew of Prague, known as the *Maharal* (*Moreinu ha-Rav Rabbi Liva*). Although nothing in Loew's vast writings concerns or even mentions the golem, his name is indissolubly linked with the creature. Perhaps, speculates Byron Sherwin, it is because of his stature as a "scholar, community leader, and national Bohemian hero" (19). Additionally, Judah Loew had achieved "fame as a wonder-worker" in Prague, and was invited by the emperor, Rudolph II, who had a personal interest in the kabbalah, to meet with him in his castle.

According to legend, Rabbi Loew and two disciples went to the banks of the Moldau River at four in the morning where they fashioned a golem on the river's clay bank. Following a prescribed ritual, the rabbi placed a piece of paper containing the words *Adonai Emet*—"the Lord is Truth"—under the creature's tongue. Thus animated, the creature stood. Loew named the golem Joseph (Yossele) because "he had implanted in him the spirit of Joseph Shida who was half-man and half-demon and had saved the sages of the Talmud from many trials and dangers" (Ausubel 608). Yet, as Hillel Kieval writes, it is important to note that the "golem legend "as far back as the 17th century Polish rendition [viewed] the source of danger [as] residing within the confines of the community; in the very process of the creation of artificial life" (16). Kieval further argues that the tale is misremembered in the twentieth century "as if it had always been concerned with the danger posed by the outside world" (16). That is to say the golem was believed to protect the Jewish people from Christian mobs who, inflamed by the notorious blood libel, posed a mortal danger to Jewish life.

Rabbi Loew's golem embodies three features: it is created to serve practical purposes; as a servant in the Loew home his task was to draw water from a well and to carry wood. Second, the golem, as we have noted, is potentially dangerous. Third, the golem can harm its creator. One of the versions of the Prague golem portrays the creature as flooding the *Maharal's* house. The rabbi is summoned, overpowers the creature—removing the name of God from under its tongue, and carries the body to the attic of the Altneuschul on the eve of Shabbat. He then decrees that only his successors be permitted entrance to the attic.

In Chabon's reworking of the Golem of Rabbi Loew tale, Joseph Kavalier, son of two secular Prague physicians, is a talented artist who studies techniques of escape with his mentor Bernard Kornblum, an eastern European *Ausbrecher* (escape artist). With the German army occupying Prague, the Jewish secret society responsible for the golem's safety enlists the aid of Kornblum in rescuing the slumbering giant before the German army can ship its remains to Berlin. The golem's remains had previously been spirited out of the *Altneuschul*—and hidden in an apartment house. The plan is to send the golem to Vilna.

The Golem of Michael Chabon

Chabon compares the novelist to the maker of a golem: "the relationship between a golem and its creator is usually viewed as a metaphor for that between the work of art—in my case, a novel—and its creator" (*Maps & Legends* 183). Chabon's novel, however, links the themes of physical escape with the escapism found in comic books, magic, and Jewish folklore tinged with mysticism. He refers to the "bitter truth of golems" writing:

> A golem, like a lie, is the expression of a wish: a wish for peace and security a wish for strength and control; a wish to know, in a tiny human way, a thousandth of a millionth of the joy and power of the Greater Creation. (187)

Literature, attests Chabon, "like magic has always been about the handling of secrets, about the pain, the destruction, and the marvelous liberation that can result when they are revealed" (155). However, literature representing the Holocaust typically eschews the possibility of truly revealing secrets. Moreover, is it possible to ever feel "marvelous liberation" when writing of the *Shoah*? Chabon's advocacy of escape from the *Shoah* is of course conditioned by time and space. He refers to himself as "a lucky man living in a lucky time in the luckiest country in the world" (154). Chabon is of course writing as an American whose worldview is not drenched in the blood of Europe.

Kavalier encounters bureaucratic difficulties seeking to leave Prague. Therefore, he joins forces with Kornblum to discover in which apartment house the golem is hidden. Disguising themselves as workers, they tell the building superintendent that the Jewish council sent them to survey the building in order to monitor the movement of Jews within Prague. By means of a ruse requiring all the building's Jewish inhabitants to put a blue Star of David in the window, the pair discover the golem's hiding place—it is the window without a star. As an aside it is worth noting that Kornblum utters the word "contemptible." But Joseph was unclear whether his mentor referred to "the ruse itself, the (Nazis) who made (their story) plausible, the Jews who had (willingly complied), or (Kornblum) himself for having perpetrated it" (45). Chabon here implicitly criticizes alleged Jewish complicity in their own demise.

Disguising the golem as a "dead goyishe giant," dressed in an oversize man's suit and secreting Joseph in the casket's concealed compartment, Kornblum has the casket loaded on a train headed to Lithuania where the golem and Kavalier subsequently arrive. At this point in the story, Chabon turns his attention from the liberated pair to focus on the subsequent adventures of Joseph. The physical remains of the golem do not reappear until the end of the novel, although symbolically the golem is present as comic book, as inspiration, and as therapeutic healer.

The novel's story takes place primarily in America. Joseph meets and falls in love with Rosa Luxemburg Sax and has a child with her. But he had left to join the navy without knowing of her pregnancy. The navy sends him to a listening post in Alaska. While there, he kills a German. By this device Chabon implies the futility of revenge for the Holocaust. During Joe's extended disappearance and silence, Sammy lives with Rosa. Together they raise Joseph's son Tommy. Joseph reappears in their lives. Rosa and Joseph reunite while Sammy seeks fulfillment of his gay lifestyle in Los Angeles. The casket of the golem, bearing Lithuanian shipping labels, mysteriously arrives at the end of the novel. Whereas the casket had been nearly weightless in Prague, in New York it is heavy, prompting Joe to speculate that the dust that once had been the mud of the Moldau contains the souls of the murdered Jews of Europe.

Chabon's use of the golem has given rise to various interpretations. Behlman contends that the figure "represents both the dead hope of Jewish life in Europe and the ever-living promise of Jewish creativity, which can be transferred to the new world" (63). Nicola Morris suggests that the golem is a "metaphor for power and powerlessness" (16-22). The creature was powerless to save the Jews of Europe, but it did save Joseph both physically and later in America psychologically. I will return to this idea shortly. Chabon himself combines the dimension of renewal and power in having Joe contrast the golem's use in literature and folklore, from Rabbi Loew to Victor von Frankenstein, with his own use of the figure.

> The shaping of a golem, to him, was a gesture of hope, offered against hope, in a time of desperation. It was the expression of a yearning that a few magic words and an artful hand might produce something – one poor, dumb, powerful thing – exempt from the crushing strictures, from the ills, cruelties, and inevitable failures of the greater Creation. It was the voicing of a vain wish, when you got down to it, to escape. To slip, like the Escapist, free of the entangling chain of reality and the straightjacket of physical laws. (582)

It is instructive at this point to contrast Chabon's golem with traditional understandings of the creature, noting several ironic reversals. The sixteenth and seventeenth century versions of the golem posit the creature as saving the Jewish people. In Chabon's reworking, the golem is saved by Joseph and Kornblum. Furthermore, in being smuggled out of Prague in a casket, Joseph replicates the act of Yohanan ben Zakkai who, Jewish folklore attests, fled Jerusalem, which was besieged by the Romans in the year 70 CE. The vital difference is, of course, that whereas Yohannan ben Zakkai founded the first rabbinic academy (in Yavneh), thereby birthing a transition from Temple religion to Rabbinic Judaism that enabled Judaism to survive, Chabon's protagonist saves only himself.

Perhaps the most problematic aspect of Chabon's golem is that his creature flees the enemy, whereas traditional assertions contend that the golem's fearsomeness causes the enemy to flee. But in 1945, a Holocaust survivor from Prague, who was not religious, told a story about the golem, which confirms the tale's power even in the face of Nazi evil.

> The Golem did not disappear and even in the time of war it went out of its hiding place in order to safeguard the synagogue. When the Germans occupied Prague, they decided to destroy the Altneuschul. They came to do it; suddenly, in the silence of the synagogue, the steps of a giant walking on the roof, began to be heard. They saw a shadow of a giant hand falling from the window onto the floor . . . . The Germans were terrified and they threw away their tools and fleed [sic] away in panic. I know that there is a rational explanation for everything; the synagogue is ancient and each and every slight knock generates an echo that reverberates many times, like steps or thunder. Also the glasses of the windows are old, the window-panes are crooked and they distort the shadows, forming strange shades on the floor. A bird's leg generates a shade of a giant hand on the floor . . . and nevertheless . . . there is something. (Idel 256)

The survivor's story, unlike Chabon's novel, affirms the golem's traditional task of scattering the enemies of the Jewish people. The golem is neither powerless nor inert. Moreover, the golem's act concerned not an individual Jew, as is the case with Joseph Kavalier; rather, the creature saves the Jewish House of Worship. This version may be a fantasy, but it is not a lie. Nor does it embrace the concept of escape from the *Shoah*.

The golem as a "gesture of hope" serves a therapeutic purpose in Chabon's novel via the medium of comic books. Kavalier muses first on the escapist role played by comics.

> Having lost his mother, father, brother, and grandfather, the friends and foes of his youth, his beloved teacher Bernard Kornblum, his city, his history- his home-the usual charge leveled against comic books, that they offered *merely an easy escape from reality*, seemed to Joe actually to be a powerful argument on their behalf. (575)

Escape from reality seemed "a worthy challenge, especially right after the war." Drawing *The Golem* occupied all of Joseph's time and helped heal him psychically.

> And as he dreamed, night after night at his drawing table, the long and hallucinatory tale of a wayward, unnatural child, Josef Golem, that sacrificed itself to save and redeem the little lamplit world whose safety had been entrusted to it, Joe came to feel that the work – telling this story- was helping to heal him. (577)

The *Golem* functions as nothing less than Joseph's "writing therapy," "secret record of his mourning, of his guilt and retribution."

Chabon's Use of Other Myths

Chabon also reworks the Talmudic myth of the Lamed Vov Zaddikim, which contends that the world exists owing to the presence of thirty-six hidden righteous men. These individuals, hidden because their generation is unworthy, are tasked with fighting evil. The Zaddikim, or "just" men, frequently need to descend into evil's depths in order to extricate Jews who have fallen into its clutches. This is termed the "descent in behalf of the ascent." Moreover, the Zaddik is one who puts things in their proper place, thereby restoring a notion of cosmic order that enables humanity to live in spite of apparent injustice or disorder.

Chabon's retelling of the myth involves inventing "The League of the Golden Key," a secret society whose members "roamed the world acting, always anonymously, to procure the freedom of others, whether physical or metaphysical, emotional or economic." The Golden Key's foes were agents of the "Iron Chain" whose aim was the enslavement of humanity. The novelist appears to suggest by this literary invention that escapism—the Golden Key—can rescue individuals from what Max Weber termed the "iron cage" of history. Tom Mayflower, the crippled apprentice to his magician uncle Max, is cured of his affliction upon receiving the golden key from the mortally wounded Max. Tom raises the key and swears "a sacred oath to devote himself to secretly fighting the evil forces of the Iron Chain in Germany or wherever they raise their ugly heads and to working for the liberation of all who toil in chains—as the Escapist."

Chabon also offers readers "Luna Moth," a feminist tale of the transformation of Miss Judy Dark, "Under-Assistant Cataloguer of Decommissioned Volumes," whose office is deep underground in the Empire City Public Library. Interrupting the theft of an important artifact, the Book of Lo, Judy is electrocuted by a live wire, becoming Luna Moth, a creature who receives instructions from the Cimmerian moth goddess Lo. Lo tells her that Cimmeria, once ruled by women, was a peaceful Queendom overthrown by men who "have been making a hash of things." Lo tells her new disciple that "she has only to imagine something to make it so." Henceforth, Judy/Luna will "haunt the night"—a time when evil often occurs—and defeat the evil ones. The fantasy scene culminates with Luna Moth rescuing the Book of Lo and freeing the kidnapped library guard. In Chabon's telling, these various myths each offer an angle of vision on the escape motif where the imagination overcomes physical death and suffering.

Conclusion

The Amazing Adventures of Kavalier & Clay illustrates both the possibilities and challenges of third generation Holocaust representation. On the one hand, Chabon seeks to acknowledge both the bond and the barrier existing between Jews on the American and European sides of the Atlantic. He recognizes that American innocence must yield before the enormity of the Holocaust. And he skillfully portrays the isolationist sentiment in America and the reluctance to antagonize Germany prior to America's eventual entry into World War II. Moreover, escaping the nightmare of Auschwitz, at least temporarily, may enable one to continue one's existence. It is, after all the case, that apart from a very few survivor memoirs, American novelists did not begin responding to the Holocaust for approximately fifteen years after the War.

On the other hand, the novel endorses a typically American embrace of the happy ending. Joe is reunited with Rosa and their son. Moreover, the protagonist is at peace psychologically and emotionally. He has, with the "help" of the golem, worked through the trauma of having lost his entire family, thereby enabling him to achieve at least a temporary *tikkun* (healing/repair). But this *tikkun* is of the self (*aztmi*). It does not address the broader and classically Jewish notion of *tikkun ha'olam* (repair of the world). Further, visiting Houdini's grave, Joe muses on the distinction between hope and belief: "No; he could be ruined again and again by hope, but he would never be capable of belief." This distinction is important but ultimately misleading. While it is certainly true that the *Shoah* destroyed the possibility of belief for some survivors, for others it was a reaffirmation of their faith. The faith and doubt of Holocaust survivors is a complex issue, and while Chabon's novel emphasizes the destruction of hope, it does so at the expense of admitting the possibility of continued faith after Auschwitz.

A further word needs to be said about Chabon's Holocaust representation. He utilizes magic and mysticism as they coalesce in the golem figure. Consequently, the *Shoah* is transformed into a metaphor and there is no distinction between the mysticism of hope and the Nazi mysticism of death. As John Podhoretz writes:

> The Jews of Central Europe, both those who were murdered and those who escaped murder, were ordinary people. In attempting to memorialize them and pay tribute to their suffering, Chabon descends into a false mysticism. It is true that their tradition featured a certain mystical strain, but it is also horrifically true that mysticism was among the forces that led to their extermination—an evil mysticism that promised the world would be purified by their removal. (71-72)

Moreover, *The Amazing Adventures of Kavalier & Clay* generalizes the *Shoah* so that Europe's murdered Jews are a nameless and anonymous group whose memory may, or may not, be for a blessing.

What is the moral responsibility of the novelist? On the one hand, while the reader's first impulse may be to recoil at Chabon's new direction in Holocaust representation, it may be that embedding the Holocaust in a broader narrative is one way to ensure that readers are reminded of the Jewish catastrophe. In the post-modern and multicultural world, novelists need to determine ways in which to navigate the shape-shifting contours between the particular and the universal in a new and challenging environment. However, I cannot avoid the uneasy feeling that it is one thing for Elie Wiesel to write: "The ghetto was ruled by neither German nor Jew; it was ruled by delusion" (12). At that time the Jews of Hungary did not understand that they were to be exterminated. It is quite another thing for Chabon to advocate escapism at a time when everything is known, at least about whom the Holocaust was designed to eliminate and why. Finally, there are two unhappy results of escapism. The first is that one cannot escape the Holocaust any more than one can escape the impact of Rome's destruction of the Jerusalem Temple. Second, escapism leads to forgetting. And forgetting is the ultimate form of Holocaust denial.

Works Cited

Ausubel, Nathan. *A Treasury of Jewish Folklore: Stories, Traditions, Legends, Humor, Wisdom and Folk Songs of the Jewish People.* New York: Crown Publishers, 1948. Print.

Behlman, Lee. "The Escapist: Fantasy, Folklore, and the Pleasure of the Comic Book in Recent Jewish American Holocaust Fiction." *Shofar,* 23.4 (2004) 56-71. Print.

Chabon, Michael. *The Amazing Adventures of Kavalier & Clay.* New York: Picador, 2000. Print.

———. *Maps & legends: Reading and Writing Along the Borderlands.* New York: Harper Perennial, 2009. Print.

Idel, Moshe. *Golem: Jewish Magical and Mystical Traditions on the Artificial Anthropoid.* Albany: SUNY Press, 1989. Print.

Kieval, Hillel. "Pursuing the Golem of Prague: Jewish Culture and the Invention of Tradition." *Modern Judaism,* 17 (1997): 1-23. Print.

Lang, Jessica. "*The History of Love,* the Contemporary Reader and the Transmission of Holocaust Memory." *Journal of Modern Literature,* 33.1 (2010) 43-56. Print.

Maliszewski, Paul. "Lie, Memory: Michael Chabon's Own Private Holocaust." *Artforum International.* 43.8 (April 2005): 1-9. Web. 12 Oct. 2009.

Morris, Nicola. *The Golem in Jewish American Literature: Risks and Responsibilities in the Fiction of Thane Rosenbaum, Nomi Eve and Steve Stern.* New York: Peter Lang, 2007. Print.

Podhoretz, John. *Commentary.* 111, no. 6 (2001) 68-72. Print.

Scholem, Gershom G. "The Idea of the Golem," in *On the Kabbalah and Its Symbolism.* Trans. Ralph Manheim. New York: Schocken, 1996: 158-204. Print.

Sherwin, Byron. *Golems Among Us: How a Jewish Legend Can Help Us Navigate the Biotech Century.* Chicago: Ivan R. Dee, 2004. Print.

Wiesel, Elie. *Night.* Trans. Marion Wiesel. New York: Hill and Wang, 2006. Print.

Alan L. Berger, Florida Atlantic University

Two Views of Jews:

Bernard Malamud, Maurice Samuel, and the Beilis Case

Carole S. Kessner

Imagine my dismay when I opened my e-mail inbox on the morning of August 19, 2009 to find two messages that a leading Swedish newspaper reported that Israeli soldiers are kidnapping and killing Palestinians in order to steal their body parts. The headline in *Aftonbladet,* Sweden's largest left-leaning daily newspaper, read "They plunder the organs of our sons;" the double page spread article was given pride of place in its "Culture" section, quoting Palestinian reports that young men from Gaza and the West Bank had been abducted by the IDF and returned to their families—but with missing organs. The reports I read online that day were in *Haaretz* and *Honest Reporting.* I was outraged—and more than a bit skeptical. It couldn't be, I thought, that in this day and age, in the twenty-first century, we were facing a blood libel accusation. But the reports about this bizarre case kept showing up all over the Internet and on YouTube; and finally on August 24, David Harris, the Executive Director of the American Jewish Committee, published a scathing letter in the *Jerusalem Post* to Foreign Minister Bildt of Sweden in which he charged, "despite many requests, you have chosen not to comment on the article's unfounded, indeed ludicrous, allegations."

This latest episode in the rampant spread of lies about Jews came at exactly the moment when I was working on a study of two books published in 1967 about a blood libel case that had occurred in Russia in 1913. Obviously, the convergence of the 2009 news and the 1967 books about a 1913 crime was enough to shake my faith in progress. How could it be that in the twenty-first century we were still fending off medieval myths about our ritual depravities? How could it be that after the Enlightenment, after the pogroms, after the Holocaust, after the great contributions of the Jews to modern civilization, such primitive accusations would not die of shame? But, it appears, they still live. Perhaps, I thought, my study of the two modern books would reveal some sort of an answer.

Maurice Samuel's history of the setup, trial, and acquittal of a Russian-Jewish bricklayer, Mendel Beilis, titled *Blood Accusation*, was published in the United States in 1966 by Alfred Knopf. In an odd coincidence, only a few weeks later Bernard Malamud's prize-winning novel, *The Fixer*, a fictional rendering of the incarceration of Mendel Beilis, was published in the United States by Farrar, Strauss and Giroux. The coincidence, if it was a coincidence, piqued my curiosity. What could have been the motivation for two major American Jewish writers to return to a story that took place in Czarist Russia half a century before, a story that could be thought of as the poor man's Dreyfus? A good place to start looking for clues might be to note the events in the few years preceding the publication of these books. In 1966, Elie Weisel's report of his trip to the Soviet Union appeared in the Israeli newspaper *Yediot Aharanot*. It would soon become his powerful book *The Jews of Silence*. In this work he reported that despite discrimination and lack of freedom, Russian Jews still wanted "to remain Jews" (vii). The book brought to the attention of the Western World the grim situation of the imprisoned Soviet Jews (1987). The Jewish community, however, really had known it before—ever since Golda Meir's trip to Russia in 1948 as the first Israeli Ambassador to the U.S.S.R. when she was smothered with acclamation outside the Moscow synagogue on Rosh Hashanah by 40,000 Jews seeking to get a glimpse of her. Their unspoken message was clear; it was not good for the Jews in Russia, and they gloried in Golda as the icon of the new State of Israel.

Two years before Elie Wiesel's report, in 1964, the musical *Fiddler on the Roof* opened on Broadway. Set in 1905, the year of the failed Revolution and six years before the Beilis case, *Fiddler* was the antithesis of the *Jews of Silence* in its unabashed romantic nostalgia and sweet sentimentality—all the warts and lesions of Czarist Russian *shtetl* life skillfully excised. In America of 1966, talk of Russian Jews, past and present, was in the air. And it would be only a few years later, in 1974, that the Jackson-Vanek human rights amendment, which denies most favored nation status to countries with non-market economies that restrict emigration, was finally signed into law. The amendment was meant to allow persecuted religious or ethnic minorities to emigrate—in particular, Soviet *refuseniks*—who while waiting for an exit permit became virtual pariahs, were dismissed from their jobs, abandoned by their colleagues, and harassed by the police. Jackson-Vanek is still in effect.

What was that twentieth century crime that sparked the literary imaginations of Maurice Samuel and Bernard Malamud? The grim tale begins in the criminal netherworld of Kiev in the Ukraine—a city with a notorious reputation—especially for Jews. Although Kiev was located within the Pale of Settlement, most Jews had been denied residence in the city; and until the 1917 Revolution, Kiev was infamous for police "hunt attacks"—hunts for Jews without residence rights. In response to the failed revolution of 1905, massive pogroms had burst onto the streets of most Russian cities, and in Kiev for several days rioters attacked both the rich city Jews and poor Jews of the suburbs while the army and the police looked the other way.

Anti-Semitism never really had disappeared from this Ukrainian city. In general, one could say that Ukraine had not been a congenial place for Jews since the Chmielnicki massacres of the seventeenth century. In turn of the century Kiev, extremist political fanatics, the Black Hundred and the Two-Headed Eagle, antecedents of later fascistic political organizations, tapped into the prevailing anti-Semitism of the general populace and attacked the Jews with primitive allegations about their religious beliefs and practices. These proto-fascist groups were encouraged by the support of Czar Nicholas and his reactionary counselors, who understood that these patriotic, pro-monarchist, anti-Semitic organizations, comprised of hoodlums and sycophants in search of career advancement, could be used as politically effective tools against the influence of anti-monarchist, Marxist, revolutionary, subversive, unpatriotic Jews.

The Beilis case began on March 12, 1911, when a Russian boy, Andrei Yuschinsky, was murdered by a gang of thugs who thought the boy was going to inform the police about their criminal activity. On March 20 his mutilated body was found in a cave outside of the city. The Czarist press quickly publicized it as a case of ritual murder, accusing the Jews of using the boy's blood in the baking of matzos. Emboldened by the accusation, at the boy's funeral the Black Hundred distributed leaflets charging the Jews with ritual murder. By this time, however, the police had actually traced the murder to a gang of crooks and their leader, a whore named Vera Cherberiak, notorious for prostitution and other criminal activities, but the Black Hundred pressured the anti-Semitic Minister of Justice to charge that it was a case of ritual murder. Consequently, the chief district attorney had to drop the police information and find a Jew on whom to pin the blood accusation. The Black Hundred was correct in its assessment that the indicted Jew would be regarded as a representative of all Jews, whom they regarded as obstructionist, anti-monarchist, leftist revolutionaries, and therefore the charge would provoke a pogrom.

In July a lamplighter testified that he had seen the murdered boy playing with two other boys on the premises of the brick factory that was owned by a Jew named Zaitsev. He also claimed that he had seen a Jew appear on the premises who grabbed Yushinsky and dragged him toward the kiln. With nothing more than this to go on, on July 21 the police arrested the superintendent of the brick factory, Mendel Beilis, and sent him to prison where he remained for over two years. Czar Nicholas was informed that the judiciary regarded Beilis as the murderer.

Unfortunately, however, the killers had provided a useful clue. Either before or after the murder—it was never clearly determined—they stabbed the body many times to suggest that its blood had been drained for ritual purposes; but they did a crude job. Later medical testimony proved that the many gashes were made in places that could not possibly have been used for the draining of blood. Undoubtedly, the killers thought that their post-murder slashes would shift the attention away from themselves. It is also likely that they hoped to incite a pogrom, which was always a good opportunity for thieves (they could loot and rape). In fact, the thugs may have been instructed by the infamous, lethal Jew-hater, the Czarist Prime Minister Peter

Stolypin, who, seeing this crime as an invitation to divert revolutionary agitation, quickly ordered the district attorney of Kiev to pump up the charge of ritual murder. This was the beginning of a legal conspiracy requiring bribes, coercion, arm twisting, lies, misrepresentations—all manner of distortions and falsehoods—as well as the cooperation of the Minister of Justice and the Director of the Police Department of the Ministry of the Interior. All the while Czar Nicholas followed the news and gave his approval.

The trial took place in Kiev from September 25 through October 28, 1913. With a jury almost totally comprised of peasants and a judge handpicked by the prosecution, Menachem Mendel Beilis, a married man with a family of five children, was framed for the ritual murder of a thirteen-year-old boy. He had been in prison for over two years, waiting for his indictment. Though every trick of cross examination, every deception, all kinds of torture were used to force Beilis to confess, he stood his ground and refused to admit any guilt. He adamantly refused to plea bargain, even though he had been urged to do so by the prosecution. He did not confess to a crime that he did not commit because he knew that if he did, it would clinch the assertion that a ritual murder had taken place, and he then would be the cause of a pogrom.

But the world of reasonable men and women were not deceived. The prosecution's case was too preposterous, from the testimony of the ringleader Vera Cherberiak, an infamous prostitute, to two bribed medical professors, as well as to Father Pranaitis, a Roman Catholic priest with a criminal record who testified using phony Talmudic sources for the lurid myriad ritual customs of Jews—especially those practices related to the use of Christian blood. One had to be unhinged or illiterate to believe the ludicrous case put forward by the prosecution.

Here is the opinion of Father Pranaitis as recorded in the indictment:

> All the rabbinical schools, notwithstanding their divergences on various questions, are united by their hatred of non-Jews, who according to the Talmud are not considered human beings but only "animals in human form." The hatred and the spite which the Jews, from the point of view of their religious law, feel toward people of a different nationality and religion, are especially strong toward Christians. Because of this feeling, the Talmud allows and even commands the killing of non-Jews. . . .The extermination of non-jews is commanded as a religious act. . . .[that] hastens the coming of the Messiah. (qtd. in Samuel 162)

Father Pranaitis goes on to explain that the *Zohar* (the prime mystical work of Kabbalah) contains a description of a ritual murder, and he asserts that he found the wounds on Yuschinsky's body "indications that the murder was carried out in strict accordance with Jewish religious prescription" (qtd. in Samuel 162).

Yes—the story is preposterous, worthy only of the gory Gothicism found in pulp magazines, DVDs, on the Internet, and on YouTube. That, perhaps, is why the case attracted universal interest. There were protests, verbal and written, by public figures, lawyers, scientists, politicians, artists, clergy, and so on. Perhaps one quotation will give the flavor. These words, written by Vladimir Nabokov *père*, father of the poet-novelist-lepidopterist, expressed this opinion:

> Beilis was tried by jury, and the first impression of everyone was unanimous: people were astonished and perplexed by the choice of jurors. [I]t consisted of practically illiterate peasants and commoners.

> During the trial the Judge declared more than once: "Nobody here accuses Judaism, we are talking of individual fanatics only." But the statements of Sikorsky [expert psychiatrist for the prosecution] and Pranaitis disprove his words. . . . Both of them spoke about Judaism, about the Hebrew faith . . . . And then came the Judge's charge, and all this complicated research into the Bible, the *Talmud*, the *Kaballah*, the *Zohar*, proved to be irrelevant . . . . This syllogism remains in all its nakedness: Beilis is a Jew, consequently Beilis could have taken part in this bloody sacrifice. . . .

> Years will go by, the memory of the Beilis trial will gradually fade away, the impressions will lose their poignancy, but the record, dry and impartial, the stenographic record, will remain. And no matter how many years will go by, the future historian of Russian justice . . . will read these ravings, these affirmations obtained from anti-Semitic literature of the lowest kind, presented under the guise of the scientific authority . . . and he will ask in amazement: "How did it come about that the Presiding Judge did not stop this expert?". . . .

> [W]e can say with complete assurance that ten or fifteen years ago such a trial would have been impossible. (qtd. in Samuel 230)

In the end, after Beilis's two years in prison waiting for the trial to begin, after hours of deliberation, the jury finally acquitted Mendel Beilis. The lamplighter and his wife, whose depositions were the original basis for the indictment, when later questioned by the presiding judge retracted their testimony and stated that they knew "nothing at all," that they had been given vodka, that they were confused by the secret police, that they were asked questions that they did not understand. No wonder that even this jury, comprised of illiterate, superstitious peasants, could not bring themselves to convict Menachem Mendel Beilis. Unanimously, they proclaimed him "not guilty." But the prosecution did have its victory. Though Beilis was acquitted of the crime, their main purpose during the long trial was to establish the fact that a ritual murder had been committed. By crafty manipulation of the kind of questions presented to the jury, with the cooperation of the presiding judge, the prosecution succeeded in having the jury put on the court record the fact that a ritual murder had been perpetrated. After the trial, because Beilis feared the revenge of the Black Hundred, he and his family left for Palestine and in 1920 went to the United States where he wrote his own account of the trial, *Story of My Sufferings* (1926).

This story, however, did fade. Though it has been compared to the Dreyfus affair that went on from1894 until 1906—only five years before Mendel Beilis was arrested—the Dreyfus affair *never* faded[1] but the Beilis case fell into obscurity. That is, until 1966, when both Maurice Samuel and Bernard Malamud wrote their books on the subject.

The first of the two, Maurice Samuel's *Blood Accusation: The Strange History of the Beiliss* [sic] *Case* is a meticulous study of all the primary and secondary sources available, including any witness or surviving family member that he could find. Samuel provides a fully detailed chronicle of the drama of this legal travesty, reconstructing piece by piece the trumped-up case by the prosecution and the brilliant case of the defense. It is a detailed book, but it reads like a riveting courtroom drama, complete with *dramatis personae*, necessary for the list of unfamiliar Russian names. But fascinating as the subject is, one does wonder what drew the author to it at the time. Surely he had not intended merely to write a best-selling murder mystery.

Perhaps a few details about the author will help. Maurice Samuel was born in Rumania in 1895. His family moved to France and then England, where Samuel was educated at the University of Manchester. There he attended class taught by Chaim Weizmann, whose biography he would later help to write. He arrived in the U.S. in 1914 and enlisted in the American army in 1917, serving in France until 1919. A gifted linguist, immediately after the war he was dispatched to the Versailles Peace Conference as an interpreter; this was followed by a similar stint with the Reparations Commissions in Berlin and Vienna. He returned to America in 1921 and later spent ten years in Mandatory Palestine. During the years between the Balfour Declaration and the establishment of the State of Israel, Samuel was one of the most influential and popular spokesman for Zionism; his major interest throughout his life, however, was the problem of living in two civilizations. He was very much at home in both the Jewish and the Anglo-American cultures, and he tried reconcile the two—but before long he saw major problems. First, was the problematic situation of the Jew in the Western World because of anti-Semitism. Moreover, he concluded that the Jewish and Gentile approaches to fundamental, existential questions were antithetical; thus his writings were much occupied with drawing distinctions between the Jewish and Christian worldviews.

During the mid-twentieth century, Samuel was lionized in the American Jewish public as a spectacular lecturer, debater, polemicist, linguist, translator, and novelist, and in an essay entitled "Remembering Maurice Samuel," Cynthia Ozick confesses that in her youth she was a Samuel groupie who followed him from lectern to lectern. She spoke of him as the best polemicist of our time for whom "the Jewish view is never yielded up through simple declaration or exposition; it is wrested out of engagement with and finally a disengagement from, an alternative world view" (Ozick 214-15). Pointing out the distinctions between the two cultures became the theme of such books as *The Gentlemen and the Jew* and *The Professor and the Fossil*. Summing up the Jewish ethos concisely, Samuel has written "to make morality and nationhood a unity, is Jewish as theme and experience" (*Light on Israel* 207).

Does this rehearsal of Samuel's deeds, accomplishments, and writings answer the question as to what drew him to this subject? Maurice Samuel, the consummate polemicist, takes no chances and shuns veiled hints; he tells his readers outright precisely how and why he came to write about the Beilis case, what relevance forty years *ex post facto* he found to issues of his time. Samuel begins with some personal details:

> I was a student at an English University . . . when Mendel Beiliss [sic] an employee in a Kiev (Russia) brick factory, was brought to trial in September 1913 on the charge of having murdered a Christian boy in order to use his blood for ritual purposes prescribed by the Jewish religion. I recall vividly, I live through again the incredulity followed by indignation that the case aroused and, finally, the sense of an insolent challenge flung in the face of twentieth century enlightenment. Above all I remember the anxiety with which the outcome of the trial was awaited; and because the reawakened feeling of participation is strong, I have permitted a personal note to enter here and there into this historical record. (*B. A.* 3, 4)

But it was not simply the personal experience that led Samuel to his project, nor was it only his lifelong concern with anti-Semitism. As an episode in "the continuing struggle between progress and reaction," he asserts, it has universal meaning:

> It is . . . an early instance of the modern governmental use of the big lie, which must be distinguished from traditional modes of lying common to governments and individuals. The big lie does not simply misstate facts: rather it aims at the subversion of the intelligence. It does not ask how plausible the lie appears in the eyes of informed people; it makes its assertions with brazen disregard for what is known and seeks, by immense clamor, by vast rhythmic repetition, to make thinking impossible. (*B. A.* 268)

Furthermore, Samuel maintains that the Beilis case was a primitive idea that was ill timed. It is a mistake, he points out, "to think that any big lie can be successfully established at any time. The big lie too must count on a certain minimum of receptivity." That, Samuel argues, is why *The Protocols* [*of the Elders of Zion*] did so much better than the blood accusation in the twentieth century. (One can only guess what he might say today about the resurgence of blood accusation in the twenty-first century.) Finally, Samuel asserts that when one studies the Beilis case in detail with all its "grotesqueries and villainies," with its disregard for scruples and inhibitions, one "perceives that it was a crude preview of the destructive possibilities of the twentieth century, a hint of the depths to which civilized man could sink" (*B. A.* 268).

Bernard Malamud's motivation and perspective on the Beilis case is quite different from that of Samuel, though it too has origins in the personal, and means to have broader significance. Malamud was one generation younger than Samuel. He was an American, born in Brooklyn in 1914 to Max and Bertha Fidelman Malamud—both immigrants from the Ukrainian shtetl Kaminets-Podolski; but he himself had no firsthand experience of European Jewry. His father owned a small grocery store, eking out a meager living in the Gravesend section of Brooklyn (an irony considering Max's lack of financial success). Bernard Malamud thought of Max as a loving but rather dull husband and father who did not observe Jewish ritual or go to synagogue because he " thought of himself as a socialist and free thinker" (Davis 8). At the age of thirteen the young Bernard discovered his mother frothing at the mouth after having swallowed disinfectant in a failed suicide attempt. Diagnosed with schizophrenia, she was sent to an institution where she died in what was probably suicide only two years later. His younger brother Eugene was also schizophrenic and lived out his life in and out of institutions.

There was little culture in Malamud's home, where his father read the Yiddish papers and spoke broken English. But he did buy his son a set of the *Book of Knowledge*—the book that introduced young Bernard to the world of cultivated English language. Malamud attended Erasmus Hall High School, City College, and received an MA in English from Columbia in 1942.He married a Roman Catholic of Italian heritage, Ann de Chiara in 1945, and in 1947 his son Paul was born. He taught evening classes at Erasmus Hall High School, all the while writing short fiction. Then, in 1949, Malamud went west to a former land grant college, Oregon State, where he taught freshman composition and wrote his first novel *The Natural*—a baseball allegory on the mythical theme of the Grail quest.

As he was preparing to write his second novel, he explained,

> I was sharing my office with a colleague who often wished aloud that he were a Jew. I understood the sentiment. I was glad I was, although my father had his doubts about that. He had sat in mourning when I married my Gentile wife, but I had thought it out and felt I knew what I was doing. After the birth of our son Paul my father came to greet my wife and gently touch his grandchild. I thought of him as I began *The Assistant* and felt I would often be writing about Jews, in celebration and expiation, though perhaps that was having it both ways. I wanted it both ways. I conceived of myself as a cosmopolitan man enjoying his freedom. (qtd. in Cheuse 6)

From these details, one is led to conclude that Malamud's relationship to his Jewishness was an ambivalent one. Like many Jewish intellectuals of his generation, he thought of himself as Jewish American—with Jewish as the adjective modifying the noun. For Samuel, the terms were reversed.

Malamud's father died in 1954 of a heart attack—the next month Malamud began work on *The Assistant*. The central figure of *The Assistant*, Morris Bober, is a *good*-hearted struggling grocery store owner with a *bad* heart. He hires an apprentice, named Frank Alpine (named to suggest St. Francis), a poor wandering Italian from out West who talks Morris into hiring him as an assistant. He steals from Morris whom he admires, tries to rape Morris's daughter Helen—whom he actually loves—and all the while insists that he wants to do good, but finds that he cannot control himself. Morris dies of a heart attack, and Frank inherits the struggling store, despite having asked and answered the question: "What kind of a man do you have to be to shut yourself up in an overgrown coffin and never once during the day, so help you, outside of going for your Yiddish newspaper, poke your beak out of the door for a snootful of air? The answer wasn't hard to say—you had to be a Jew" (103). In the end Frank converts to Judaism, and after Passover, which is after the fact, he is circumcised.

If Malamud's first novel was an allegory of the Grail myth, *The Assistant*, too, is derived from traditional material. In this case his novel is a parable, a Christian "*midrash*," on a New Testament text—Paul's *Letter to the Romans*—in which the major themes of the *Letter* are resurrected in the novel: such ideas as the re-interpretation of the Hebrew Law from the law of Moses to the Christian law of love; circumcision after the fact; Paul's own confession of his many sins that he has been unable to control. The characters in the novel correspond to the groups Paul speaks of in his letter—Jews, Greeks, and Barbarians; and in chapter I of the *Letter*, Paul states his main theme, which is his desire to wipe out the distinctions between Jews and Gentiles. If these parallels are not sufficiently convincing, there is one clinching argument for the textual influence: the words of the Orthodox Rabbi's eulogy at Morris Bober's funeral. After saying that he knows that Morris Bober "worked among the Gentiles, and sold trayfe, and not once in 20 years comes inside a synagogue," he still would call Morris a Jew because "he lived in the Jewish experience, which he remembered with a Jewish heart. . . .He was true to the spirit [not the letter] of our life—to want for others that which he also wants for himself. He followed the law which God gave to Moses on Sinai . . ." And then in a sentence that directly quotes Paul—the rabbi says, "He suffered, he endured, but with hope" (Malamud 275). The relevant text here is chapter 5:3-5 of Paul's *Letter to the Romans*: "we rejoice in our sufferings, knowing that suffering produces endurance, and endurance produces character, and character produces hope." The plain meaning is that suffering is an ennobling experience—through suffering and the strength to withstand it comes moral improvement, and thence redemption. Philip Roth, often an admirer of Malamud, has wryly commented that "a less hopeful Jewish writer than Malamud might not have understood Alpine's transformation into a Jewish grocer . . . as a sign of moral improvement, but as the cruel realization of Bober's revenge, 'Now suffer, you goy bastard, the way I did'" (October 3, 1974).

"Suffering servant" saintliness may not have been Roth's style, but a more likely voice of approbation might be Martin Buber—obviously suggested by Malamud's decision to name his protagonist Morris Bober. Buber even may have provided Malamud with a model for Morris. In 1951, Martin Buber contributed an essay to an anthology entitled *Two Types of Faith* called "A New Type of Faith" in which he asserts the appearance of Paulinism without Christ. The essay focuses on Paul's *Letter to the Romans*. Buber writes, "The periods of Christian history can be classified according to the degree in which they are dominated by Paulinism, by which we mean, of course, not just a system of thought, but a mode of seeing and being which dwells in the life itself. In this, our era is a Pauline one to a particular degree. In the human life of our day . . . Christianity is receding, but the Pauline view and attitude is gaining mastery in circles outside of Christianity." Buber claims that the Pauline view has penetrated Jewish thought, and he proposes a type that instantly evokes the image of Morris Bober. In this new Paulinism, Buber explains, "the redeemed Christian soul stands over against an unredeemed world in lofty impotence" (Buber 162, 3).

When Bernard Malamud began to search for a subject for his next novel he wrote to a friend that he was "tense, anxious, somewhat depressed" as he thought about writing his new book:

> [My] doubt centers on this new novel I have in mind. I had originally wanted to center a story (because I've never done any such thing) around people like Sacco and Vanzetti, which I, like many people, felt was one of the great tragedies of American life in the twentieth century. However, I've decided that the reality is greater than any fiction; that is to say, I doubt fiction could equal the effect of the incident . . . so I settled for a combination of a blood ritual incident in pre-Soviet Russia, plus something like the Dreyfus incident. A man is put in prison, and there he must suffer out his existence with *what* he has and, in a sense, conceive himself again. It is, as you see, my old subject matter. (qtd. in Davis 235)

It would turn out to be his old subject matter—suffering, endurance, redemption—with a slightly new twist: the passive sufferer is placed in the context of history.

Interestingly, Leonard Shapiro, reviewing Maurice Samuel's book in the *The New York Review of Books*, writes, "I wish Mr. Samuel had told us rather more about Beilis—a gentle, almost saintly man, whose resignation and patience in the face of the most appalling persecution was very moving to all who witnessed it. Perhaps there is little more to be disclosed about him. But he remains a shadowy figure during his two-and-a half years in prison and his the thirty-four-day trial" (32).

Shapiro's words sound like an advertisement for *The Fixer*, for that is precisely what Malamud did; he concentrated his eye on the shadowy figure, fleshed him out, and brought him into the foreground—bleak as it is. The very vagueness, however, was an artist's dream. Freedom to invent. In fact, Malamud himself has asserted that he had used some of Beilis's experience, but not the man himself, "partly because his life came to less than he had paid for it by his *suffering and endurance* [italics mine], and because I had to have room to invent" (qtd. in Davis 240). Placing the mantle of suffering on Yakov Bok, Malamud invents a personal situation quite unlike that of the real Mendel Beilis, who was married and the father of five children, who lived openly as Jew and on good terms with his fellow workers at the brickworks in Kiev even though the factory was located in a section of Kiev that was restricted for Jews, except if they had a special permit, which Beilis had. Bok's situation is quite different. The first part of the book is all invention; Bok, a simple man, is alone—his fictional wife Raisl, who is barren, has left him, and he decides to flee the narrow and bleak life of the shtetl. Packing his tools (he is a fixer—handyman), his books, including his beloved volume of the heretical Jewish philosopher Spinoza, and his prayer articles, he takes off for the big city, accidently (but symbolically) dropping his bag of prayer items in the Dnieper river. Again, unlike Beilis, Bok has no residence permit, so he tries to pass himself off as a Russian and takes a Gentile name. He lives by himself near the brickworks and is shunned by the other workers who despise him. The fixer's *tsuris* begins with his decision to pass himself off as a Russian when he is arrested. Under pressure he admits that he is a Jew: "He had stupidly pretended to be somebody he wasn't, hoping it would create 'opportunities', and had learned otherwise—the wrong opportunities—and was paying for learning" (72).

The rest of the novel is closer to the facts, to the terrible suffering he undergoes in imprisonment in his cell—which grows smaller and smaller as he awaits the indictment—with the anguish, the physical torture, with the obscene actions of his jailers, with the corruption and anti-Semitism of the officials at the trial and in the jail. At one point he rejects the God of Israel altogether and says, "Don't talk to me about God. . . . I want no part of God. When you need him, he is farthest away" (256). In the course of the book he summons all his powers merely to survive. Near the end of the book his guard reminds him of one saying he always used to repeat from memory: "But he who endures to the end will be saved." The guard adds, "It's either from Matthew or Luke, one or the other." By novel's end, Yakov Bok has suffered *in extremis* and has endured—but in what sense has he been saved? On the last page he says, "One thing I've learned . . . there's no such thing as an unpolitical man, especially a Jew" (335). This is moral illumination, but not salvation.

Malamud, it would seem, turned to the Beilis narrative [2] because he saw in it a vehicle for his personal vision of redemptive suffering, the central theme of both *The Assistant* and *The Fixer*. In these works, moreover, the transformative power of passive suffering and endurance is presented in terms of the individual experience. Personal salvation, however, has never been a central concern of Judaism. Yes—there *is* the powerful text of the "suffering servant" in Second Isaiah (40-66), which seems to present the Jewish case for redemption *after* much suffering, but not *through* it. More importantly, the "suffering servant" is not a specific individual, but an allegorical figure representing the suffering of the nation Israel during the Babylonian captivity and exile; he does not suffer passively and accept Israel's condition, but powerfully challenges God; finally, in Second Isaiah, salvation does not mean personal moral illumination, but rather, the restoration of the people to its land, Zion, which will take place in history, on this earth. Malamud's conception of the meaning of redemption is, therefore, inconsistent with traditional Jewish ideas. Maurice Samuel's conception of redemption is quite consistent with Jewish ideas: it is collective; it will take place in history, on this earth, and in a specific location: *Eretz Israel* (the land of Israel). And if mankind wills it, in our time.

Notes

1.　The memory of, and interest in, the Dreyfus affair is apparent in three recent publications: *Why the Dreyfus Affair Matters,* Louis Begley, Yale UP 2009; "Trial of the Century," Adam Gopnik, *The New Yorker,* 28 Sept. 2009; and *For the Soul of France: Culture Wars in the Age of Dreyfus.* Frederick Brown, New York, Knopf 2010.

2.　Before Malamud settled on Beilis as the subject of his novel, he had considred not only Sacco and Vanzetti, but also Caryl Chessman and Martin Luther King.

Works Cited

Buber, Martin. *Two Types of Faith: The Interpenetration of Judaism and Christianity.* Trans. Norman Goldhawk. New York: Syracuse UP, 2004. Print.

Cheuse, Alan, and Nicholas Delbanco, eds. *Talking Horse:Bernard Malamud on Life and Work.* New York: Columbia UP, 1977. Print.

Davis, Philip. *Bernard Malamud: A Writer's Life.* New York: Oxford UP, 2007. Print.

Malamud, Bernard. *The Fixer.* New York: Farrar, Straus and Giroux, 1966. Print

———. *The Assistant.* New York: Dell, 1957. Print.

Ozick, Cynthia. "Remembering Maurice Samuel," *Art & Ardor: Essays by Cynthia Ozick.* New York: Knopf, 1983. 110-16. Print.

Roth, Philip. "Imagining Jews," *New York Review of Books.* 3 Oct. 1974. Print.

Samuel, Maurice. *Blood Accusation: The Strange History of the Beiliss Case.* New York: Knopf, 1966. Print.

———. *Light on Israel.* New York: Knopf, 1968. Print.

Shapiro Leonard. New York Review of Books. 1 June 1967. Print

Weisel, Elie. *The Jews of Silence.* 3rd ed. New York: Schocken, 1987. Print.

Carole S. Kessner, SUNY Stony Brook

Crossing Boundaries:

Memory and Trauma

Myra Sklarew

Simon Schama wrote, in *Landscape and Memory*, that he learned from his teacher how history is not to be found only in the text but through the archives of the feet (24). In my eleven lengthy journeys throughout Lithuania beginning in 1993, I was, like many others, searching out my Jewish roots in a country that I never imagined I would visit. But my American feet took me back into the villages once inhabited by my family. And to the very places of massacre where their lives came to an end. At first it seemed only in the compressed silence of poetry could such experience find its language. Or in testimony of survivors, despite the view of some historians about the unreliability of testimony. I began to realize that it was this very unreliability that contained what was to be learned, the variations in the descriptions of specific traumatic incidents. And I discovered that an image from my childhood that I had not understood—the sight of my mother and father sitting in stunned silence on the stairway between the first floor of the house and the second—took on new meaning as I wandered in the forests and villages of this place where our family had lived for so many centuries and where the stories of childhood had taken root. For this was the moment, in 1941, when a letter arrived with a plea for help, but by the time the letter was in their hands, it was already too late. Sixteen years have passed since I first walked in Lithuania. I was privileged to know those survivors, rescuers, and witnesses who talked with me and became my friends.

After the war, the writer Chaim Grade returned to the Vilna Ghetto: "I go home, and gliding behind me comes the ghetto, with all its broken windows, like blind people groping their way along the walls" (429). He imagines that the dead have come back to study their books and scrolls, for he finds scattered pages from sacred books. "Perhaps the tears that drenched the Techinas will live again for me, perhaps my own boyhood face will shine out as so many years past, and I will be able to go on dreaming over a book of wonder tales" (429). Perhaps that is what we all wish for, that the stories will not be lost but will reveal themselves once more.

Just as the partitions between disciplines in science and medicine are being dismantled to our great benefit, so the wide gulf between literary exploration of experience and scientific investigation may be diminished, letting in more light through this synthesis. And rather than dismissing the narrative of testimony, may it be the basis for new insight in a way similar to what literature has to teach us. At least that is the effort in this work.

> It's not the echo of bullets at the edge of the forest,
> it is a swarm of silver bees on the way to the hive of our orchard.
>
> Algimantas Mackus

If we could rewrite history, we would do as Lithuanian poet Algimantas Mackus instructs us: we would transform bullets into living creatures, used not to destroy life, but to propagate it. Perhaps that wish is behind the great variety of historical "truths" that have emerged in Lithuania since World War II with regard to the deaths of approximately 95% of Lithuania's Jewish population. Most were killed during the opening months of the German occupation in 1941. It was said that the killing was done by Germans with Lithuanian collaborators or by Lithuanians at the instigation of the Germans or orchestrated by the Germans even before their arrival in Lithuania or done to avenge Jewish sympathizers during the previous Russian occupation––1940-1941—when numbers of Lithuanians were exiled to Siberia. Now, far more detailed information is available thanks to the courage and willingness of researchers to confront this history. Saulius Suziedelis, in "The Burden of 1941," writes that

> how we imagine the past is an important, perhaps even the most decisive, catalyst in the formation of collective identity, especially national consciousness. In as much as the purpose of commemoration, the affirmation of a particular vision of a shared history, is the reinforcement of group loyalty, the exercise of the various solemn national remembrances is, at heart, a political act. By its very nature, the act of remembrance is hostile to critical analysis—shades of gray are unwelcome. This is particularly true of historical events characterized by mass violence. Wars, revolutions and genocides have winners as well as losers, perpetrators as well as victims, and it is natural that irreconcilable memories will clash. (47)

In the sixteen years since this project began its journey, much has changed in Lithuania. Initially, in 1993 after the long silence under Communism, the "party line" regarding wartime activities had not quite made its way to the rural villages. Those who were willing to talk did not offer reasons for the murders that had taken place in every small hamlet, but they could describe the events. A witness I interviewed in 1994 in Vandzhigola, Lithuania recalled:

> The Jews were taken to the church, locked up without food or water. I was a widow with two small children. I took food and water to them. I was locked

up with them but I pleaded to be released. They did nothing wrong. At first they were taken at night so we would not see. To the forest where they were shot. Later, when no one spoke up, the killers became more courageous and took them in daylight.

Now information about the Holocaust is being taught in the schools and through public international conferences, newspaper articles, museum exhibitions, and education projects. A national task force has been established to provide a program for Holocaust remembrance, education, and research. The Holocaust in Lithuania is no longer a secret, though its causes are still strongly debated as is the issue of responsibility, and "not a single person who collaborated with the Nazis has been convicted in independent Lithuania," according to Irena Veisaite (Levinson 491).

In the overall study, two main streams have emerged. The first has to do with multiple versions and perceptions of the same events by different subjects. It is based on memories told immediately after the War and memories told approximately fifty years after events took place, and in some cases as written memoirs. Interviewees were from villages and cities, as well as DP camps, and included survivors, witnesses, rescuers, and collaborators. In some cases testimony from those born after the war who now live in the U.S. and other countries was included. The events constitute situations of extreme cruelty and barbarism, in some cases threshold events that paved the way for the eventual large-scale murders. The second stream has to do with the application of what is now known in neuroscience about the construction of memory to the study of Holocaust testimony. The major task here is the integration of what I have collected and learned over these years in order to determine whether this approach can shed any new light on traumatic experience and the narrative and nature of memory. The reliability of traumatic memory is another issue of considerable controversy and importance, as is understanding how the synthesis of incoming information with preexisting information takes place.

Whereas previously it was thought that experience entered memory the way we might put a book on a shelf and simply retrieve it when we needed to, it is now clear that memory is far more complex. This study entails the formulation of questions that explore specific cognitive and affective issues having to do with the modulation of incoming stimuli and the formation of memory during trauma. For instance, it has been observed that traumatic memories often do not initially have a narrative or sequential story but occur as sensations—auditory, visual, or affective. And even after a person creates a narrative in order to tell what he or she has experienced, when the memory reoccurs, it comes back piecemeal, as it had originally, sometimes as charged affect without being attached to a specific incident, sometimes as an auditory memory without a visual component.

One important question that arises in this work is the degree to which this inability to process and integrate information interferes with such processing and integration of non-traumatic experience later in life. S. S., a man who survived selections and Aktions, ghetto life and concentration camps, forced marches and the deaths of those close to him, asks, "What did I learn about memory? Memory is adjustable." A man with a meticulous memory, when comparing his experience of a specific event involving the fate of a small child with that of his companions, re-members the event and its outcome differently from his companions. He describes what he calls the "modification of the gate," not only for the past and past memory, but for what is actually permitted to be taken in now, today—a kind of vigilance that does not permit certain kinds of information to be experienced or even to gain entry. "Not only do you have to rid yourself of the images, but of the language which might contain the images."[1]

The issue of language suddenly blocked from consciousness is a crucial area worthy of study. That trauma can obliterate the words we use to communicate with one another, the words we use to name our known world, the words of childhood, raises the question of what else is kept apart from consciousness. What aspect of encoding, storage, and retrieval of memory has been disrupted? And why, in some cases, is language the single-most manifestation of memory loss. Survivor M. B., sixteen years old at the start of the war, fluent in Lithuanian, completely lost the lan-guage by war's end. It is interesting to note that her fluency in Italian, Polish, Russian, German, Yiddish, and Hebrew—languages learned in early childhood apart from Italian—is intact to this day. Her clear and specific memories of Aktions, selections, conditions in the concentration camp, and forced marches seem to be readily avail-able to conscious memory; yet the striking loss is language itself.

Another survivor who has lost his knowledge of Lithuanian speaks of hav-ing heard Lithuanian spoken but not being able to see the Lithuanian collaborator as Jewish neighbors in an adjoining room were taken away. It is as if the language itself, on the other side of a wall, had become the agent of death.

Shalom Eilati[2] was a survivor of the Kovno Ghetto thanks to the heroism and courage of Lithuanians who took him in shortly after the Children's Aktion during which some 5,000 children met their deaths. On April 12, 1944, he went out with his mother to forced labor, crossed the river in a boat from Slobodka to Kaunas, and was instructed to walk up a hill without looking back. There he was to be met by a woman who would take him to the family where he would be safe. He did not see his mother again. And later he writes, "Like Moses in the bulrushes I was cast by Mother onto the shore of life. She gave me life twice, but was unable to save her own even once" (Eilati manuscript 203-4).

He describes witnessing the Great Aktion where some 10,000 people were taken, following a selection, from the Ghetto to the Ninth Fort, a former Czarist fortress, and murdered. The morning after the selection, Shalom Eilati, walking in the square where the selection had taken place, comes upon "strangely shaped lumps among the mounds of rubbish" (Eilati manuscript 71), but when he draws nearer, he realizes that these are dead bodies. As he stared at them, he heard the "distant sounds of shots," and suddenly noticed clusters of people climbing a hillside in the distance surrounded by guards. The road, "visible to all as it rose diagonally from left to right, was already mostly full of people. Had I not," he writes, "looked up to find the source of the gunfire, their march would have been completely unheard and undetected" (Eilati manuscript 72). Suddenly the information he was receiving—the sounds of gunfire, the images of the people—exploded incomprehensibly into a full registration: these people were going to their deaths at the Ninth Fort. It was at this moment that his childhood ended—"its innocence, the privilege of being unafraid" (Eilati manuscript 73). Since then, he has only to see a drawing or painting with a diagonal line rising from left to right in the background, and he is transported there again (Eilati manuscript 75).

The cues or triggers that call forth the visceral memory—in Shalom Eilati's experience a diagonal line or certain sounds—cannot be stilled by cognitive awareness that a selection and murder of thousands of innocent people is not about to take place in the present. As Charlotte Delbo speaks about how the skin of memory comes away, how in dreams she feels physically as if she is back there, in Auschwitz, "frozen to the marrow, filthy, skin and bones" (Delbo 3). In a sense, the cues that cause the repetition of the experience resemble the original experience in that Shalom Eilati describes hearing the sound of the footsteps, of the guns shooting, seeing the angle of the road *before* registering the meaning of what was happening. The body, the senses, have registered the information in fragments, but it has not yet been fully integrated, not even years later.

In 1977 Shalom Eilati spent the summer in Washington, D.C. and decided to visit the White House. People waited on the south lawn for their turn to enter, amid the sounds of an orchestra playing, flag waving, a choir singing. As one group entered, another exited. "They moved quietly," he says, "without raising their voices. Suddenly something was very familiar to me, very close. Surprised, I found I was choking anew, after so many years, at the scene of the big Aktion in Democrat's Square. Shocked and upset, I left the place immediately, in a turmoil" (Eilati manuscript 77-78).

Later, in November 1995, after the assassination of Prime Minister of Israel Yitzak Rabin, Eilati set out before dawn and encountered tens of thousands of Israelis who had walked during the night to the place of the killing to pay their respects. People, "eight or ten abreast, moved forward slowly, too slowly. Coming the other way are those who have already been there; they too are silent, their faces grave.... As for me, as soon as I began waiting in the silent crowd, a feeling of suffocation fell upon me, of deep oppression, that grew as I moved forward in line. As if 54 years and one week had not gone by since the Big Aktion. I turned around and went home" (Eilati manuscript 78). It is interesting to note how Eilati puts his need for vigilance to practical and adaptive use in his adult life. He has become a decipherer of military aerial photographs as a member of the army reserves in Israel. "Like ancient diviners examining the liver of a young calf, I bend over the stereoscope, examining the minute clues sketched in the emulsion of the film before me. Like those haruspices, Estruscan soothsayers, I too look for signs and portents, trying to prognosticate events before they materialize. Thus I can be on constant lookout, observing the horizon for events still beyond it, know in advance things that may happen before too long...I no longer like surprises. Those bronze shell casings that fell onto the grass…were early omens that continue to affect my life to this day, like a long-sustained underlying bass note" (Eilati manuscript 33). At times when he walks in Jerusalem, he tries to recapture "the first intoxicating walk with his mother into the city to the bus station before the war." However, attached to this memory is the memory of the massacre at the Lietukis Garage where the buses were washed. He refers to his walks in Jerusalem like this: "Streets turn to paths, walls of stone close upon you. I catch glimpses of spacious inner courtyards…A green lemon tree, sane and tranquil, awakens a latent yearning. An uncontrollable thought rises: 'If I must hide, let it be here, surely they can't reach me here'" (Eilati manuscript 40-41).

Here we can observe a number of aspects of memory: the triggers that enable us to gain access to memory; the ways that memory is encoded in multiple sites and is constructed and retrieved through a series of operations—hormonal, neuronal, the action of neurotransmitters. Perhaps most important with regard to the appearance without warning of these triggering events is recent study by neuroscientists on the function of the amygdala and hippocampus, regions in the temporal lobe. It is thought that the amygdala mediates the emotional valence of incoming information and that the hippocampus provides the space/time context. In trauma, excessive stimulation interferes with "integrated narrative memory" at the same time that it "strengthens the vividness and endurance of fragmented perceptual and emotional memories" (Kraft 94). The same stress hormones that enhance emotional memory tend to diminish or suppress hippocampal function and the space/time context. Thus we have memory that is fragmented, enduring, and without context. It is formed, as well, without the "supervision" of the cerebral cortex, the executive function of the brain.

All of this is for good reason under normal circumstances. If we took the time to weigh and consider whether a certain action was sensible and what its long-term consequences might be, we might very well not survive in a crisis situation. Thus the ability to respond to danger instantaneously is an adaptive one. An example: one day recently I walked out of the front door of my house to the mailbox, crossing the garden, and as I returned I heard an ominous sound, a crunching of wood breaking. Without determining where it was coming from—apart from the sure knowledge that it was above my head—I simply ran as fast as I could toward the house. It might have been wiser to look up and to determine at what angle the huge branches, torn off by the wind, would fall. But had I done so, taken the time to let my neocortex ascertain the full situation, it might have been too late to get out of the way of the falling branches. In this case my body took the advice of my amygdala: flight! No time for the neocortex to get into the act.

Joseph LeDoux, professor at the Center of Neural Science at New York University, recalls Darwin's experience putting his "face close to the thick glass-plate in front of a puff-ader in the Zoological Gardens, with the firm determination of not starting back if the snake struck at [him]; but as soon as the blow was struck, [his] resolution went for nothing, and [he] jumped a yard or two backwards with astonishing rapidity. [His] will and reason were powerless against the imagination of a danger which he had never experienced" (112). Not the cortex talking here, but the adaptive survival function of the amygdala. "Emotional reactions," LeDoux tells us, "are really reactions that are important in survival situations. The advantage is that by allowing evolution to do the thinking for you at first, you basically buy the time that you need to think about the situation and do the most reasonable thing." LeDoux points out that freezing when danger appears is what animals and people generally do first (or flight in my case). He notes that the "connectivity of the amygdala with the neo-cortex is not symmetrical. The amygdala projects back to the neo-cortex in a much stronger sense than the neo-cortex projects to the amygdala." Thus the earlier incidents—falling tree branch and puff adder—likely induced a response from the amygdala first, getting the body into play before cognitive function had a chance to weigh the pros and cons of a proper course of action. According to LeDoux, "the amygdala's ability to control the cortex is greater than the ability of the cortex to control the amygdala," which may explain "why it is so hard for us to will away anxiety; emotions, once they're set into play, are very difficult to turn off " (Brockman).

Thus the difficulty of therapy in cases of extreme trauma. The role of the neocortex in controlling the amygdala is like "trying to find your way from New York to Boston by way of country roads rather than superhighways." At a later point, the occurrence of anything suggestive of the original experience is capable of eliciting profound fear responses by reactivating these powerfully potentiated amygdala circuits.

Some contemporary examples might serve to illustrate this phenomenon. In 1970 when I first started teaching at the university, my first students were young men returning from the war in Vietnam. They were, in general, unrehabilitated. Some were addicted to drugs, some appeared to be in shock, still dazed by the world they had recently left. One veteran always stood at the back of the hallway, nearest the stairway, while we waited for the preceding class to leave the classroom. It was as if he needed to be sure he had a clear escape route. I had not known the details of his experience in Vietnam but after an assignment reading Dante's *Inferno*, he dropped by my office one afternoon and handed me a packet, telling me that he had not been able to talk about his experience in Vietnam, nor to write about it until now, that Dante and the descent into the Inferno had given him a route for his expression. He asked that I read his writing, and I told him that I would as soon as I had time to do so. Of course I took the pages home that same evening and read every word. What I learned was that he had been part of a special reconnaissance group that took the forward positions, which put his men in grave danger. That he was, at a certain point, airlifted into a helicopter from a ring of fire, that all of the men in his unit had been killed. That he could identify a trip wire fine as a hair that might be attached to explosives. That when he saw the film *Platoon*, and came to the part where the men in Vietnam came across a metal box and began to open it, he screamed in the movie theatre for them to stop, that he knew it would contain explosives. He described the terrible longing they had to find signs of the enemy, to touch something the enemy had used. He was tuned to danger, at the ready to read whatever environment he was in for the least sign that might require sudden action for survival, even though he was now safe in America and the necessity for this hypervigilance was no longer required.

And now, during the Iraq War, a young man on a brief army leave comes home to America and goes to a shopping mall with his family. He describes his terrible unease, that he is without his machine gun, that no one is guarding the entrances and exits of the mall, that people are moving about in large numbers and no one seems concerned. In Iraq, every face and motion must be interpreted. Their lives depend upon this knowledge. He speaks of being afraid that he will feel this terror and the need for vigilance for the rest of his life.

Kristen K., who survived as a child during World War II by hiding in the sewers beneath Lvov, Poland for fourteen months, lived in a tube five feet high by four feet wide, amid sewage and sewer rats. When I asked, during a telephone interview on May 18, 1995 (auspices of the U.S. Holocaust Memorial Museum), how that experience manifested itself in her present-day life, she described visiting a new house and feeling fearful about going down to the basement. But then, when exploring the attic, she thought immediately that this might be a good place to hide. She points out how hard it is, after living on instinct during those years, to feel free of the need to do so. Cognitive function assures her that she is safe and the earlier need to fear for her life is no longer necessary. Yet the ingrained emotional response says otherwise.

In the case of extreme trauma that continues over a long period of time, the inhibitory mechanisms that would normally turn off the stress hormones, like epinephrine, cortisol, or norepinephrine, fail to do so. And the provision of context in place and time is diminished or absent altogether. Bessel van der Kolk's findings support the earlier studies of Joesph LeDoux where "intense affective stimulation may thus inhibit proper evaluation and categorization of experience" (van der Kolk 234). Thus we see hypervigilance and triggers—dissociated mental imprints—that can be set off at any moment and without warning.

This subject has engaged a number of researchers including Bessel A. Van der Kolk, James McGaugh, and Joseph LeDoux. These findings offer insight into the intrusive fragmented memories that survivors report where they feel that they are not simply telling what happened in the past but are back there, living once again through the actual experience.

Bessel van der Kolk has talked about the body's memory in "The Body Keeps the Score." S. S. describes returning to the concentration camp Dachau, walking into the barracks that had been reconstructed, and just by looking at the wooden planks, he began to itch. Walking by the crematorium "brought back the smell, brought back the experience in Stutthof Concentration Camp where he was made to clean up after the killings in the crematorium there." M. B., prior to being interviewed by the Shoah Foundation, began to hunger for bread, as she had hungered in the concentration camp for the small ration of bread they were allotted, insufficient for survival. For several weeks before the interview, she ate little else but bread, a literal repetition of the earlier situation in extremis. She notes that as she could pass for a Lithuanian, she had been the breadwinner for her extended family in the Ghetto. She also mentions that at the time of liberation, pointing to the palm of her hand, she was given a small piece of bread and how she saved it, eating only small bits so that it might last for several days. Doing so saved her life, as many who attempted to eat larger quantities of food, after years of starvation, died as a result. And in terms of repetition, Leiser W. acknowledges that the fact that he keeps his belongings in five separate places and often carries them from place to place in his current life (quite difficult as he is nearly blind and elderly) is an echo of his years in the Kovno Ghetto where he was, as a child, a messenger boy, carrying messages to partisans, carrying food secretly back into the ghetto, constantly hiding objects and himself.

As a young boy, shortly after the Nazi invasion, he was taken with all the men and boys in his building on Laisves Aleja in Kaunas, Lithuania to the basement of the building at four in the morning and all were shot to death, including his father. He was wounded but escaped. His younger brother was burned alive in a hospital in Slobodka along with all the patients, doctors, and nurses. His mother gave birth at that time to an infant son. He was made to help with the delivery and to bury the placenta. The baby died a few days later. He survived Dachau Concentration Camp and years later had his first experience swimming in the sea. As he entered the water, he had the feeling that he was entering a sea of blood. A striking effect of his wartime experiences is that he does not sleep for more than an hour or two at most during any night. It is not that he is afraid of having nightmares, but that he is concerned about what he might do if he lost control during sleep, a form of vigilance unlike others that I have encountered.

Sara Ginaite-Rubinson, imprisoned in the Kovno Ghetto during the war, joined the underground Anti-Fascist Fighting Organization resistance movement. After escaping the selection and the Great Aktion (collective murder at a former Czarist fortress in Kaunas where close to 10,000 Jews were killed in a period of forty-eight hours during October 28-29, 1941), she was determined that she must reject the way the Nazis had arranged her death. "If it was my fate to die," she said, during a talk on Holocaust Remembrance Day, April 24, 2006 in Earl Bales Park, Toronto, "I would die on my own terms." On one occasion, she escaped secretly from the Ghetto in order to make contact with other partisans and collect information. She safely crossed the bridge from Villiampole to Kaunas, met with her contact person, and on her return realized that she was being watched. She proceeded to make her way back across the bridge. The man, though with a limp, followed her and eventually caught up with her. "Nervously, I looked at the Neris River below me. If I'm unable to escape from him, I thought to myself, I'll jump into the river" (117). She managed to return safely to the Ghetto, though not without travail. Of that time and experience she writes: "The memory of running across the bridge, of wanting to jump into the river, continued to haunt me. To this day, I can't erase that scene from my memory. I still can't cross a bridge alone, afraid that I'll get the urge to jump into the water" (117). Though the cause of the trauma no longer exists, and the author of these words knows this on a cognitive level, the power of the emotional memory is still operative.

A curious form of forgetting that has been observed is the loss of memory about events that are not on the surface traumatic ones but times of relative safety. For example, E. L. describes surviving the war in concentration camps and forced marches, always keeping in mind the image of her father, the deep belief that she will see her father again, if only she can manage to stay alive. Of that first meeting between the child and her absent father, E. L. remembers nothing. Throughout her life she has attempted to recall those first precious moments of reunion, but though her memory for multiple details of her experiences seems to her to be completely intact, this memory is a lacunae. Entirely erased. Or unavailable to conscious recall. The other strange lapse in memory for her is the name of the friend with whom she went through the entire experience of the concentration camp.

Eta Hecht remembers in great detail—despite the fact that at the time she was four and a half years old—the Kinderaktion where the majority of the children in the Kovno Ghetto were rounded up, dragged from their hiding places, put on lorries, and killed at the Ninth Fort. She was one of the very few whose hiding place behind a stairway and under a mattress—to this day she has a fear of suffocation—was not discovered by the Germans. In a period of a few weeks she was required to learn Lithuanian (her only language at the time was Yiddish) and to relinquish her Jewish identity so that she could be hidden with a family that had agreed to take her in. She was sedated, put in a tool sack, and carried out of the Ghetto on her mother's back as her mother went to forced labor, and given—in a prearranged plan—to a woman who would deliver her to the family. At a certain point that family felt it was too dangerous to keep her and she was given to another family out in the countryside. Though she was with the second family for some eighteen months, and though there were other children in that family, she has almost no recollection of anything that took place during that time. As if in stop-time, what was forgotten is bounded on either side by rich memories of her family before and with the reconciliation with her parents afterward. These examples represent only a few of the many unanswered questions.

In sum, the partitions that have been erected between disciplines are giving way. Psychoanalytic theory is being examined in light of neuroscience. Molecular biologists are teamed with bio-engineers, physicists, and biochemists to provide insights about immunology. The tools of immunology are being applied to the study of consciousness. We no longer think of memory as a vast immutable library housed in our gray matter that preserves a literal representation of the world, but rather as a dynamic process calling upon multiple areas and systems in the brain. Never before have we had the tools to make the profound connections that are possible today. This project links current thinking in the neurosciences about memory formation with Holocaust testimony taken in recent years as well as testimony from some who, because of the relative isolation of Lithuania, harbored memories and conceptions that had gone unchallenged during the years following the War, untested by discussion with others or by any national source of information about the past. Such experiences and internal narratives had essentially evolved in a walled-off place and surfaced in interviews, particularly in rural areas of the country.

Some years ago, while studying a collection of plays edited by Sarah Blacher Cohen and Joanne Koch, *Shared Stages: the Drama of Blacks and Jews*, I noted that the book raised the question of who can speak for us, for our experience. One of the great functions of art is to probe the inner life of humans and to illuminate it so that others may register its depths, its shallows, its misdemeanors. Revelations that cannot penetrate the barriers of everyday life can sometimes provide a bridge through drama or music or film and then begin "to set the stage for significant new dialogues in the real world" (2), as the editors observed. This project, crossing various boundaries, brings a complex set of approaches to bear on a core issue—how memory is encoded, stored, and retrieved under the conditions of extreme trauma that were experienced during the Holocaust. The hope is that it too, as in literature and the arts, can provide a bridge to deeper understanding and a basis for a new form of dialogue.

Notes

1. In order to protect the identity of witnesses and survivors, they will be identified throughout only by initials or first names.

2. All references to Shalom Eilati are taken from the unpublished manuscript of *Crossing the River*, University of Alabama Press, 2008.

Works Cited

Brockman, John. "Parallel Memories: Putting Emotions Back Into The Brain: A Talk with Joseph LeDoux." *Edge: 3rd Culture*, 17 Feb. 1997. Web. 11 Nov. 2009. www.edge.org.

Chiger, Krystyna, with Daniel Paisner. *The Girl in the Green Sweater.* New York: St. Martin's, 2009. Print.

Cohen, Sarah Blacher, and Joanne B. Koch. *Shared Stages: Ten American Dramas of Blacks & Jews.* Albany: SUNY Press, 2007. Print

Delbo, Charlotte. *Days of Memory.* Marlboro, VT: The Marlboro Press, 1990. Print.

Eilati, Shalom. *Crossing the River.* Tuscaloosa: U of Alabama P, 2008. Print. (Quotations are from the unpublished manuscript translated into English by Vern Lenz.)

Ginaite-Rubinson, Sara. *Resistance and Survival: The Jewish Community in Kaunas 1941-1944.* Ontario: Mosaic Press, 2005. Print

Grade, Chaim. "Sanctuaries in Ruin." *Great Yiddish Writers of the 20th Century.* Ed. Joseph Leftwich. New Jersey/London: Jason Aronson Inc., 1987. Print.

Kraft, Robert. *Memory Perceived: Recalling the Holocaust.* Connecticut/London: Praeger Press, 2002. Print.

LeDoux, Joseph. *The Emotional Brain: The Mysterious Underpinnings of Emotional Life.* New York: Simon & Schuster, 1996. Print.

Levinson, Joseph. *The Shoah in Lithuania.* Lithuania: Vilna Gaon Jewish State Museum, 2006. Print.

Mackus, Algimantas. "Jurek: VIII." Web. 11 Nov. 2009. http://efn.org/~valdes/mackus. html.

Schama, Simon. *Landscape and Memory*. New York: Knopf, 1995. Print.

Suziedelis, Saulius. "The Burden of 1941," Lituanus 47:4 (Winter 2001). Print.

van der Kolk, Bessel A., et al. *Traumatic Stress*. New York/London: The Guilford Press, 1996. Print.

Myra Sklarew, American University

Malamud's Early Stories:

In and Out of Time, 1940-1960,with Humor, History, and Hawthorne[1]

Sanford E. Marovitz

Bernard Malamud's humor is always ironic and usually grim, dark, evoking the type of comic image conveyed by a grinning skull. Often his humor evolves from someone's deservedly or undeservedly being victimized—Schwartz the Jewbird, for example, or the mourners Gruber and Kessler—death and implicit death, but in either case the grinning skull looks on unseen. Although in many of his stories a suggestion of tragedy exists behind the humor, in others whimsy predominates, as in "Angel Levine" and "The Girl of My Dreams." Whimsy is a device that Hawthorne also employs, even in stories based on historical accounts. A perfect example is "Wakefield," in which Wakefield leaves home one day and without a word to his wife does not return for twenty years, when he suddenly steps inside the house while walking past it on a rainy afternoon as if he had been gone no longer than a few hours. According to the narrator the story has a truthful foundation, but in Hawthorne's art, as at times in Malamud's, it is pure whimsy.

As Malamud's ironic humor, both the woeful and the whimsical, is characteristic of Hawthorne's, so may the same be said of the earlier author's predilection for history as a prominent thematic concern in developing his fiction. History provides a foundation of actuality on which to base even most of their more fanciful stories no matter how far from historic reality the two authors may stray. Eventually the reader's awareness of history will keep the incidents and characters linked to that foundation, grounded effectively enough to make the most preposterous possibilities seem viable and acceptable, at least for the duration of the story. Undoubtedly, it is largely if not wholly for that reason that Poe insisted a short story be limited in length to what can normally be read in a single sitting; a longer story, he believed, would override its effect on the imagination of readers and make it incredible before the conclusion was reached. Like Hawthorne, Malamud rarely if ever allowed that to occur.

Whether rapping the conscience or tapping the fancy, Malamud's humor, again like Hawthorne's, leaves one pondering over the unpredictable reversals that ironic twists bring to the end of their tales. For instance, Hawthorne's young Goodman Brown loses his Faith but receives her pink ribbon to remind him of his loss; Feathertop, with a pumpkin head and broomstick back, has the witch-given appearance and manner of a nobleman, but on seeing himself reflected in a mirror for what he really is, he collapses and becomes a scarecrow again; mentioned already is Wakefield, who in a momentous unanticipated decision reappears at home after two decades as if he had never been away. Similarly, in Malamud's "The Last Mohican," the woebegone Fidelman's manuscript is stolen and lost for good before he realizes how worthless it is; Mitka's erstwhile dream-girl in "Girl of My Dreams" is suddenly transformed from a "lone middle-aged female" with a "bulky market bag"[2] into a young writer's inspiration; and Schwartz the schnorring Jewbird is flung outside by the "Anti-Semeet" Cohen to die in filth as an obnoxious Jewish pest. What Robert Alter says about the latter story—"Without the grubby realism in which the fantasy is embodied, the bird would be only a contrived symbol and the story would lack conviction" (31)—applies to much of Malamud's early fiction and to many of Hawthorne's tales as well. Pathos is an element in the ironic conclusions of all these stories; pathos and humor together generate the effect sought by both authors a century apart, and history has a prominent thematic role in much if not most of their fiction. As the etymology of the words themselves imply, *history* and *story* are intrinsically linked, both having evolved from the same root.

Although Malamud's first known story as a mature author was written in 1940, it was not published until three years after his death. Based on the appalling conjunction of history and anti-Semitism near the outset of World War II in Europe, "Armistice" is neither whimsical nor comic but heavily ironic, and the grim humor is increasingly evident as the linkage between its two parallel situations in France and New York becomes apparent. Sarah Blacher Cohen might have had this story in mind when she wrote that the humor of Jews in particular "has been a balance to counter external adversity and internal sadness" (4). Malamud himself suggests as much, when he says that when the author writes his story, it puts him "in high spirits and good form. If he's lucky, serious things may seem funny" (*Stories* xii). But, of course, the humor would likely be lost on looking into the dark eye sockets of the grinning skull. As in much of his fiction to follow for nearly half a century, the heavy shadow of contemporary events hangs heavily over the narrative. "Armistice" first appeared in print as part of a group of then uncollected stories published with Malamud's unfinished novel, *The People*, in 1989. When he wrote it, the U.S. had not yet struck out against the German onslaught in Europe that would soon expand into World War II, but Malamud was already profoundly disturbed over the plight of the Jews there as the Nazis gained control over one country after another.

Anti-Semitism is behind the relentless distress that pervades "Armistice."

Like Malamud's father, Morris Lieberman in that story is a grocer with a small city store who fears not only for himself and his son, Leonard, but for Jews everywhere. It opens with Lieberman's memory of a horrific act of violence he had witnessed as a youth during a pogrom against the Jews in his native Russia, an act that initiates the fright and stress that underlie the rest of the story. He had seen "a burly Russian peasant seize a wagon wheel that was lying against the side of a blacksmith's shop, swing it around, and hurl it at a fleeing Jewish sexton. The wheel caught the Jew in the back, crushing his spine. In speechless terror, he lay on the ground before his burning house, waiting to die" (*People* 103). This graphic description shocks readers and remains with them to the end of the story, continually reinforced by radio broadcasts of the Nazi advance in Europe and underscored by the gloating approval of their success by Gus Wagner, a German-American sausage salesman peddling his wares to the grocer.

Morris is literally addicted to the radio broadcasts; he cannot break away from the war news that informs him about what he fears to hear but to which he compulsively listens hour by hour. His son, Leonard, pleads with him to stop, as do the other salesmen with whom he trades, all of whom insist that the war in Europe has no relation to the U.S., but they cannot convince him. As France gives way, Morris feels lost, and Gus's periodic stops with baskets of sausages bring his increased crowing over the inevitable French surrender. When it occurs, Marshall Pétain signs an armistice for "peace with honor" according to Hitler's demands and becomes the notorious leader of Vichy France. With this news, Morris is devastated (*People* 105). Malamud must have been drafting his story as these events were occurring in June 1940 or immediately afterward, while holding a civil service position in Washington, D.C., at the age of twenty-six (*People* vii-ix).

To complicate further Morris' conflict with Gus, the salesman attempts to cheat him by making small errors in his bill for meat purchased, but Leonard's checking the figures exposes his chicanery. An argument that ensues over Morris's reason for a French victory—whether to support democracy or protect the Jews—reveals Gus as an anti-Semite. When Morris calls the salesman a Nazi, Gus, already angry over being caught cheating on his bill, admits his admiration for the victorious German army and curses at Leonard, leading the grocer to hug and kiss his frail son protectively. Knowing he has pushed too hard and fearing to lose future sales, Gus places several sausages on the table and leaves, saying he can wait for payment.

The story does not end there, however. Whereas it begins with Morris's shocking memory of anti-Semitic persecution, it concludes with a description of Gus driving from the store in his truck, musing disgustedly over the Jews holding and consoling each other. "Why feel sorry for them?" he asks himself. Sitting straight with the steering wheel firmly in hand, Gus imagines himself driving a "massive tank" with terrified Parisians on the sidewalks watching him pass. "He drove tensely, his eyes unsmiling. He knew that if he relaxed the picture would fade" (109).

The armistice to which the title of the story ostensibly refers is the one Pétain signed to end the fighting, allegedly to restore "peace with honor," and to give the

Nazis control over France, but on a lesser scale it also represents an unspoken truce between Morris and Gus, who despise but need each other. Morris and Leonard, always defensive, can live with it because they know where they stand in a hostile world. Gus Wagner, in contrast, whose surname recalls the renowned German nationalist composer and anti-Semite, Richard Wagner, cannot come to terms with his stifled humaneness. He has suppressed his sympathy in favor of an arrogant, domineering façade governed by his imagination, itself fueled by the news of glorious German conquest that he shares in name only. Unnatural restraint keeps him from sympathizing, from sharing the kind of affection that enables the grocer and his son to fear, suffer, and love openly. Gus knows this but will not face it; instead he allows the news of Nazi victory to feed his ego and dominate his relations not only with two frightened and relatively helpless Jews, but with his own inner self. For him alone there can be no armistice until he surrenders to compassion and faces the truth about himself, but whether he can or will do it is left an open question.

From this story on, Malamud often drew from history and current events, applying them realistically as complementary forces in developing the romantic themes of his fiction. In this respect, as he progressed into writing several of the stories included later in *The Magic Barrel* and the other collections that followed, his method of composition resembled Hawthorne's. Malamud has openly acknowledged that "a line" from that early predecessor exists in his own work (qtd. in Solataroff 151) and embedded in that line is history. Although Hawthorne employs America's Colonial and Revolutionary past as settings for many of his best known tales and romances, Malamud usually turns to events of the twentieth century to complement his stories. Nonetheless, recognizing that historical nexus offers insight into the similarities between the two authors in their conceptualization of romance in fiction and should support the acceptance of Malamud as a mainstream American author rather than more narrowly a Jewish one, as he has often been categorized, to his chagrin.

Both authors also shared the experience of living in Rome, experience they carried into their writing although it affected them in decidedly different ways. Hawthorne was too much the conservative Bostonian to feel comfortable amid the less inhibited life he saw around him in Rome, whereas Malamud was fascinated by the culture. Yet both felt the strangeness at first of being immersed amid surroundings that exposed the layers of millennial Roman history and prehistory in the form of myth and legend. If Hawthorne embodied such myths most notably first in *A Wonder Book* and *Tanglewood Tales*, and later in his portrait of Donatello in *The Marble Faun*, Malamud used the old streets and buildings as the setting for such stories as "The Lady of the Lake" and "The Last Mohican," which despite their Italian locale, are thematically Jewish.

Instead of Greek and Roman myths, Malamud drew from biblical history for imaginative truths on which to build, not in Italian stories, but in such New York ghetto tales as "The First Seven Years" and "Angel Levine." "The First Seven Years," for example, is set in a small cobbler's shop during the period of mass Eastern-European immigration. Feld, a Polish immigrant living with his wife and daughter, Miriam, owns the shop; his trusted assistant, Sobel, also a Polish immigrant, has worked for him about five years. Feld worries about his nineteen-year-old daughter; instead of showing interest in college and dating, she has turned to the thirtyish Sobel as her mentor; a prolific reader, he recommends and lends classic books to her accompanied with written expositions and critiques. When Feld arranges a date for Miriam, Sobel rushes enraged from the shop and does not return, leaving her aging father to work alone. Only after pleading uselessly does he realize that his assistant has been laboring not for money, but for Miriam. Initially incredulous and outraged, he responds harshly, but on learning that Miriam accepts Sobel's devotion, Feld relents and asks him to work for two more years until she is twenty-one; then he leaves before receiving an answer. Early the next morning he finds Sobel in the shop "seated at the last, pounding leather for his love" (*MB* 16).

As its title suggests, the story is based loosely on the scriptural account of Jacob's desire to wed Rachel, the younger daughter of his mother's brother, Laban, who consents to their marriage if Jacob will agree to give him in return seven years of labor. Jacob concurs, and when the time has passed, Laban hands him his veiled daughter. Not until the following morning does Jacob discover that he has been deceived into marrying Rachel's elder sister, Leah. According to the law of the land, Laban tells him, the eldest daughter must be the first to marry. Only after seven more years may Jacob take Rachel as his wife. Again the noble Jacob agrees, and after the next seven years have passed, he and Rachel are wed. The romantic plot of Malamud's story advances within a time frame that compresses biblical and relatively recent American history. Again like Hawthorne, Malamud has expanded a plausible setting to incorporate an improbable event of biblical consequence when he parallels the courtship and marriage of a cobbler's assistant and his silent sweetheart with a great Hebrew patriarch and matriarch; by doing so, he has blessed an ordinary ghetto couple with an almost heavenly glory without losing touch with reality. In neither the Genesis version nor in "The First Seven Years" does the courted maiden speak to her father about the pending betrothal, a detail that tightens the correspondences between the two relationships.

Like "The First Seven Years," "Angel Levine," also in *The Magic Barrel*, has roots in the Bible. Although angels are more closely associated with the Christian than the Hebrew Scriptures, references to Gabriel and Michael do appear in the Book of Daniel, but only generically are they related to the black angel in "Angel Levine." In this story Manischevitz the tailor, a man of faith, is confronted in his living room by one Alexander Levine, a shabbily clothed black man claiming to be a Jewish angel sent by God. If Manischevitz requests his help, Levine can assist him, but he cannot restore the health of the tailor's dying wife without being acknowledged as an angel. When the tailor's doubt precludes this, Levine leaves, saying that if needed he may be found in Harlem. As his wife declines further, Manischevitz gives in and finds Levine in a Harlem honky-tonk. Derided there as white and Jewish (*MB* 54), and dissuaded anew by the ungodly atmosphere, he leaves but ultimately relents and hesitantly addresses Levine as an angel of God. On returning to Manischevitz's dingy apartment building, Levine climbs the stairs to the roof, and the tailor soon spots him aloft on large black wings. Stepping into his apartment, Manischevitz sees his wife out of bed, dust mop in hand. "A wonderful thing," he tells her; "Believe me, there are Jews everywhere" (*MB* 56). As Robert Alter points out with reference to the shabbiness around Cohen's apartment on the Lower East Side in "The Jewbird," so Malamud's realistic description of the Harlem setting, where Manischevitz seeks Levine amid the hostility of a low-class cabaret, has a validating effect on the fanciful conclusion.

"A wonderful thing," indeed, is this story, which creates its effect in a multitude of ways. It is fanciful and fantastic; it depicts profound suffering and sordid conditions yet qualifies them with poignant humor, leaving readers with relief and the pleasant sensation of having tasted the bittersweet. It is also socially rewarding through its humanistic representation of interracial harmony, especially when one considers it as having been published only a year after the Supreme Court ruled that segregated public schools are unconstitutional (*Brown vs. the Board of Education of Topeka*, 1954) and a few months before Rosa Parks refused to relinquish her bus seat to a white passenger in Selma, Alabama (December 1, 1955). But Malamud's seemingly hopeful vision of Black-Jewish relations in "Angel Levine" was no harbinger of changes soon to come. As Cynthia Ozick has pointed out, the "redemptiveness of 'Angel Levine'" and "the murderous conclusion of *The Tenants*" (1971), Malamud's vitriolic novel of interracial conflict, are thematically at odds although separated by only thirteen years (qtd. in Field and Field 83). Yet a careful reading of "Angel Levine" shows even in that story of the 1950s that Malamud was not as sanguine as Ozick had believed about an early resolution to interracial conflict in the U.S. because he depicts Manischevitz in Harlem as the object of both anti-Semitic and anti-white derision and scorn. In 1963 Malamud focuses more specifically on such hostility in another story, "Black Is My Favorite Color," which implies little hope of assimilation or even harmonious racial relations in the near future. *The Tenants*, then, does not mark a change but a reinforcement of his earlier views.

Yet it would be a great exaggeration to assess "Angel Levine" chiefly in terms of black-and-white, which would be the result of confusing a part of the thematic design for the whole. Essentially, it is a moral tale on the order of "The Minister's Black Veil" and many of Hawthorne's other timeless stories, a tale of renewed faith that overrides Manischevitz's despondency and reconfirms his trust in God as he sees his wife's health miraculously restored. He knows that such things occur only by miracle, yet it happens. As Levine's black wings lift him heavenward, a dark feather seems to flutter down before Manischevitz's eyes, but it turns white and proves to be only a snowflake. This imaginative touch recalls a scene in Hawthorne's "Young Goodman Brown," where a pink ribbon, apparently belonging to Brown's wife, Faith, floats down beside him as he walks to a witches' meeting in the forest, but Malamud reverses the implication. Instead of losing faith as Brown does, Manischevitz's faith is sustained; nevertheless, the fanciful auctorial device in both stories operates similarly by drawing on the supernatural to support a moral position, for Brown a rejection of faith and for Manischevitz a confirmation of it. Moreover, in both tales history provides an authentic, if subordinate, foundation for the timeless moral truth as Goodman Brown loses his Faith among the Puritans and Manischevitz maintains faith amid the Blacks' chaotic struggle for civil rights in secular America.

A brief look at three of Malamud's early stories, then, reveals how he deepens their central situations and moral issues by alluding to complementary events and figures in history, contemporaneous as well as past. As a young man he could see history in the making as he took in the daily news reports on Jewish persecution with the Nazis gaining control over much of Europe, facts that he included in "Armistice" to compound Wagner's anti-Semitism as a revelation of his unacknowledged defensiveness and alienation in a community where love predominates. In "The First Seven Years," he draws from the biblical narrative of Jacob and Rachel, and in "Angel Levine," he alludes to the interracial hostility and anti-Semitism that have not yet been eradicated in the United States.

However, those three titles are not the only ones among Malamud's early stories in which comic irony depends, often heavily, on history—past, contemporaneous, and literary—to achieve its full effect by complementing and intensifying his central conflicts. During the mid-1950s in Rome, for example, he unexpectedly brings visions of the Holocaust into "The Lady of the Lake" near the end with a revelation that blatantly exposes to the hero himself, Henry Levin, alias Henry R. Freeman, his simple-minded hypocrisy. Refusing to acknowledge his Judaism, Levin becomes the victim of his own folly as Isabella, his beloved Jewish signorina, with the heretofore hidden blue numbers tattooed at Buchenwald newly exposed on her breast, disappears forever among a stand of white marble statues. In another of his Roman stories, "The Last Mohican," also in *The Magic Barrel*, Fidelman, a dubious author, is bemused over his own presence in a city steeped in history: "under his feet were the ruins of Ancient Rome. It was an inspiring business, he, . . . born a Bronx boy, walking around in all this history. History was mysterious, the remembrance of things unknown, in a way burdensome, in a way a sensuous experience. It uplifted and depressed, why he did not know, except that it excited his thoughts more than he thought good for him" (*MB* 162). In Rome he meets Shimon Susskind, figuratively "a Jewish refugee from Israel," "always running" (*MB* 158), whose increasingly irritating antics as a Jewish trickster eventually prove oracular to Fidelman, for they teach the unwitting Giotto-scholar manqué that he, like Freeman/Levin, cannot come to terms with history until he knows himself.

Malamud's "The Elevator," written in Italy in 1957 but unpublished until after his death, exhibits in a seriocomic manner the overwhelming effects of American arrogance, imposition, and wealth on an ancient culture. This is as serious a matter in Rome as are interracial hostility and anti-Semitism in the U.S., yet as in "Angel Levine," the story ends whimsically. In this relatively unfamiliar narrative, George Agostini, an Italian-American, has come to Rome with his family to work for an office in the U.N. and after a trying search has leased a satisfactory apartment, small but large enough, his wife insists, for a full-time maid, Eleonora. George becomes upset when Eleonora begins weeping for no apparent reason until he learns that the owner of the building where they live forbids her to use the elevator instead of the stairs when carrying laundry up and down between the first and fifth floors. When the landlady refuses George's request to let Eleonora ride, he grows irate and breaks his lease. Angrily herself she says bitterly:

> Oh, you Americans. . . . Your money is your dirty foot with which you kick the world. Who wants you here, . . . with your soaps and toothpaste and your dirty gangster movies!

> I would like to remind you that my origin is Italian, George said.

> You have long ago forgotten your origin, she shouted. (*People* 199)

Soon afterward, however, she relents because she needs the rent money and allows Eleonora to use the elevator, but the permission comes at the cost of her pride, pride in the ages-old culture she had known before the war. She tells him:

> You have no idea how bad things have become since the war. The girls [i.e., maids] are disrespectful. Their demands are endless, it is impossible to keep up with them. They talk back, they take every advantage. They crown themselves with privileges. It is a struggle to keep them in their place. After all, what have we left when we lose our self-respect? (200)

She "wept heartbrokenly" and departed, leaving George depressed over what he considered his inept handling of the controversy. The next line, however, which closes the story with reference again to the maid, sharply contrasts with George's mood and the landlady's: "On her afternoon off Eleonora rode up and down on the elevator" (200). The tragedy of war and the undermining of a culture that had developed over millennia are completely suppressed by her childish delight in transforming the elevator from the subject of argument and grief into a toy, and the final victory is hers.

But closer to home in one of Malamud's earliest stories, "The Place Is Different Now" (1943), Wally Mullane, a homeless Irish lad, views the passage of time in a city neighborhood from the perspective of a lost soul who futilely attempts to live as freely as he once did at home with friends around him. Like Susskind years later, but lacking the intelligence of the "Jewish refugee," Wally is always broke, threatened, and beaten or running because time has passed him by. He cannot cope, for having remained his old self in a new time, he can only complain repeatedly between blows that "the place is different now" (*People* 153).

Clearly, in this story and much of Malamud's other early fiction, time brings the making of some and the stultification or breaking of others but the outcome is always determined by character, not by characterization and not by personality, but by *character*. In "The Girl of My Dreams," the dowdy, maternal Olga (who calls herself Madeleine, the name of her daughter, who died at twenty) tells a downcast

Mitka, as he puts her on a bus for home, that when she saw him for the first time and he did not walk away disappointed over her age and appearance, she knew immediately that he "is a man of character." She advises him to continue writing and not be discouraged because "Character is what counts in the pinches, of course mixed properly with talent" (*MB* 41). Mitka is elated as the story ends:

> He thought of the old girl. He'd go home now and drape her from head to foot in flowing white. They would jounce together up the stairs, then . . . he would swing her across the threshold, holding her where the fat overflowed her corset as they waltzed around his writing chamber (4).

Hawthorne understood this sudden shift of mind, and so did Malamud, in whose marvelous stories, however fanciful they may be, the effects of time, whether woe or whimsy, are always as *character* dictates.

Notes

1. A shorter version of this essay was published in the *NOBS Newsletter* (Winter 2008), and I am grateful to the editor for permission to include a substantial revision of it in this memorial collection for an old friend and distinguished scholar, the late Sarah Blacher Cohen.

2. Malamud, *The Magic Barrel* 36; hereafter cited textually as *MB*.

Works Cited

Alter, Robert. "Jewish Humor and the Domestication of Myth." Cohen 25-36. Print.

Astro, Richard. and Jackson J. Benson, eds. *TheFiction of Bernard Malmud*. Corvalis:Oregon State UP, 1977. Print.

Cohen, Sarah Blacher, ed. *Jewish Wry: Essays on Jewish Humor*. Bloomington: Indiana UP, 1987. Print.

Field, Leslie A., and Joyce W. Field, eds. *Bernard Malamud: A Collection of Critical Essays*. Englewood Cliffs: NJL Prentice-Hall, 1975. Print.

Giroux, Robert. "Introduction." Malamud. *The People*. vii-xvi.

Hawthorne, Nathaniel. *The Works of Nathaniel Hawthorne*. 2 vols. Boston: Houghton Mifflin, 1882. Print.

Malamud, Bernard. "Angel Levine," *Magic Barrel*. 43-56.

———. "Armistice," *The People*. 103-09.

———. "The Elevator," *The People*. 191-200.

———. "The Girl of My Dreams," *Magic Barrel*. 27-41.

———. "The Last Mohican," *Magic Barrel*. 155-82.

———. *The Magic Barrel*. New York: Farrar, Straus & Cudahy, 1958. Print.

———. *The People and Uncollected Stories*. New York: Farrar, Strauss & Giroux, 1989. Print.

———. "The Place is Different Now," *The People*. 143-53.

———. *The Stories of Bernard Malamud*. New York: Farar, Straus & Giroux, 1983. Print.

Ozick, Cynthia. "Literary Blacks and Jews." Fiel and Feld 80-98.

Solotaroff, Robert. *Bernard Malamud: A Study of Short Fiction*. Boston: Twayne, 1989.

Sanford E. Marovitz, Kent State University

One Clove Away From a Pomander Ball:

The Subversive Tradition of Jewish Female Comedians

Joyce Antler

"Let the fat girl do her stuff!" yelled the audience one night as a young Sophie Tucker came on stage. Even then, Tucker knew that size didn't matter "if you could sing and make people laugh" (Tucker 11). Tucker is one of six veteran comedians profiled in the Jewish Women's Archive's documentary film, *Making Trouble,* who used not only her body, but her subversive Jewish wit to make people laugh. Of the group, only writer Wendy Wasserstein didn't go on stage herself, but joins the other funny women in this film by dint of her legacy of thought-provoking, trouble-making, female characters. Like the others, Wasserstein doesn't so much laugh at women, but at the things that women find strange and funny. She wanted to give them their dignity, rather than render them as caricatures. "Women who shopped at S. Klein's and Orbachs," Wasserstein comments. "Women who knew their moisturizer," like Gorgeous Teitelbaum, the bloozy matron of *The Sisters Rosensweig* (*MT*).

Fanny Brice, Molly Picon, and Gilda Radner mugging it up may not seem dignified, and certainly Joan Rivers clowning about fallen vaginas looking like bunny slippers is anything but (*MT*). However, these comedians' performances show that Jewish women can be proud of the comic tradition in which they have been trailblazers. While the predominance of Jews in American comedy is well-known (one frequently cited statistic is that the minute proportion of Jews in the United States made up 80% of the comedy industry), Jewish *women's* comedy has largely gone unnoticed.[1]

Exceptions to this critical failure include, most prominently, Sarah Blacher Cohen, whose pioneering studies of Jewish comedy included a formative article, "The Unkosher Comediennes: From Sophie Tucker to Joan Rivers," published in her 1987 anthology, *Jewish Wry: Essays on Jewish Humor,* and June Sochen, whose essay, "Fanny Brice and Sophie Tucker: Blending the Particular with the Universal," appears in Cohen's 1983 collection, *From Hester Street to Hollywood: The Jewish-*

American Stage and Screen. Cohen's piece on "unkosher comediennes" featured such "brazen offenders of the faith" as Sophie Tucker, Belle Barth, Totie Fields, and Joan Rivers, all of whom gleefully violated the Torah's conception of feminine modesty. "As creatures of unclean lips," Cohen wrote, "they make dirty, they sully, they corrupt," but they also shattered taboos and liberated their audiences (105). Focusing on Brice as well as Tucker, Sochen portrayed the theme of the female "victim" in addition to the "aggressive" type created by Tucker and later *vilde chayes*, the "wild women" that Cohen writes about in her "unkosher" article.

Some two decades later, the Jewish Women's Archive film, *Making Trouble*, showcases a trajectory of three generations of funny Jewish women, including Molly Picon, Gilda Radner, and Brice from the gentler side of the comedy spectrum, as well as Tucker and Joan Rivers as representative vulgarians. Additionally there is playwright Wasserstein, who thought of herself as a comedy writer, highlighting the significant role played by Jewish women authors in developing Jewish humor.

Fulfilling the Archive's mission of chronicling and transmitting the hidden story of Jewish women's contributions to American history and culture, *Making Trouble* proclaims that yes, Virginia, there has been a veritable *tradition* of Jewish women's humor. From Yiddish theater and film, to vaudeville and burlesque, to nightclubs, improv and stand-up clubs, radio, television, the Broadway stage, and Hollywood cinema, Jewish women have made us laugh in a myriad of performance venues. In each of these arenas, they challenged conventional modes of joking. When they speak up, stand-up, or even sit-down (like the four younger comedians in *Making Trouble*—Judy Gold, Jackie Hoffman, Corey Kahaney, and Jessica Kirson, who guide us through the film as they chat in New York's famed Katz's Delicatessen), these women create humor by speaking through their female sensibilities. Writer Ann Beatts, interviewed in the Gilda Radner segment in *Making Trouble*, joked that none of the writers on *Saturday Night Live* (*SNL*) saw the humor in a line that a character was a few cloves away from finishing a pomander ball. None of the *SNL* men knew what a clove was (although executive producer Lorne Michaels guessed that it was a spice), much less a pomander ball, but the two women on the show found humor in this obscure term and a way to joke about women's things in a male world.

It is not that Jewish woman's appreciation of humor has gone unnoticed—think of Sarah, who laughs when God informs her of the imminent birth of her son despite her advanced age. And Sarah names this son "Itzhak" or "Isaac," meaning he who laughed.[2] But the role of Jewish woman as professional comic has been largely overlooked. This was brought home to me some years ago, when I dedicated my book on Jewish women's history, *The Journey Home*, to my two daughters, calling them "*badkhntes* of the next generation." At the time, Yiddish language experts discouraged my use of the word, telling me that there was no feminine form for *badkhen*, the Yiddish word meaning jester or clown. The *badkhen*, who had amused Jews in Europe for hundreds of years with his witty rhymes, composed on the spot at weddings, was a formative influence on the creators of Yiddish theater and may be seen as the forerunner of today's stand-up comedian. However, this important Jewish icon, as well as the important tradition he started, has been considered wholly male.

Coming to America meant breaking the Old World pattern whereby men usually performed comedy, as *Making Trouble* makes clear. Jewish women became prominent comic artists in the immigrant generation, with such comedic talents as Tucker, Brice and Picon. Their comic routines expressed the experiences and desires of many second-generation Jews while making the transition to mainstream audiences. Gertrude Berg, who began her long broadcast career on NBC radio in 1929, is another example of a Jewish woman who entertained audiences with a peculiarly ethnic humor.

In every successive generation, Jewish female comedians helped shape the contours of American comedy. These comic pioneers were followed by a new cohort, schooled in the academy of improv clubs, and liberated by feminism, which led them to invent new forms of comedy, more satirical and openly rebellious than their predecessors. Elaine May, Joan Rivers, Gilda Radner, Roseanne Barr, and Elayne Boosler were among these innovators.

A third generation of Jewish female comics came to prominence in the 1990s and fill mainstream and alternative comic venues today. These women, who came up through stand-up clubs and often appear on late night TV, HBO, Comedy Central, and in films and theater, are more diverse than previous cohorts of female comics, including such talents as Susie Essman, Wendy Leibman, Rita Rudner, Sarah Bernhard, Rain Pryor, Carol Leifer, Lisa Kron, Amy Borkowsky, Page Hurwitz, Cathy Ladman, Sherry Davey, Julie Goldman, Betsy Salkind, Susannah Perlman, Cate Lazarus, Jesse Klein, and Sarah Silverman. These comics can be as aggressive and bawdy as their male peers, but they emphasize women's strengths in ways that set them apart from many earlier women comedians.

When we look at the historical trajectory of Jewish women comics, we find them in every generation in every corner of American culture. Like male Jewish comedians, they have demonstrated superb verbal skills and the masterful use of irony, satire, and mockery, including self- mockery. Their heritage as Jews—especially, the Diasporic experience of living between two worlds—gave them a sharp critical edge and the ability to express the anxieties and foibles of contemporary culture. Yet there is something unique about female Jewish comics that makes them distinct from male peers.

As the "pomander ball" exchange reveals, many of these comedians center their humor in a specifically female—and often feminist—point of view that showcases issues of particular relevance to women. Whether they have been explicitly bawdy in sexually frank and often unladylike routines in the manner of a Sophie Tucker, Belle Barth, Pearl Williams, Patsy Abbot, Bette Midler, or Joan Rivers—or presented more innocent challenges—think Molly Picon, Fanny Brice, Gilda Radner, and Goldie Hawn—these comedians have stretched the boundaries of conventional thinking about comedy and about gender roles. The laughter they engender is powerful and subversive.

Perhaps this is because women's humor often deals with the incongruities and inequities of a world based on gender distinctions. When women use humor to express and laugh at their visions of the world, they cannot help but challenge the social structures that keep women from positions of power. Some do this explicitly, others turn the spotlight inward, and the gender issues are expressed in self-deprecating ways. But because expectations are that men do the joking and women receive (or are targets of) humor, for women merely to take the mike as comic performers upsets role norms. Their humor challenges the structures that keep women from power by turning our attention to things that matter to women. Comedian Kate Clinton has called feminist humorists "fumerists," a term that captures the idea of simultaneously being funny and wanting to burn the house down (Barreca 38-40). In her influential 1976 work, "The Laugh of the Medusa," the French (Jewish) theorist Helene Cixous talked about the revolutionary potential of women's humor, urging them "to break up the 'truth' with laughter . . . in order to smash everything, to shatter the framework of institutions, to blow up the law" (258).

Jewish female comedians have successfully stretched the boundaries of conventional comedy and gender roles—even when they didn't *intend* to burn the house down. "A performing Jewish woman is a force to be reckoned with," says June Sochen, "and possibly feared" ("From Sophie Tucker" 69). They have been not merely funny, but transformative.

Mollie Picon: "Yonkele"

Molly Picon, born Margaret Pyekoon on the Lower East Side of New York City in 1898, began her theatrical career performing with a Yiddish repertory troupe in Philadelphia, where her mother moved after her father abandoned the family. Picon went on to become the first great international star of the Yiddish theater. Presenting humorous interpretations of the plight of first- and second-generation Jewish immigrants, audiences recognized "in her highly magnified or distorted humor the stuff which makes up their own lives" (Romeyn and Kugelmass 27). Tiny (4' 11") but sprightly (at age eighty, she was still performing somersaults), Picon starred in a variety of venues as well as Yiddish theater—radio, television, Broadway, Yiddish and American film.

Most often Picon played young girls who dressed or behaved like young boys, parts written for her by her Polish immigrant husband, director and producer Jacob ("Yonkel") Kalich, whom she married in 1919. Kalich convinced her to pursue a career in the Yiddish theater, rather than the Broadway stage, to which she aspired, and took her to the great Yiddish theaters of Europe, "to perfect my Yiddish, to get my star legs." Performing across the continent in original works by Kalich, Picon was launched to stardom in her role as the thirteen-year-old boy, "Yonkele," in the play of the same name produced by Kalich in Vienna in 1921. Between 1922 and 1925, she played similar characters in such Yiddish plays as "Tzipke," "Shmendrik" ("Loser"), "Gypsy Girl," "Molly Dolly," "Little Devil," "Mamale" ("Mommy"), "Raizele," "Oy is Dus A Madel" ("What a Girl"), and "The Circus Girl." Even in middle age, Picon continued to reinvent her transgressive, tomboy character, which audiences loved. Her most famous film was the 1936 *Yidl Mitn Fidl* (*Yidl with His Fiddle*), in which the thirty-eight-year-old actress played a girl disguised as a teenage boy so she and her father can earn a living as traveling musicians. In fact, said Picon, she played the "Yonkele" role at least "3,000 times": "Deep down within me, I was Yankele [sic]. I still am" (jwa.org "Molly Picon").

Fanny Brice: "Playing the Clown"

Fanny Brice (born Fania Borach) was "one of the great, great clowns of all time," in the opinion of famed film director George Cukor (Grossman xi). Appearing in burlesque, vaudeville, drama, film, musical revues (including nine Ziegfeld Follies between 1910 and 1936), and on radio (she had her own "Baby Snooks" radio show from 1944 through her death in 1951), Brice's career lasted more than four decades. Biographer Barbara Grossman observes that the star built her career on "manic mimicry and exuberant buffoonery," both rooted in Yiddish parody. When early in her career Brice went to Tin Pan Alley, songwriter Irving Berlin gave her a new lyric, "Sadie Salome," with the words: "With your face, you should sing this song," and urged her to adopt a Yiddish accent. Brice learned the accent especially for the part—the most successful of all her stage appearances—and it became a trademark of her routines in burlesque and musical comedy. Soon after she began appearing on the Ziegfeld stage, and although Brice did not conform to feminine beauty standards, the Follies proved to be a wonderful vehicle for her parodic talents. "If she could not be the prettiest girl on the stage," says Grossman, "she would be the funniest" (*MT*).

Brice's broad physical humor and mimicry differed from the ingenuousness of Molly Picon's child/woman roles. Brice specialized in representing incongruity: she played the American Indian/Jewish girl "Rosie Rosenstein"; an evangelist and neophyte nudist, both Yiddish-accented; a Jewish girl, "Sascha," who became a Sultan's wife; and "Mrs. Cohen at the Beach," a "consummate *yente*," who nagged her children. Whether Indian, Arab, or any ethnic personage, with her Yiddish accent and dialect Brice constantly stepped out of character, commenting on the absurdities of the action going on. And she announced that she was Jewish.

There was a serious side to Brice's comedy. With numbers like "Second-Hand Rose," "My Man," "Oy, How I Hate that Fellow Nathan," she mocked men's unreliability, and also herself. Audiences related to her witty put-downs of men and marriage, or to expressions of disappointment and unhappiness, because they knew these portrayals sprang from Brice's life. "In anything Jewish I ever did, I wasn't standing apart, making fun of the race," Brice said. "I *was* the race, and what happened to me on the stage is what could happen to them...." (Sochen, "Fanny Brice and Sophie Tucker" 49).

Combining a "'traditional' feminine concern for others, albeit in a funny vein" with a style and persona rooted in her Jewish environment, Brice tapped into current issues relating to all people, despite her pronounced ethnicity (Sochen, "From

Sophie Tucker to Barbra Streisand" 73). Yet by 1923, she wanted to play more universal roles and underwent a nose job to alter her appearance, an event that made the front page of *The New York Times*. But the desired parts never materialized. Brice had apparently "cut off her nose to spite her race," Dorothy Parker quipped, all to no avail (Grossman 149). Audiences preferred her as she was—a talented, outrageously funny, good-humored, Jewish comic. Brice "immediately connected with her audience," says June Sochen, in a way that was both woman—and Jewish—centered, offering "a different reading of the known material...she found the humor, the silliness, and the humanity beyond the stereotype" ("From Sophie Tucker to Barbra Streisand" 73).

Sophie Tucker: "Yiddishe/Red Hot Mama"

Sophie Tucker (born Sonya Abuza) has a special place in the tradition of Jewish women's comedy. Because of the longevity with which she held the limelight (over sixty years in the industry), and also because of her trademark transgressiveness, she was called the "Queen of Show Business."[3] Using humor and self-mockery, Tucker sang "hot" torch songs with titles like "Nobody Loves a Fat Girl But How A Fat Girl Can Love," "That Lovin' Soul Kiss," "Everybody Shimmies Now," "Vamp, Vamp, Vamp," and "Who Paid the Rent for Mrs. Rip Van Winkle when Rip Van Winkle Was Away." Her message was that all women, even "big, ugly" ones needed sex and love.

At the very time when vaudeville and burlesque were becoming increasingly subdued as they reached out to broader family audiences, Tucker managed to elude mass entertainment's censorship; her supposed "ugliness" and her size permitted her to challenge social norms of femininity and "good girl" behavior. Eddie Cantor quipped that Sophie Tucker "sings the words we used to write on the sidewalks of New York" (qtd. in Cohen 107).

Tucker hadn't meant to become a comedian. She left home at seventeen, leaving her one-year-old baby with her mother, Jennie in Hartford, for a show business career as a singer. The neighbors in Hartford were shocked: "they said only a bad woman would do such a thing. I must be a bad woman—a whore, in the unvarnished language of the Scriptures" (Tucker 44).

Slowly, Tucker built her career, singing in rathskellers, becoming a well-known blackface "coon singer"—one of the few women to black up among the likes of performers like Eddie Cantor and Al Jolson. But she was uncomfortable in blackface because it masked her true identity. Sometimes Tucker pulled off a glove to show that she was white, and there would be a surprised gasp, "then a howl of laughter." She would throw in some Yiddish words, too, to "give the audience a kick," and to show that she was white *and* Jewish (Tucker 64).

The idea of becoming a comic performer came to Tucker by accident. One day a theater manager sent her on without blackface, telling her that her trunk was lost. Dressed in a tightly laced black princess gown (like a "baloney in mourning," she cracked), with a long train of red chiffon ruffles, she slipped during her bows and caught her heel in the ruffles of her dress (Tucker 64). "Down I went on my fanny like a ton of bricks," she recalled (44-45). The applause was deafening; even the cast shrieked with laughter. Sophie the comedian was born.

It was not only as a raunchy "Red Hot Mama" that Tucker reached the heights of stardom. Her most famous song was "My Yiddishe Mama," introduced into her repertoire after the death of her mother, Jennie Abuza, in 1925. Jennie's death was deeply traumatic for Tucker, until her accompanist wrote "My Yiddishe Mama" for her, and the effect was cathartic. Tucker sang it throughout the U.S and in Europe, and there was never "a dry eye in the house."

A generation of young Americans grew up listening to Tucker's records, often forbidden them by their parents, in secret; others went to her live nightclub performances. She was an effective "Red-Hot Mama" because audiences believed she told the truth about her own experiences. In England, even among the royals, she was a special favorite. ("Hi ya, king!" Tucker irreverently quipped to one of her most ardent fans.) The "Last of the 'Red-Hot Mamas'" died in 1966. Although not a "nice Jewish girl" by the standards of her mother's generation, she was one of America's first "popular culture" feminists and among its most celebrated Jewish comic voices.

With Sophie Tucker's death and the demise of Gertrude Berg's long-running "Goldberg" situation comedies a decade earlier, the baton passed on to a new generation of female comics. A new style of female Jewish comedy—fast-paced, hip, and deeply satirical—emerged to replace the pioneering women comics of the previous generation. The new style of comedy was ushered in by a group of talented satirists, male and female—Lenny Bruce, Mort Sahl, Shelley Berman, and the extraordinary Mike Nichols and Elaine May. Though Nichols and May performed for merely four years, ending their collaboration in 1961, they left their mark on comedy for years to come.

The female Jewish comics that came up through the Second City route—Elaine May, Joan Rivers, and Gilda Radner—hit their stride in the 1960s-1970s. This comic wave was joined in mid-stream by another group of Jewish women comics emboldened by the feminist movement—particularly during the 1980s when the increased confidence of feminism allowed women to laugh at themselves in new ways—and to laugh at others.

Joan Rivers: "Rita" and "Heidi Abromowitz"

"I am not the ideal Jewish woman," Joan Rivers admits in a comedy act filmed in *Making Trouble*. "I love to take [my audience] to the edge," she says. "I love to get them upset. And ruin their value system" (*MT*). Known for her aggressiveness and her "unkosher" bawdy style, in Sarah Cohen's words, Rivers (née Joan Molinsky), Phi Beta Kappa Barnard graduate and daughter of a Brooklyn Jewish doctor, has been performing for over forty years. Making her television debut on Johnny Carson's *Tonight Show* in 1965, she went on to host a daytime talk show, became the first solo guest host of the *Tonight Show*, and by 1986 had her own late night show on the new Fox Network. In 1990 Rivers won an Emmy for Outstanding Talk Show

Host. She also authored two successful books, *Having a Baby Can Be a Scream* (1975) and *Life and Times of Heidi Abromowitz* (1984) and wrote and starred in a well-reviewed Broadway drama based on the life of Lenny Bruce's mother, *Sally Marr and Her Escorts* (1994).

Rivers struggled for many years to find her comic style. She bombed in the Catskills, feeling she was not "ethnic enough," and disliked the model followed by pioneer women comedians of the time, like Phyllis Diller, who were, "basically doing a woman's version of men's acts" (Rivers 293). Working with her comic "soul-mate," writer Treva Silverman, who appears in the Rivers' segment of *Making Trouble*, Rivers began to find her comic voice. Elaine May served as role model for both women: "an assertive woman with a marvelous, fast mind and, at the same time, pretty and feminine. We did not know any other women like that" (Nachman 601).

Rivers's breakthrough came at Second City, where she started in 1961—"the best girl since Elaine May" (Rivers 291). But Rivers was not the typical "compliant," "uncompetitive" Second City girl, and she found the troupe's unwillingness to treat her as an equal deeply troubling. Nonetheless, she feels she was "born as a comedian" at Second City, "no Second City, no Joan Rivers" (Rivers 274). Seeing Lenny Bruce perform for the first time in Greenwich Village became another turning point. From Bruce she learned that "personal truth can be the foundation of comedy, that outrageousness can be cleansing and healthy.... I had found the key," Rivers recalled. "My comedy could flow from the poor, venerable schlepp Joan Molinsky" (qtd. in Nachman 607-8).

Rivers created a character named Rita, the "urban ethnic loser girl who cannot get married," who she believed became the secret of her success, allowing Rivers to "turn autobiography into comedy and touch all women." Rita *was* Joan Rivers in all her desperation: "I'm not married and life is awful, so what's wrong with me?" And finally, "I'm married: Why is everything still wrong?" Rita worked because "people recognize insecurity and respond to it," said Rivers, because "everybody is like me" (Rivers 277).

Rivers understood that she was part of a new transitional comedy generation that was leaving the one-line joke litany of traditional comics far behind. Nichols and May had been the pioneers of the new style—a much more "personal comedy" that described "humor behavior by describing our own behavior." Rivers used this style to talk openly about her emotional travails and also about sex. "I was becoming a nice Jewish girl in stockings and pumps saying on stage what people thought but never said aloud in polite society" (Rivers 341). Mentioning the word "tampons," she has said, was the greatest challenge of her career. But whereas Sophie Tucker (along with the streetwise raunchiness of Pearl Williams, Belle Barth, and Patsy Abbot) performed in the limited space of nightclubs and comedy LP albums, Rivers did her parodies on national TV, testing the medium's limits. Despite her edgy routines, she never downplayed her Jewishness, even though her agent often warned her that she was "too Jewish" and "too New York" for much of the country (*MT*).

The self-deprecatory style that became the Rivers trademark coexists with a much more aggressive humor that targets others, often with great cruelty. Sarah Blacher Cohen feels that Rivers resembles the traditional *yente,* "a woman of low origins or vulgar manners," a "scandal-spreader and rumormonger," although her biting sarcasm is not indiscriminate, but directed at celebrities and "people of high degree" ("Unkosher Comediennes" 118). But Rivers offers a contrast to these routines through her "Heidi Abromowitz" character—her "comically spiteful portrayal of the nice Jewish girl's direct opposite....the sexual transgressor...the whore with the heart of gold." "Devoid of moral constraints," says Cohen, "she can take the lid off her id and fly away on the wings of an ego. And we, who are grounded by our multiple repressions, are temporarily seduced into flying away with her" ("Unkosher Comediennes" 121). Over her long career, Rivers also introduced feminist characters, with hostile jokes aimed at gynecologists and others in the male power structure who demeaned women.

Whichever the routine, Rivers spits out mocking, nervy jokes that Cohen sees as full of "unkosher" *chutzpah.* To her critics, however, she is merely "abrasive, tasteless, profane." Rivers defends herself against such charges."You have to be abrasive to be a current comic," she says. "If you don't offend someone you become pap" (qtd. in Cohen "Unkosher Comediennes" 119). For Rivers, humor serves as a "medium of revenge" by which comedians "deflate and punish" rejection (Nachman 600). "Comedy is power," she says. "The only weapon more formidable than humor is a gun" (Rivers 23-24).

Gilda Radner: "Jewish Jeans"

Gilda Radner (the family name was originally Ratkowsky) decided to be funny as a teenager, when she knew she "wasn't going to make it on her looks."[4] Thirteen years younger than Rivers, Radner produced humor that was very different from her predecessor's, though Radner, too, got her start at Second City (the Toronto company). With her fellow Second City players, Radner was a member of the "Not Ready for Primetime Players," which became the first cast of *Saturday Night Live,* debuting to rave reviews in 1975. Radner became an audience favorite with her ingenious, loveable female characters—among them, dowdy schoolteacher Emily Litella; dorky adolescent Lisa Loopner; lispy newscasters Roseanne Roseannadanna and "Baba Wawa" (Barbara Walters); and Rhonda Reiss, a Long Island Jewish "princess."

A self-proclaimed "total child of television" who grew up admiring the female comedians of an earlier age, Gilda provided a new template for female comics. Described as a "thirty-three-year old who had a band-aid on her knee," Gilda combined the innocence of a little girl with a hip, fresh satirical zaniness that charmed audiences and her fellow players alike. "She was so happy on camera," Steve Martin observed; she was "the sweetest, kindest, funniest person....you really came to love her" (Antler, Lauren).

The authenticity in Radner's performances was not that she played herself, but that the vulnerability in all of her characters—true part of the core Gilda Radner—shone through. There was nothing hostile about her. Rather, she excelled in physical comedy in the fashion of a Fanny Brice, and the versatility of her portrayals recalled her own heroine, Lucille Ball.

Radner did not shy away from doing Jewish characters, though some, like her famous "Jewish Jeans" ad parody, created controversy. With lines like "She shops the sales for designer clothes/she got designer nails and a designer nose," some thought it was "too Jewish," too "Jappy." But in *Making Trouble*, writer Marilyn Suzanne Miller notes that it is Gilda, the Jewish Jeans girl in the spoof, whom the other multicultural singers aspire to be: *she* is their goal; the Jewish woman has triumphed. Like the other comics in the film, Radner is not afraid to wink at the audience, proclaiming her Jewishness. She always referred to herself as "this Jewish girl from Detroit." Radner hated the idea, however, that "if you were Jewish and a comedian, you had to be unattractive." She fought her own battle with bulimia for much of her life, but insisted, as the film makes clear, that she was a "beautiful girl" with "great legs and I am also funny: Live with it!" (*MT*).

Wendy Wasserstein: "Sisters Rosensweig"

Pulitzer-Prize winning dramatist Wendy Wasserstein, the first woman to win a Tony for a single-authored work, may seem like an unusual choice for inclusion in a film about Jewish comedians. But Wasserstein always thought of herself as a comedy writer, understanding comedy to be a "broader category than just fun and jokes" (*MT*). Her comic voice is loud and strong in her dramas, and she enjoyed writing for TV comedy series and humorous essays as well. In *Making Trouble*, Wasserstein stands for all the Jewish writers who created comedy, including Ann Beatts, Rosie Schuster, Treva Silverman, and Marilyn Suzanne Miller, all of whom appear in the film.

Born in Brooklyn, Wasserstein briefly attended the Yeshivah of Flatbush before switching to an exclusive Manhattan private school for girls. She graduated from Mt. Holyoke College, drawing on the incongruities of her experience at this all-female, upper-crust, WASP school in her first play, *Uncommon Women and Others*, produced off-Broadway in 1978. *Isn't It Romantic?* opened in 1981, *The Heidi Chronicles*, winner of the Pulitzer Prize, a Tony Award, and a host of other prizes, appeared in 1988 and was followed by *The Sisters Rosensweig* in 1992. *The Sisters Rosensweig*, Wasserstein's most explicitly Jewish play, worried colleagues who thought that it might not play well in middle America. "Believe it or not, I've heard there are sisters beyond the Mississippi," the author replied, and kept the play's title and focus (*MT*). *The Sisters Rosensweig* tells the story of three sisters, who greatly resemble Wasserstein and her own two sisters, who spend a weekend in London to celebrate the birthday of the eldest. Sara, cool and self-controlled, an expatriate and atheist, is a high-powered international banker who has renounced all possibility of romance as she moves into her fifty-fourth year. The "funsy," clothes-conscious, garrulous Gorgeous, slightly younger, is a housewife, mother, and temple member from suburban Boston, where she is a talk-show personality. Pfeni, single and forty, is the "wandering Jew" of the family—an itinerant journalist who roams the world in search of causes and stories.

By the time the play has ended, the identities the playwright establishes for the sisters evaporate, and they are revealed in surprising ways. Wasserstein takes us inside Gorgeous's seemingly superficial materialism, showing as much compassion for her struggles as for those of her more intellectual and achievement-driven sisters. "I grew up with the Dr. Gorgeouses of the world," says Wasserstein, "I loved them" (*MT*). She and Madeline Kahn, the talented Jewish comedian who played the role on Broadway, believed that audiences would identify with the character—many of them *were* Gorgeous, Wasserstein thought. (The character actually drew on her mother, Lola, and her own sister, nicknamed "Gorgeous.") Gorgeous would not be "a joke," not the extreme JAP rendered by so many other comic writers, but a character with familiar Jewish traits, at last rendered sympathetically.

Wasserstein should be seen as a true social "reformer," as June Sochen argues was the case with comedians like Tucker and Brice. Through their comedy, these women offered audiences "unpopular views in a popular mode," aspiring to "change their audience's...values." (Sochen "From Sophie Tucker to Barbra Streisand" 80). And although Sarah Blacher Cohen worried that feminism and comedy might be mutually exclusive—feminism could lead to a "rigid sense of political correctness that has a dampening spirit on humor," she thought—Wasserstein's plays show the compatibility of comedy and feminist thought (qtd. in Wallenstein).

The Radical Potential of Humor: Contemporary Jewish Women Comedians

Jewish female humorists are more widely accepted today than ever before. The documentary, *The Aristocrats*, in which 100 comedians are asked to give their renditions of the same obscene joke, is dominated by Jews. Although there are relatively few women comedians in the film, many of them are Jewish—Wendy Leibman, Susie Essman, Rita Rudner, Judy Gold, Cathy Ladman, and the sardonic Sarah Silverman. In addition to these comics, Jewish women comedians performing today include Jackie Hoffman, Cory Kahaney, Sarah Bernhard, Rain Pryor, Carol Leifer, Lisa Kron, Amy Borkowsky, Jessica Kirson, Sherry Davey, Julie Goldman, Betsy Salkind, Cate Lazarus, Susannah Perlman, and Jesse Klein.

Why are Jewish women comics so prominent today? Why do there seem to be so many of them, and why are they everywhere?[4] One factor is the tremendous growth in comedy clubs that took place after the late 1980s. Comedy clubs have been joined by a wide network of small theaters and underground, alternative, "hipster" comedy rooms and clubs—spaces where stand-up comedians, sketch comedy, and improv groups can perform. In addition, there is the festival route for stand-up, improv, sketch comedy, and short films.

This interactive world allows many younger comics to gain a foothold. Opportunities in television, especially in cable TV, where young comedians are recruited for stand-up, sketch comedy, and improv shows as performers and writers, have enlarged the possibilities for comedians. Working in multiple genres, lucky comedians today can be experimental and commercially successful.

A second factor is that women have so many more role models today than ever before. In the post-feminist era, women have become prominent in all the professions—in business, law, and medicine, as directors, theater producers, and actors, *and* in all capacities in television, especially cable TV, and in performance art. Young comics see before them a plethora of female comic role models. A quarter century of performances of *Saturday Night Live* comedians and highly visible female comics of all ethnicities have broadened the theatrical types that women play. This contrasts with the experience of the early improv comics, for whom the only role models were women who played "angels in the house," "mothers," and "whores," or were zany screwballs such as Lucille Ball, stern spinsters like Eve Arden, or, in Joan Rivers' view, women comics acting too much like men.

The flourishing of gay culture has also stimulated female comedy—there are many lesbian comics performing today, including Jewish lesbian comics, and these women have innovated fresh, forceful material. According to Susie Essman, who plays the foul-mouthed Suzy Green in *Curb Your Enthusiasm,* "really good lesbian stand-ups...are happier with power, not like straight [comedians] trying to be nice young ladies" (Friedman).

Finally, there is the prominence of comedy itself in today's world. The great success of Jon Stewart's *The Daily Show, The Colbert Report*, and the Comedy Central channel point to the central role that comedy now plays. Many people believe that these shows are the only place where they can get their news—and the truth. All of these factors have empowered contemporary women comedians, including many Jewish comics, and have helped to catapult them into comic success.

The careers of the four "Katz's Deli" comedians in *Making Trouble* suggest the kind of issues and performance styles that characterize contemporary Jewish women comedians. They also reveal that despite the many new arenas for female comics, it remains the case that to be Jewish and female in the still "all boys club" of comedy can be daunting. Katz's Deli comic Cory Kahaney was often told to keep her acts "Jew-free," but she never hid her Jewish identity (Wallenstein). "It's a very big thing among Jews when someone's Jewish," Jackie Hoffman notes in the film. "So whatever comic or whoever in the performing world was Jewish, it was a huge deal." The *Making Trouble* pioneers helped these women find their voices and comic styles.

Judy Gold: "Mommy Queerest"

Judy Gold won two Emmy Awards for writing and producing *The Rosie O'Donnell Show*, a Cable Ace Award for her HBO special, and was twice nominated as funniest female stand-up by The American Comedy Awards. More recently she has had hit solo shows, *25 Questions for A Jewish Mother* and *Mommy Queerest.*[5]

Often Gold's performances are little more than a stream of Jewish mother jokes. "My mother is the most annoying person on the face of the earth," she jokes, "a miserable human being. You can say something to her and she cannot only make it negative, she makes it about herself. What are you having for New Years, filet mignon? I'll be eating shit." Her mother's just-published autobiography, she has quipped, is titled "*I Came, I Saw, I Criticized.*" A lesbian who is raising two sons with her one-time partner, Gold often says that she feels sorry for her kids because they have two Jewish mothers. She jokes that as a child, every time she left the house, her mother feared something was going to happen; when once she came home forty-five minutes late, her mother had already called the police and was serving them her homemade *rugaleh* in her living room. Judy's tardiness led her mother to attach an egg-timer to her belt to remind her to get home on time. No fun and games in this family: Mrs. Gold's favorite read-aloud story to the young child was the pop-up version of the *Diary of Anne Frank.*

As an easily recognizable Jewish shtick, Gold's routine has an immediate pay-off, calling forth a reflex response that allows spectators to laugh at this "insider" humor. Gold believes that her humor challenges rather than reifies stereotypes, illuminating the real women behind them. Audiences respond to her Jewish mother jokes because of the fact that they *are* stereotypes. Making the stereotypes excessive through insult humor may actually explode them, revealing through exaggeration that despite the kernel of truth that may lurk within, the caricature is anachronistic and incorrect.

"To be a great stand-up," Gold says, "you have to tell the truth and you have to draw upon your own experience.... Otherwise there's no passion." And comedians often must take on aggressive styles of humor that are staples of the comedy club circuit. Gold explains. "Stand-up comedy is not a feminine profession at all ... it's very 'aggressively' male." Susie Essman, who stars in the HBO show *Curb Your Enthusiasm*, argues that stand-up is far more aggressive than doing sit-coms. Joan Rivers "*had* to be self-deprecating," she observes, "because you couldn't be an attractive, funny woman. It was too threatening." Gold echoes her thought: "There's nothing more threatening to a man than a female comic" (Cohen, D.). Even today.

But times are changing. Essman believes that comics like Judy Gold are changing them, and maybe "younger guys [audiences and comedians] are nowhere near as sexist, maybe because their moms are out in the workplace." And women comics are getting more comfortable with the power of comedy. However confrontational, says Essman, "when you're standing on stage alone with the mike—the phallus symbol ... it **is** incredibly powerful" (Cohen, D.).

Jackie Hoffman: "The Kvetching Continues"

Jackie Hoffman is an eight-year veteran of Chicago's Second City improv group, an Obie award best-actress-winner, and much acclaimed for her performance as the pregnant co-worker friend, Joan, in *Kissing Jessica Stein*. Hoffman also won awards for her performance in *Hairspray* and is a regular performer on late night TV and comedy specials. She has done many one-woman shows, often with Jewish themes—for example, "The Kvetching Continues," "Jackie Hoffman's Hanukkah," and "Jackie's Kosher Khristmas." Hoffman also played in *The Sisters Rosensweig* and the rock musical *Xanadu*.

Like Gold, Hoffman uses Jewish mother routines in her shows. Since every word to an older parent might be the last, she says that she frequently ends her calls by telling her mother she loves her. Her mother calls her too, leaving messages frantic with worry whenever Jackie doesn't immediately answer. Then she calls the police to describe her missing daughter. "She's not married. She has a filthy mouth. If she took her hair out of her eyes she'd be a beautiful girl." In another joke, Hoffman describes the language tapes she played to learn Yiddish. Rather than the standard phrases for language instruction, these tapes conveyed key phrases of Jewish life: "Her daughter gives her heartache. I feel sick." Like Gold's mother, Hoffman's mother is supportive, despite the hostile-seeming jokes. "She always says, 'If it weren't for me, you wouldn't have any material.' My mom's mantra is 'Don't give up the pay-check!'" (Antler, J., *You Never Call* 248).

Cory Kahaney: "JAP: Jewish Princesses of Comedy"

Cory Kahaney is a popular New York comedian who created the hit multi-media show, *JAP: Jewish Princesses of Comedy*, a tribute to Jewish comic "queens"—Belle Barth, Pearl Williams, Betty Walker, Jean Carroll, and Totie Fields—who paved the way for "all females in comedy," in Kahaney's view (Corykahaney.com). Clips of the legendary queens are combined with individual sets by contemporary comedians—including *Making Trouble's* Jessica Kirson and Jackie Hoffman. Kahaney was a grand finalist on NBC's *Last Comic Standing* and has appeared in many comedy specials on Comedy Central and HBO. Kahaney also conceived and developed *The Radio Ritas*, a nationally syndicated talk radio show for Greenstone Media, a company created by Gloria Steinem and Jane Fonda to provide radio programming for women.

Kahaney allows that she was inspired to do comedy by her own Jewish mother's humorous impersonations and her family's regular trips to Grossingers, where they loved the comedy acts. One of her signature routines pokes fun at her own parenting of her teenage daughter, whom she raised as a single mother. "The other day, she emptied the dishwasher, which is like an annual act," Kahaney says. "And she asks, 'Do I get a cell phone now?' And I said: 'What happens when you take out the garbage? Do you get a Mercedes?'"(qtd. in Antler, J., *You Never Call* 253-54).

Jessica Kirson: "My Cookie's Gone"

The youngest of the Katz's Deli comics in *Making Trouble*, Jessica Kirson, a social worker from New Jersey before she turned to comedy, has appeared on Comedy Central, Nickelodeon, the *Tonight Show*, and the Logo Network. Kirson tours with her one-woman show, *My Cookie's Gone*—her answer to a homeless person who asks her for food ("do I look like I have leftovers?")—and makes fun of "fat, ugly" girls like herself who complain about getting hit on. Like the others, Kirson also jokes about her mother—"My mother is a therapist. She had clients in the house, so

I always had to be quiet. I was like Anne Frank in my own house." Her jokes come at a frantic pace—she seems "out of control, like a more sarcastic version of early-career Robin Williams," wrote a *Variety* reviewer, and she "subverts some of stand-up's biggest cliches" about marriage, beauty, sex, ethnicity, and race. "I'm an angry Jew, and you'll get to hear about it," she tells her audiences. "But I feel like an angry black woman" (qtd. in Blankenship; Kirson videos).

Not all of the six *Making Trouble* pioneers nor the four younger "deli guides" would label their comedy "feminist." But in drawing on their own experiences for humor, they expressed and helped to shape perspectives about issues of concern to women. Women have special secrets and shared bonds they tell us, like pomander balls, dieting and purging, the travails and joys of dating, marriage, and sex, being mothers and daughters. Much that defines their authenticity is also related to their experiences as Jews, and the dual emphasis on their Jewish backgrounds and female identities made them distinctive in the comedy world. Their struggles fill the screen in *Making Trouble*, along with their many triumphs, and always there are the jokes. We learn that laughter provides a way not only to cope with the tensions and conflicts of daily life, but to transcend them.

The gift of comedy that emanates from these Jewish women has been to make us transcend our own daily lives as well and to see, through humor, alternative visions of who we could be if we, too, had the courage to challenge—and mock—the strictures that hold us back.

Notes

1. See "Behavior: Analyzing Jewish Comics," *Time*, 2 Oct. 1978; Samuel S. Janus, "The Great Jewish-American Comedians' Identity Crisis," *American Journal of Psychoanalysis* 40, no. 3 (Sept. 1980): 259-65.

2. Like her namesake, scholar-playwright Sarah Blacher Cohen loved to make people laugh. Even her academic presentations were filled with jokes, some of them surprisingly racy: she enjoyed offering audiences the choice of "the most vulgar or the least vulgar" versions of her talks. See Irwin Richman, "11th Annual Conference Recap," The Catskills Institute (27-28 Aug. 2005), http://catskills.brown.edu/confrep/11.html.

3. The following account of Sophie Tucker is taken from Joyce Antler, *The Journey Home*, 137-43, and *You Never Call! You Never Write!*, 17-21; and Joyce Antler comments in *Making Trouble*.

4. Thanks to Lauren Antler for her insights on this question.

5. This discussion of Judy Gold is taken from Antler, *You Never Call! You Never Write!*, 249-52.

Works Cited

Antler, Joyce. *The Journey Home: How Jewish Women Shaped Modern America*. New York: Schocken, 1998. Print.

———. *You Never Call! You Never Write! A History of the Jewish Mother*. New York: Oxford University Press, 2007. Print.

Antler, Lauren. "Gilda Radner." *Notable American Women: A Biographical Dictionary, Completing the Twentieth Century*. Cambridge: Harvard University Press, 2004. Print.

Barreca, Gina. "Real Stories, real laughter, real women." *Ms.* Summer 2004. Web. 1 Oct. 2009.

Blankenship, Mark. "The J.A.P. Show." *Variety,* Spring 2007. Web. 1 Oct. 2009.

Cixous, Helene. "The Laugh of the Medusa." *New French Feminisms.* Eds. Elaine Marks and Isabelle de Courtivron. New York: Schocken Books, 1981. Print.

Cohen, Debra Nussbaum. "Funny Girls: Gorgeous, female, and profane—that's today's successful female stand-up Jewish comics." *Jewish Women International.* 2006. Web. 1 Oct. 2009.

Cohen, Sarah Blacher, "The Unkosher Comediennes: From Sophie Tucker to Joan Rivers." *Jewish Wry: Essays on Jewish Humor.* Ed. Sara Blacher Cohen Detroit: Wayne State University Press, 1987: 105-24. Print.

Corykahaney.com. Web. 9 Sept. 2009.

Epstein, Lawrence J. *The Haunted Smile: The Story of Jewish Comedians in America.* New York: Public Affairs, 2001. Print.

Friedman, Dan. "High School Reunion: The Actress and the Editor Visit Mt. Vernon High, 36 Years Later," *Forward.* 30 Oct. 2009. Web. 21 Oct., 2009.

Grossman, Barbara. *Funny Woman: The Life and Times of Fanny Brice.* Bloomington: Indiana University Press, 1991. Print.

Jessicakirson.com. Web. 4 Oct. 2009.

"Jessica Kirson: My Cookie's Gone Special." Web. 4 Oct. 2009.

Making Trouble: Three Generations of Jewish Women in Comedy. Dir. Rachel Talbot. Jewish Women's Archive. 2006. Film.

"Molly Picon." Web. 16 Sept. 2009. http://jwa.org/historymakers/picon.

Nachman, Gerald. *Seriously Funny: The Rebel Comedians of the 1950s and 1960s.* New York: Pantheon, 2003. Print.

Rivers, Joan. *Enter Talking.* New York: Delacorte Press, 1986. Print.

Romeyn, Esther and Jack Kugelmass. *Let There Be Laughter: Jewish Humor in America.* Chicago: Spertus Press, 1997. Print.

Sochen, June. "Fanny Brice and Sophie Tucker: Blending the Particular with the Universal." *From Hester Street to Hollywood: The Jewish-American Stage and Screen.* Ed. Sarah Blacher Cohen. Bloomington: Indiana University Press, 1983: 44-57. Print.

———. "From Sophie Tucker to Barbra Streisand: Jewish Women Entertainers as Reformers." *Talking Back: Images of Jewish Women in American Popular Culture.* Ed. Joyce Antler. Hanover: Brandeis/University of New England Press, 1998: 68-84. Print.

So Laugh a Little. Jewish Women's Archive. Performance at Copacabana, New York City. 14 March 2005.

Tucker, Sophie. *Some of These Days.* New York: Doubleday & Co., 1945. Print.

Wallenstein, Andrew. "From This She Makes A Living?" *Hadassah Magazine,* June/July 2006. Web. 1 Oct. 2009.

Joyce Antler, Brandeis University

Alienation and Black Humor in Philip Roth's *Exit Ghost*[1]

Elaine B. Safer

> An aged man is but a paltry thing,
> A tattered coat upon a stick, unless
> Soul clap its hands and sing, and louder sing
> (Yeats, Sailing to Byzantium ll 9-11)

Ever since Portnoy, most of the protagonists in the many novels of Philip Roth have been outsiders (i.e., persons estranged in some way from their environment). This basically serious theme is illuminated by the ever-present—and sometimes macabre—black humor in which it is cast. Indeed, one way to read Roth's *oeuvre* is to trace the many variations—and the growing depth—in which he treats personalities distanced or even divorced from their settings.

Take the case of the assimilated Jew, "Swede" Levov, and his daughter, Merry (*American Pastoral*, 1997). Swede's American dream and sense of belonging crash when Merry—estranged from her family and from contemporary America—becomes an anti-Vietnam War militant, a bomb planting terrorist, and later, a Jain ascetic. Swede's wife deceives him; his brother bursts out in a tirade expressing utter contempt for him; his fantasy of living the life of a country gentleman in the affluent WASP countryside of Old Rimrock turns to dust and ashes: "Whirling about inside him now was a frenzied distrust of everyone" (357). The narrator sums up the result: "The breach had been pounded in . . . [his] fortification . . . and now that it was opened it would not be closed again" (423).

Or take the case of that totally asocial puppeteer, Mickey Sabbath (*Sabbath's Theater*, 1995) who will not—cannot—commit suicide because: "How could he leave? How could he go? Everything he hated was here" (451). Or Coleman Silk (*The Human Stain*, 2000), the light-skinned African American who feels that his blackness makes it impossible for him to be a full-fledged member of society, and who therefore "passes." Although accepted as a white man, he remains an outsider at the college at which he teaches. And, not fortuitously, his warmest human bond is formed with another outsider, an abused and deeply depressed woman, the unforget-table Faunia. Silk has deconstructed his past by denying his race and his family; and he eventually also destroys his new present by resigning from Athena College when accused—falsely and grotesquely—of racism. He dies, belonging nowhere at all.

Yet another facet of alienation—that of a group—appears in *The Plot Against America* (2004), a "what if" novel, a novel that speculates on what would have happened if the pro-Nazi Charles Lindbergh had become president of the United States in 1940. The narrator's Jewish family become outcasts, lost souls, not because of anything that they have done, but because of what society thinks of them. Although Herman Roth pre-books a room for his family at a hotel in Washington, D.C., the manager tells them that another person has registered for the room. Herman calls the police in protest, mentioning that the Gettysburg Address in the Lincoln Memorial says "All men are created equal." The policeman responds: "But that doesn't mean all hotel reservations are created equal" (54-55). Young Philip feels that he and his family are outsiders (Safer 54-55).

The estrangements described above are primarily the result of the hostility or rejection that the individual encounters in his/her environment, although the response—*vide* Coleman Silk—also plays a role. But alienation can also be the result of an act of will. David Kepish and his friend George O'Hearn build up a rather repellent theory in which the good life consists of a refusal to make personal commitments: Love is the experience that instead of making you whole "fractures you. . . . You're whole and then you're cracked open. . . .attachment is ruinous" (99-100). Whether their self-regarding ethos will survive when, unexpectedly, genuine feelings threaten to overwhelm Kepish is the central question. Roth's art is so subtle that the reader really cares to know the answer. But Roth sensibly withholds it.

The feeling of sinfulness, unworthiness, and estrangement that can be caused by the imposition of rigid rules—first by a father, later by an institution—and the consequent inability to function as a full and self-regarding member of society are described in *Indignation* (2008), Roth's twenty-ninth novel. Not surprisingly, the narrator and victim is a dead man. Were he still alive the victory of the repressive rules would not yet be complete.

The analysis and description of estrangement is taken a step farther in *Exit Ghost* (2007), where the focus is on Roth's old alter ego, Nathan Zuckerman. This is a novel that powerfully concentrates on the relation between aging, letting go, illness, and alienation. This time narrator Zuckerman, instead of telling the tale of others, as he does in eight other novels, focuses on his own story. In this novel, the ninth (and Roth says last) Zuckerman novel, the protagonist is seventy-one. A prostate operation has left him impotent and incontinent. He no longer dares to swim in a public pool. In social situations he refrains from actively engaging with others so as to avoid emotional trauma. He has become something of a hermit, having buried himself in the Berkshires for the last eleven years. Writing is his only solace. Ostensibly, his alienation is a conscious but imposed response to the accident of a botched operation. But as we read further, we begin to wonder whether there is not more to it than that.

The various dimensions of his own estrangement are illustrated by his interaction with four characters: his neighbor, Larry Hollis; his former adored Amy Bellette; Richard Kliman, a would-be biographer of the deceased novelist E. I. Lonoff, whom Zuckerman reveres; and Jamie Logan, whom Zuckerman meets in answer to an ad for swapping two residences and who, unexpectedly, re-awakens Zuckerman's passions. Each, except possibly Kliman, has his or her own problematic issues of relating to the world, and each definitely—including Kliman—serves to throw light on those of Zuckerman.

Larry Hollis, a successful lawyer, commits suicide at age sixty-eight so as to avoid having his daughters witness his agony as he dies from cancer (13). Larry's suicide shows Zuckerman a way out that, despite his infirmities, he will not consider. In many respects, choosing life seems to be a virtually "heroic" act on the part of Zuckerman, a man who feels estranged from his peers because of physical disabilities, especially the incontinence that forces him to wear diapers. We need to appreciate the effort he makes to survive—at the same time that we see comic elements in the contrast between his theories on being separated from actively living versus his inescapable involvement in life once he returns to New York City.

But the choice involves not only heroism, but also a grand illusion. Zuckerman chooses to live, but his life is to be of writing about living rather than baring himself to challenging experiences. He tells readers that for some few people "the unlived, the surmise, fully drawn in print on paper, is the life whose meaning comes to matter most" (147).

Amy Bellette, like Zuckerman, lives a life of estrangement. She—the beautiful woman Zuckerman had once adored—now at seventy-five is a victim of brain cancer. Amy isolates herself not by moving to the Berkshires like Zuckerman, but by living in the past when her beloved "Manny" Lonoff left his wife to live with her. For Amy, everything after Lonoff's death has been "inconsequential" (172). She evinces some involvement with others when she writes a letter to the *New York Times* criticizing a reviewer for reading literature into an author's life. But not much; she never mails the letter. Amy, in spite of her losses, and Zuckerman, in spite of his physical decay, chooses to live rather than take the path of Larry Hollis.

The third character, Richard Kliman, sharpens Zuckerman's estrangement from his younger self. One sees the contrast between Kliman's youth and Zuckerman's elderly fear of suffering the loss of his faculties: memory, energy, as well as his upset over impotence and incontinence. Zuckerman broods over "those grand grandstand days when you shrink from nothing and you're only right" (48); "All of us are now 'no longers' while the excited mind of Richard Kliman believes that his heart, his knees, his cerebrum, his prostate, his bladder sphincter, his *everything* is indestructible and that he, and he alone, is not in the hands of his cells" (256). Zuckerman is aware that young people such as Kliman "are not 'no longers'" like the elderly. Instead they are "not-yets," with a future (256-57). Note that Kliman is depicted as a decidedly unattractive figure; when Zuckerman sees him as his former self, he may not like what he sees, but he also misses and feels alienated from the energy and vitality that this former self possessed.

It can be argued that humor in the novel is itself a form of alienation. For example, Roth seems to make Zuckerman's infirmities of old age increasingly ludicrous—thus, perhaps, skirting the pain somewhat by telling a joke. At seventy-one, a physical wreck, Zuckerman has returned to New York City to undergo the medical procedure that doctors say will cure his incontinence. Once he comes to the city, the past begins to impinge on the present, and he retreats by creating imaginative fantasies, elaborations that provide a counterpart to his paltry existence. These fantasies revolve around Jamie Logan and they comprise the major part of the novel. These are Zuckerman's last attempts to struggle out of the slough of despond, to reverse by an act of will the growing indifference that has engulfed him.

John Freeman and others have pointed out that Philip Roth, who is seventy-seven, "doesn't see the humor in aging. But *Exit Ghost* readers will" (Freeman L11). Freeman states: "Many of the scenes in *Exit Ghost* are laugh-out-loud funny, in a bleak, cackling way" (L11). Sarah Kerr calls the tone "both funny and hostile."

All these comments point to the tone of black humor in which the tales of Zuckerman's estrangement are suffused. It is a tone that combines pain and pleasure. There is a frenzied, brittle quality to this grim humor. On a psychological level, laughter at this dark edge of the humor continuum can be explained as a "grotesque-comic sublimation," when the "function of the comic is to overcome anxiety" (Reich 166). But, ultimately, we might not perceive any of this as "humorous" were it not for the fact that we know—because it is part of the common human experience—that Zuckerman's struggles and his attempts to make meaningful decisions are part of a great delusion. He thinks he sees himself as an outsider. But his actions contradict this notion.

Hermione Lee observes that *Exit Ghost* "is a book of haunting" (56). And, indeed, haunting memories give the novel an elegiac tone (Kakutani E6). Concomitantly, irony also is evident because Zuckerman exerts his imagination to develop imaginary dialogues between "He" and "She." Zuckerman writes five playlets to create a counter life to his own experiences in the city. The incongruity between the wish fulfillment dialogues and Zuckerman's real actions creates dark humor. Such humor bounces from the comic to the grotesque edge of black humor.

Zuckerman is deluded in thinking that he can write about life while being distant from it. The novel evolves from this initial delusion to Zuckerman's attempt to reverse his self-imposed exile from the world and to re-enter the life of sex and politics. The contrast between his desire for a peaceful and reasonable existence, on the one hand, and, on the other, full participation in an essentially unreasonable world provides a comic framework; but the issue itself—can alienation be switched on and off at will—is quite serious.

Zuckerman, though very intelligent, is deluded about his own nature. In many respects, he is an obtuse narrator. He is an intellectual who one minute connects his eleven-year retreat in the Berkshires to that of Rip Van Winkle and the next minute—in spite of his lack of knowledge (since 9/11 when he stopped reading newspapers [69-70])—thinks of entering into a political discussion as well as a sexual relationship. Both endeavors become part of the imagination and drama of the mind of this elderly man. The incongruity between his thoughts and his actions contributes to the novel's comic irony and also to its tragic poignancy.

In 2004, after being away from New York City for so many years, Zuckerman finds himself back in a world where youthful energy prevails. However, as mentioned above, Zuckerman believes that the life of the writer provides the meaning that "matters most." The experience of the writer provides the distance needed to remove oneself from frustrations in everyday life. For this reason, Zuckerman plans to leave for the Berkshires the next day—after he undergoes the medical procedure.

In an episodic and fragmented style, Zuckerman tells the reader how for years he has refused to engage in the turmoil of sexual and political upheavals. Since the election of George W. Bush, he has "decided no longer to be overtaken every four years by the emotions of a child—the emotions of a child and the pain of an adult. At least not so long as [he is] holed up in [his] cabin" (69). He insists: "I could manage to remain in America without America's ever again being absorbed in me. . . . America . . .exploited by an imbecile king . . . a king in a free country" (69-70). Zuckerman's vehement words contradict his continual protestations of disinterestedness. For years, Zuckerman has pretended to himself that his separation from the world he lived in was an act of will. He has tried to think of himself as an estranged individual, a disembodied spirit, like the first person narrator Marcus Messner in Roth's 2008 book *Indignation*.

But there is a vital difference. Marcus tells us that he died on the battlefield in the Korean War. He narrates the novel from beyond the grave (54): "And even dead, as I am and have been for I don't know how long, I try to reconstruct the mores that reigned over that campus and . . . the series of mishaps ending in my death at the age of nineteen" (54). Zuckerman, however, is a live person who merely thinks of himself as a disembodied spirit, distancing himself from the corporeal. The point of view Zuckerman wishes to attain is that of a person who can escape from his body and recreate himself as a character in art. The apparent absurdity of this notion develops dark humor in the novel. However, it is left to the reader to decide whether this desire to create an artifact can lead to valid artistic results (as it does for Yeats's narrator in "Sailing to Byzantium"), or whether it is the psychological aberration of a decaying individual.

Back in New York City after his eleven years of self-exile, Zuckerman stands in front of his hotel and wonders "where to reenter for an hour or two the life left behind" (14). He thinks of taking a train to Ground Zero, but realizes that since he has "withdrawn as witness and participant both," he could not go: "That would have been wholly out of character for the *character* I'd become" [italics added] (15). Instead he goes to the Metropolitan Museum of Art, "whiling away the afternoon like someone who had no catching up to do" (15). Zuckerman feels confident that he has achieved emotional separation from the wounds experienced in the past. He believes that he has successfully estranged himself from life's turbulence and confusion and that he has extricated himself from frustration with regard to sex and also to politics.

Now, in New York City, Zuckerman casually buys a copy of *The New York Review of Books*. A significant detail is that novelist Zuckerman does not peruse the different book reviews in the paper. Instead he starts reading the classified real estate advertisements and comes across an ad for swapping homes. He gets excited; he feels that the ad is "pointedly addressed" to him: "RELIABLE writing couple in early thirties wishes to swap homey, book-lined 3-room Upper West Side apartment for quiet rural retreat one hundred miles from New York. New England preferred." Eagerly, Zuckerman calls and tells the advertiser—Billy Davidoff—that he "could be there in minutes" (29).

When Zuckerman meets Billy and his attractive wife, Jamie Logan, he is aroused with desire. This happens despite his theorizing about the excitement of the life "fully drawn in print on paper," and despite the awareness of his physical infirmities. In the Davidoff apartment, Zuckerman confesses to the reader: "[Jamie] had a huge pull on me, a huge gravitational pull on the ghost of my desire." He explains, "This woman was in me before she even appeared" (66). Zuckerman bounces from the philosophical stance of preferring the peaceful life of the mind to suddenly getting involved emotionally in desiring Jamie Logan. He tells us: "And so I set out to minimize the loss by struggling to pretend that desire had naturally abated, until I came in contact for barely an hour with a beautiful, privileged, intelligent, self-possessed, languid-looking thirty-year-old . . . and I experienced the bitter helplessness of a taunted old man dying to be whole again" (67).

It is election night at the Davidoff's apartment; Zuckerman wants to join these people in their angry discussion of George Bush, who is re-elected president. But he is unprepared for discourse on politics or on anything current because, in the Berkshires, he had virtually taken himself out of history. Jamie exclaims: "Have you ever lived through an election like this one? With the magnitude of this one?" He responds, "Some. This one I haven't followed . . . I told you the other night—I don't follow such things." She responds: "So you don't care who wins?" He: "I didn't say that" (82).

The otherwise intelligent Zuckerman confides to the reader his fear that Jamie will think he is ignorant: "All the things I *thought* to tell her would likely strike her as cant. I *thought* to repeat, It's amazing how much punishment we can take. . . . I *thought* to say, It's bad, but not like waking up the morning after Pearl Harbor was bombed. . . . It's bad, but not like waking up the morning after Martin Luther King was shot . . . after the Kent State students were shot . . . We have all been through it. But I said nothing" [italics added] (86). He fears to speak because he lacks information about current events. His outdated references would be to the 1960s and earlier. Zuckerman seems to be a caricature of Rip Van Winkle. The reward for renouncing the world is to court ridicule.

There also is poignant irony in the descriptions of Zuckerman as he tries to engage in verbal battles with Richard Kliman. Zuckerman, who compares himself to Rip Van Winkle, is no match for the crude and aspiring Richard, who not only seems to have the wherewithal to get his biography on Lonoff published, but who also, in Zuckerman's wild imaginings, seems to be picking up an old relationship with Jamie. Zuckerman is outraged that Kliman wants to reveal what seems to be the dark secret of E. I. Lonoff's youth: his incest with his half sister: "So you're going to redeem Lonoff's reputation as a writer by ruining it as a man. Replace the genius of the genius with the secret of the genius. Rehabilitation by disgrace" (101). Emotions rising, in spite of himself, Zuckerman threatens to stop the book from ever getting published. He tells the reader: "When I heard my voice rising, I did not rein it in" (103). He is pleased that Kliman and Jamie have "the effect of rousing the virility in me again, the virility of mind and spirit and desire and intention, and wanting to be with people again" (103). However Kliman cuts Zuckerman's enthusiasm for the fray by shouting "You stink . . . you smell bad! . . . . You smell of decay! You smell of death!" (104). And Zuckerman ironically tells the reader, "What could a specimen like Kliman know about the smell of death? All I smelled of was urine" (104).

It is difficult to describe the tone of this passage. It is a tone that epitomizes the dark humor one experiences in *Exit Ghost*. We find ourselves laughing out loud, but we also feel horrified at Zuckerman's experience because we can envision it for ourselves. In this passage the ludicrous and the fearful seem to merge. Psychoanalyzing such laughter, Annie Reich explains it as a "grotesque-comic sublimation," when the "function of the comic is to overcome anxiety," giving the comic a "double-edged character," and bringing about the nervous laughter of black humor (Reich 166). But what makes the humor black is that the reader knows that now Zuckerman has lost his battle to reverse his purportedly voluntary alienation. He gives up. His bravado collapses, and he slumps back into despondency, deciding to go back to his life of estrangement, leave the city, and head for the Berkshires. Later that night, Zuckerman exposes his weaknesses to the reader, especially his losing the most important thing for a writer—memory. He is sadly aware that his "memory [is] beginning to fray" (106-7): "Without the chore book, I could . . . easily forget whom I had spoken to about what as recently as yesterday" (105-6).

At their next meeting, Jamie speaks to Zuckerman, asking him to help Richard Kliman with his biography by giving him information about Lonoff. Zuckerman is beside himself with agony. He ruminates:

> I left without daring to touch her. Without daring to touch her face, though it was within my reach . . . Without daring to place my hand on her waist . . . Without daring to say whatever words a man mutilated as I was says to a desirable woman forty years his junior that will not leave him covered in shame because he is overcome by temptation for a delight he cannot enjoy and a pleasure that is dead. (122-23)

Zuckerman returns to his hotel and retreats into his creative imaginings: the dialogues of "He" and "She," which he had started after first meeting Jamie Logan and

Billy Davidoff in their apartment. This is almost his last attempt to reverse his previously embarked upon course of self-willed alienation. One wonders if this is the
Zuckerman who has estranged himself from the active life.

The playlet begins:

> She: "I understand why you're coming back to New York, but why did you
> go away in the first place?"
> He: "Because I began to get a series of death threats in the mail. Postcards
> with death threats. . . ."
> He: "You don't know how attractive you are."
> She: "Why did you come here today?"
> He: "To be alone with you. . . ." (124-31)

After writing the dialogue, Zuckerman thinks about the exchange with Jamie "that
had not taken place . . . and was an aid to nothing, alleviated nothing, achieved
nothing, and yet . . . it had seemed terribly necessary to write the instant I came
through the door, the conversations she and I don't have more affecting even than
the conversations we do have" (147). The reader appreciates the ironic self deception
in Zuckerman's statement. As Clive James observes: "For Zuckerman . . . potency is
gone. Has desire gone with it? You bet your life it hasn't" (James E34).

In the fifth and last playlet, "He" and "She" become more daring. He opts for
love and invites "She" to his hotel room. "She" accepts, but author Zuckerman finds
that fictional possibility too threatening. He has the protagonist pack his bag, leave
New York City, and return to the Berkshires. Alienation has won.

So what do readers take away from the book? And why do the evaluations
that it has received fluctuate so wildly? Comments range from Clive James—"This
book is latter-day Roth at his intricately thoughtful best" (14)—to Michael Dirda,
". . . as a work of art it feels unfocused, never quite drawing together its various
threads"(10). For Carol Iannone, "Exit Ghost is marred by wearisome repetition"
(91). James Wood, on the other hand, praises the novel's "plain, hard style," Roth's
ability to make "subtle poetry by using ordinary words in unexpected ways" (94).
Bharat Tandon observes: "There are few American writers who write with such
power of the loss of powers" (22).

The weakness may be easy to explain: the essential absurdity of Zuckerman's
scheme of life before meeting Jamie has already been alluded to.

But why, then, does the book grip the reader's imagination? Like many other
Roth novels it adumbrates a very serious aspect of the human condition: the estrangement one feels from others and often from oneself: We age and our relation
to our surroundings inevitably changes. For many, no for most, it means that the
world puts great pressure on us to withdraw from active participation in the processes of daily life. This, in turn, may cause us to feel isolated, estranged. Only with
great luck or great strength of character can this pressure be resisted.

It may, therefore, be argued, plausibly, that the incontinence and impotence
with which Roth burdens Zuckerman reinforce but do not cause the latter's isola-

tion. The more basic cause is the simple brute fact that life comes to an end gradually if not suddenly, and that it is indescribably hard to come to terms with this. Or, if not indescribably, at least describable only by a great artist.

Notes

1. My thanks go to Allison Elizabeth Myers for helping with the research and Enrique Lerdau for offering several important suggestions.

Works Cited

Dirda, Michael. "Nathan Zuckerman, Now 71, faces Mortality—and Sex—One Last Time," *The Washington Post.* 30 September 2007: BW10. Print.

Freeman, John. "Zuckerman's Last Act," *St. Petersburg Times* (Florida). 30 September 2007: L11. Print.

Iannone, Carol. "Review," *Exit Ghost. Commentary.* 124.4 (Nov. 2007): 90-93. Print.

James, Clive. "Falter Ego," *The New York Times.* 7 October 2007: E14+. Print.

Kakutani, Michiko. "Seeking A Moral At the End Of the Tale," *The New York Times.* 2 October 2007: 1+. Print.

Kerr, Sarah. "Nathan Farewell," *The New York Review of Books.* Web. 6 Dec. 2007. http://www.nybooks.com/articles/20852.

Lee, Hermione. "Interview," "Age Makes a Difference," *The New Yorker.* 1 October 2007: 56-62. Print.

Mustich, James. "Philip Roth. Indignation: A conversation with James Mustich, Editor-in-Chief, Barnes & Noble Review." Web. 3 Nov. 2008. http://www.barnesandnoble.com/bn-review/note.asp?note=19972727.

Reich, Annie. "The Structure of the Grotesque-Comic Sublimation," *Bulletin of the Meninger Clinic* 13. 5 (1949): 160-71. Print.

Roth, Philip. *American Pastoral.* New York: Houghton Mifflin, 1997. Print.

———. *The Dying Animal.* Boston: Houghton Mifflin, 2001. Print.

———. *Exit Ghost.* Boston: Houghton Mifflin, 2007. Print.

———. *The Human Stain.* Boston: Houghton Mifflin, 2000. Print.

———. *The Plot Against America.* Boston: Houghton Mifflin, 2004. Print.

———. *Sabbath's Theater.* New York: Houghton Mifflin, 1995. Print.

Safer, Elaine. *Mocking the Age: The Later Novels of Philip Roth.* New York: SUNY, 2006. Print.

Tandon, Bharat. "Philip Roth and the Consolations of Denouement," *The Times Literary Supplement.* 28 Sept. 2007: 21-22.Print.

Wood, James. "Parade's End: The Many lives of Nathan Zuckerman," *The New Yorker.* 15 October 2007: 94-98. Print.

Elaine B. Safer, University of Delaware

Potok's *Asher Lev*:

Orthodoxy and Art: The Core-To-Core Paradox

Daniel Walden

The epigraph to *My Name is Asher Lev*, "Art is a lie which makes us realize the truth," a quote from Pablo Picasso, is a kind of metaphor, one of the controlling ideas of the book. The essential conflict is revealed in the first pages of the book:

> My name is Asher Lev, *the* Asher Lev, about whom you have read in newspapers and magazines, about whom you talk so much at your dinner affairs and cocktail parties, the notorious and legendary Lev of the *Brooklyn Crucifixion*.

Yet, he went on, "I am an observant Jew." The result is that I am labeled

> a traitor, an apostate, a self-hater, an inflictor of shame . . . a mocker of ideas sacred to Christians, a blasphemous manipulator of modes and forms revered by Gentiles for two thousand years.

> Well, I am none of those things. And yet, in all honesty, . . . I am indeed, in some way, all of those things. (1-3)

The novel is an explanation, a defense, for a long session in demythology. As Potok once said about Picasso's *Guernica*, "That's the redemptive power of art. The artist, in strange fashion, redeems the horror of reality through the power of his or her art" (Kauvar 70).

In a 1956 interview, Chaim Potok said, "Today is the first time in the history of the Jewish people that the Jews actually constitute a fundamental element of our umbrella civilization" (Hinds 89). But, as a result of being in the cores of two cultures simultaneously and having to fight the battle of how to fuse them, we are in a between period. What will happen, he concluded, is "very difficult to discern, but it is something that will come out of our fusion with the best of Western humanism unless we're inundated by the periphery of things Jewish and things secular" (Kauvar 87).

In his many novels and in his essays, Potok tried to explore how people confront ideas different from their own. The central metaphor of *The Chosen* (1967) is combat of various kinds, about two components of the core of Judaism, or any tradition, one component looking inward and one looking outward to solve its problems. The baseball game, for example, is a metaphor for a kind of combat, for a war, of spiritual as well as material differences. The central metaphor of *The Promise* (1969) is about the confrontation with text criticism. *My Name Is Asher Lev* (1972) is about an observant Jew's confrontation with Western Art. *Davita's Harp* (1985) is about Davita using her imagination as a way of coming to terms with unbearable reality. The central metaphor in *The Book of Lights* (1981) is the mystery and the awe that some of us sense in the grittiness of reality (Kauvar 67-68).

The world that Potok created in his books was a small esoteric world, much like that of Faulkner's small-town Mississippi. It was about good people involved in situations that they want to come to terms with in a positive way. Potok's art was filled with aesthetic vessels, motifs that reflected a conflict between art and any established institution. The modern artist's voice is really an antagonistic one. Asher Lev typifies what happens when an observant Jew wants to enter the mainstream of Western art. Or, in reverse, the artist who wants to remain an observant Jew confronts a significant problem. The moral quotient of the artistic endeavor is at times necessary and never enough; the aesthetic element, however, to Asher Lev, was at all times necessary and sometimes sufficient.

My Name is Asher Lev owes its beginning to an event in his childhood when his yeshiva inexplicably hired an artist to give a course in painting to the children. Normally, orthodoxy and an orthodox school viewed painting as a taboo; it was against their interpretation of the Second Commandment, it was against Jewish tradition, and his father thought it a terrible waste of time. But Potok saw Asher Lev as the metaphor for his own conflicts. By the time he was twenty, he was the inheritor of two utterly antithetical commitments: modern literature, employing interpretations, told him no institution was sacred, while the religious tradition he inherited said that there are things that are intrinsically sacred (Abramson 59, Lindsay 28-29).

My Name is Asher Lev tells of a clash between the secular and the Orthodox Jewish cultures. Born with a supreme gift, Asher is an artist with a prodigious talent. Though his father, who travels for the Rebbe, the dynastic inheritor or leader, the head of the Ladover Hasidim (modeled on the Brooklyn Lubavitcher Hasidim), cannot understand Asher's talent or obsession, it is the Rebbe who realizes that Asher Lev's gift cannot be suppressed, and he arranges for him to study with a famous secular Jewish sculptor and artist, Jacob Kahn. For Kahn, art is a religious calling. "I do not know what evil is when it comes to art. I only know what is good art and what is bad art," he tells Asher. Asher, forced to choose between art and Jewish tradition at age thirteen (when he would have taken on the responsibilities of a Bar

Mitzvah) chose to try to follow his gift while breaking away from his father's brand of fundamentalism, but not from Judaism (191-95).

According to Asher, his father, an Orthodox Hasidic Jew, suffered "aesthetic blindness." When Asher's father responded with a question, what about "moral blindness?," Asher could only reply that he was not hurting anybody (304). His father answered that one day he would hurt someone with that kind of attitude. Potok explained that there's a good case for art as delectation, for the sheer joy of an aesthetic experience. Like Danny Saunders in *The Chosen*, Asher Lev put personal fulfillment before the needs of the Jewish community. The point is art, for Asher, influenced by Jacob Kahn, has nothing to do with the Jewish community—that is the problem. As Asher read from a book his mother gave him, *The Art Spirit*:

> Every great artist is a man who has freed himself from his family, his nation, his race. Every man who has shown the world the way to beauty, to true culture, has been a rebel, a "universal" without patriotism, without home, who has found his people everywhere. (203)

When he met Jacob Kahn, the famous sculptor, modeled on Jacques Lipschitz, Kahn described him as a prodigy in *payos* (side curls). But Kahn, trying to describe the difference between a workaday artist and a great artist, said, "Art is whether or not there is a scream in him wanting to get out in a special way" (212). "This is a tradition," he tells Asher; "it is a religion, Asher Lev....It is a tradition of goyim and pagans. Its values are goyisch and pagan. Its concepts are goyisch and pagan. Its way of life is goyisch and pagan. In the entire history of European art, there has not been a single *religious* [my emphasis] Jew who was a great painter (212)." Chagall was not a religious Jew.

Jacob Kahn went on: "As an artist you are responsible to no one and to nothing, except to yourself and to the truth as you see it" (218). Then, as he drew for Asher the street, Place Emile-Goudeau, and the building he and Picasso had lived in, he exclaimed, "God, how poor we were. And how hard we worked. We changed the eyes of the world (218-19)."

One day Asher and Kahn went to the Metropolitan Museum of Art. They walked through centuries of nudes and Byzantine and western Crucifixions. When Asher complained, Kahn instructed him: "I am not telling you to paint crucifixions. I am telling you that you must understand what a crucifixion is in art if you want to be a great artist. The crucifixion must be available to you as a form. Remember that Picasso, at a moment in his life when he was wracked with anguish...drew a crucifix....He wanted to express his feeling of torment and suffering, and he drew a crucifix" (Potok, "Role" 11).

Asher was now painting nudes and crucifixions. In the midst of his internship with Jacob Kahn, he met with the Rebbe. In the Rebbe's view, he was entering the world of the Sitra Achra, the "other side" (244). Asher, at this time, was also drawing or painting his mother and himself, although he did not always give the mother and child their faces. But he was slowly appreciating, understanding, what his mother meant when she said: "It hurts me to be caught between my husband

and son" (276). When she asked him, "How do you paint, Asher?" he answered, "I paint my feelings. I paint how I see and feel about the world. I express my feelings in shapes and colors and lines. But I paint a painting, not a story" (295). And another time she reiterated what she was going through: "You have no idea what it's like to be standing between you and your father" (299).

The problem with his father was a situation of long standing. To Aryeh, art was "trivial"; a Jewish man was supposed to study the Torah and the Talmud. The trouble was, as Asher knew, his father's Hasidic yeshiva education gave him no frames of reference for the concepts of art. Asher's world of aesthetics was as bewildering to his father as his father's insatiable need for travel for the Rebbe, for the Jews, for his people, was for him.

It is Asher Lev's mother, Rivkeh, who understands both her husband's view and her son's obsession and talent. It is Rivkeh's angst and suffering that impinges on Asher's consciousness and thus leads him to his greatest work.

Influenced by the centrality of religion and yet the questioning in the writings of Evelyn Waugh, James Joyce, Flannery O'Connor, and Thomas Mann, Potok has tried to mediate between the languages, traditions, and beliefs of (liberal) Orthodox Judaism while encountering the world of modern art. Thus, Asher's notorious paintings of the "Brooklyn Crucifixion," the only form he recognized in Western tradition, that portrays the suffering of mankind, protracted suffering (significantly, Potok was painting a crucifixion at the time), were explained by a reference to Picasso, by no stretch of the imagination a traditional Christian, who painted a crucifixion in a moment of deep anguish. To show his mother's suffering, and his own, to depict the values he got from his parents—honesty, integrity, and a fine work ethic—the crucifixions reflected the ways in which those values affected his parents' attitudes. To his parents, crucifixions were what they were to most Jews: centuries of pogroms, suffering, anti-Semitism, rivers of blood.

As Asher Lev began to think about the "Brooklyn Crucifixion," it was his guilty feelings toward his mother that were constantly before him. When he drew his mother's profile in the dust on a bench near Picasso's house in Paris, it was the emotional cost his mother sustained that he was thinking about. In the anguish of his mother he was symbolically reacting to his father.

The first Crucifixion owed a debt to Michelangelo's Pietás, one in the Sistine Chapel, the second in Florence, both of which Asher saw and copied assiduously again and again. Asher destroyed the first attempt when he realized that the woman supporting the twisted arm of Jesus slightly resembled his mother. In the next one, which he also destroyed, he left out the standing figure of Nicodemus, perhaps because it reminded him of his father. Eventually, having decided that to show his mother's torment and anguish, he had to use the model of the crucifixion, because "there was no aesthetic mold in his own religious tradition into which he could pour a painting of ultimate anguish and torment," he went ahead. His first "Brooklyn Crucifixion" was good but incomplete. The second "Brooklyn Crucifixion" was complete. He had portrayed the loneliness, the anguish, the torment of Rivkeh Lev. As Adena Potok told me:

Chaim painted only the first of the two. He did so in order to see for himself how such a representation would take shape on canvas. The second he left to his and the reader's imaginations. Of course, the first did not appear as an illustration in the book, so to all intents and purposes it, too, was left to the imagination of the reader. (Interview)

Asher's first painting was a good one. But it did not include a clear crucifix; it did not completely fulfill his vision; and he recognized it was incomplete.

It would have made him a "whore," as he put it, to present this one, a fraud, as complete. He wanted to handle the Crucifixion theme without it being a cliché. When his parents saw the two "Brooklyn Crucifixions" on the gallery wall, they were horrified. To them crucifixions represented rivers of blood. To Asher they were aesthetic vessels representing suffering, specifically his mother's suffering.

The fact is that sometimes Asher Lev was able to make an accommodation between his Orthodoxy and Western art, and sometimes he was not. He had to make choices. When asked about the Crucifixions, Potok explained it is not a halachic problem. Halachically, one can paint all the Crucifixions one wants. That is, "you are not violating Jewish law so long as you don't paint them for purposes of worship" (qtd. in Ribalow 11-12). Potok, like Asher, had to fight his way up through the yeshiva once he committed himself to writing. "Yes, the love-hate is one of the prices you have to pay for a core-to-core cultural confrontation. My goal is to express my own particular vision of the world," Potok said. On the one hand, he believed Jacob Kahn's admonition that "Art is not for people who want to make the world holy." On the other hand, at certain points, particularly the ideational elements of the world, one is going to come into serious conflict. Asher came from the core of the Jewish tradition, and at the same time he was committed to Western art. The Jewish tradition has its own aesthetics and its own sense of morality. It has a different sense of the aesthetic nature of reality; its aesthetics are in the service of humanity, the commandments. The aesthetics of Asher Lev, artist, are just aesthetics for the sake of beauty, for the sake of enhancing the world so that it becomes a different place in which to live. Great artists pay a terrible price for what they do. Asher Lev knew that if he chose to become an artist, it was incumbent on him to become a great artist, the only way to justify the harm that his choice did to everybody else's life. He chose, he was happy, but he suffered, all for those who might be grateful for the honest mirrors that they were shown of themselves (Lindsay 28-30).

Asher finally understands the power of the artist: "Power to create and destroy, Power to bring pleasure and pain. Power to amuse and horrify. There was in that hand the demonic and the divine at one and the same time" (Potok, *Asher Lev* 348). From that time on he would go forth to encounter the reality of experience. It would be a quest, a journey of reconciliation. As Asher said at the beginning of this *kunstlerroman* (the novel of an artist's education), "I am an observant Jew," but he was also pointed toward becoming a great artist, which might mean his own core-to-core paradox.

Works Cited

Abramson, Edward. *Chaim Potok*. New York: Twayne, 1986. Print.

Hinds, Lynn. "An Interview with Chaim Potok." Walden. *Conversations* 88-91.

Kauvar, Elaine. "An Interview with Chaim Potok." Walden. *Conversations* 63-87.

Kremer, S. Lillian. "Daedalus in Brooklyn: Influences of *A Portrait of the Artist as a Young Man* on *My Name is Asher Lev*," *The World of Chaim Potok* . Ed. Daniel Walden. Spec. issue of *Studies in American Jewish Literature* 4 (1985): 26-38. Print.

———. "An Interview with Chaim Potok," Walden. *Conversations* 31-45.

Lindsay, Elaine. "An Interview with Chaim Potok," Walden. *Conversations* 28-30.

Potok, Adena. E-mail to Daniel Walden. 26 May 2009.

Potok, Chaim. *My Name is Asher Lev*. New York: Knopf, 1972. Print.

———. "Role of the Jewish Artist as Jew, as Citizen, as Craftsman," *Congress Bi-Weekly*. 15 March 1974: 3-12. Print.

Ribalow. Harold. "A Conversation with Chaim Potok," Walden. *Conversations* 1-27.

Sternlicht, Sanford. *Potok: A Critical Companion*. Westport: Greenwood Press, 2000. Print.

Walden, Daniel, ed. *Conversations with Chaim Potok*. Jackson: University Press of Mississippi, 2002. Print.

Dan Walden, Penn State

Heaven Is Full of Windows

Steve Stern

Had Gussie Panken looked up from her machine, a movement that could get her salary docked a dollar, she would have seen what the lazy Sadie Kupla saw in the window overlooking Washington Place. The late March breeze was causing the orange curtains to billow, the serrated orange curtains, though the open windows along Washington Place had never had any curtains. Then the wisps of orange turned into waves, a rumbling swell that poured over the sills into the shop, engulfing the bins of scraps, torching the bales of unfinished waists heaped atop the oil-soaked tables. By the time Gussie had turned to see what Sadie was screeching about—her shrieks echoed in a chorus all up and down the long rows of work tables—the fire was advancing like a mob of ragged hooligans. Gussie's first impulse was to do nothing; she was tired and this wasn't the first time she'd been the victim of hooligans—hadn't they driven her family out of their home back in Dlugacsz, forced them to cross an ocean to a rat-hole flat on Broome Street, where she lived with a crippled father and her bed-wetting little brother who must nevertheless be honored as a prince? She felt her charging heart secrete a poison that paralyzed her limbs, but only momentarily, until she too was swept up in the hysteria that harried her fellow seamstresses from one end of the shop to the other, like sticks in a box tilted this way and that.

At the door to the Greene Street stairwell, which opened inwardly, the knot of workers rushing to escape was stalled, and unable to squeeze through the narrow gap, they began in the thickening smoke to claw and flail at one another. Then the crowd had reversed itself, stampeding through eddies of flame past wicker baskets combusting in horse-fart poofs, and Gussie found herself carried along in the tide. At the door on the Washington Place side of the shop, which was always kept locked by management for reasons known only to them, a burly fellow with a handlebar mustache hurled his weight against the metal plating, leaving it concave though the door never budged from its jamb. Others pounded the door with their fists, a shuddering that reverberated in Gussie's gut until she retched, sinking to her knees. From the floor, her eyes smarting, lungs beginning to wheeze in pain, she groped among the remnants on the table above her for a swatch of lawn to cover her face.

Showers of sparks seemed to blend with the curses and cries for help like flights of hornets making an eerie drone. Windowpanes above a nearby airshaft splintered in popgun bursts, a party of workers swarming through their ruined frames out onto the fire escape. Then in seconds the whole rusted structure had pulled away from the wall, and the people, releasing a noise like a sepulchral moan, dropped out of sight as on a raft sinking below waves.

"Mama," said Gussie, unable to hear the sound of her own voice, not beckoning her mother so much as scolding her for having died of diphtheria three years ago back in Dlugacsz.

Somehow she was on her feet again, blundering blindly alongside the tables on top of which the more athletic girls hopped and jigged in an effort to elude the saw-toothed conflagration. Arriving at the Greene Street vestibule just in time to see the freight elevator descending, she blinked through stinging tears at what was at once real and not real: A clutch of employees who hadn't made it on board the elevator thrust aside the accordion grate and, licked from behind by tongues of flame, plunged after the departed car into the yawning shaft. She saw a pretty girl spinning like a top to try and unravel the fiery helix of fabric she'd wound about her for protection, and another with a torch in place of her hair. One shouted something in broken English about having to meet Gaspar behind Bottle Alley; another crooned idiotically in Yiddish: "Ev'ry little movement has a meaning all its own." Unaware that her own skirt had started to smolder, Gussie now wanted only to breathe. A wall of fire flapped like sheets on a line, then blew apart in a dragon's exhalation that chased the seamstress back toward the windows along Washington Place. In each of them were figures silhouetted against the failing afternoon light, who disappeared only to be replaced by others who also instantly disappeared. Jostled and caromed against from all sides in the choking atmosphere, Gussie half-stumbled, half-fell in the direction of the tall windows. Unconscious of having made a decision, she avoided the casement in which the girls tussled as if vying with one another to board a packed trolley, the window from which a tangle of girls tumbled like a flickering pinwheel over the ledge. Instead she elected to mount the sill upon which a young man in a waistcoat stood helping the girls to step one by one into space. With sleeves rolled he bussed them tenderly on the cheek, then lifted them under their arms, as in a dance, before letting them drop.

Now it was Gussie's turn, and with the aid of the gallant young man she had mounted the sill, stepped onto the ledge, and stood vaguely aware of the sirens, the roar of the multitude below, their howls of alarm indistinguishable from cheers. She saw the ladders extending several stories shy of the ninth floor, the plumes of water spraying so far from their marks. Letting go of the lawn hankie, which the wind carried over the sooty skylights and water tanks etched against a cobalt sky, Gussie imbibed the cool evening air of her oblivion and felt her fear abruptly dispelled. In its place was pure rage.

Plain Gussie Panken, born to be a spinster, dried up and unshtupped at twenty-three: "What did I have? Mama's carbuncle brooch when it wasn't in hock, and her dog-eared copy of *The Duties of the Heart.* Freda Fine has a beau plus a book signed by the theater idols Thomashefsky and Kalisch, and my pious Papa tells her, 'Our Gussie will get in paradise her *Duties from the Heart* autographed by God.'"

Over her shoulder the shop was a garden of flame, every flywheel, driveshaft, and burning maiden limned in undulant gold. "Ptui on God," spat Gussie, feeding the blaze.

It came then, the gingerly peck on the cheek from the young man, a fresh-faced boy really, despite his tarnished brow, with downcast eyes and a shock of sable hair; he kissed her and endeavored to lift her under her sweat-soaked arms. "That's it?" she asked, still immovable. Then wiping the drool from her lips, she clapped her hands over his cheeks and kissed him full on the mouth: a scandal! She grinned at his astonishment, impish Gussie, who also blushed, then heaved a sigh over the ineffectual husband he would make—a pisher who stole kisses from ladies in extremity. She sighed as well at the dingy hall they would rent for their wedding, the tallis shop they would open on Orchard Street and later set fire to for the insurance, the hungry baby mauling her breast and the dim one lolling under foot on the greasy floorboards, the extra weight she'd put on fore and aft that added to her burden, the shoes she had to cut slits in to relieve the pressure on her bunions, the gray hairs that would come to signify this frustration and that disappointment and the joys (surely there would be a little joy) that she'd survived. Then Gussie, decked out now in an incandescent gown, wrapped her fingers—perforated by a thousand needles but still very strong—about the hand of the chivalrous boy and leapt from the ledge without the help of anyone on earth.

A cop covering the broken bodies with a tarpaulin noted the half-incinerated girl with her goggle eyes and crooked mouth holding hands with a dark-haired lad, and observed ironically to his mate, "A match made in heaven."

Steve Stern, Skidmore College

Saul Bellow's Enigmatic Love

Norma Rosen

On a summer afternoon I approached the old farmhouse where I was scheduled to meet my teacher, Saul Bellow. He sat on the porch in a rocking chair with a book in his lap. I was nervous about how he would respond to my stories. What else could I do but trip on the wooden stairs? He looked up and grinned in sympathy.

He was fresh from a great novel's success. *The Adventures of Augie March* had just won the 1954 Pulitzer Prize, and I wondered why he would bother coming here to the Bread Loaf Writers' Conference in Vermont to teach. He was handsome as a movie star. Large brown eyes, wide mouth, head thrown back to enjoy his own laughter—an image familiar now from book photos. But then! He gleamed. The presence of "Saul," as we students democratically called him, added a giddiness to the already over-excited atmosphere, the boundless aspirations of writing students.

Those in the know that summer said Saul was recently divorced. So was I, as it happened, but I was not gleaming. I had come to Bread Loaf in the hope that someone would lift my disillusion by telling me that my writing, at least, was good.

Saul opened my folder, studied it again for a second. There was no other chair. I sat on the porch steps to wait for his comments.

At dinner the night before, I had had to pass him to get to my place. He shoved his chair from the table and said, "I seem to recognize you." I was pleased but blank. "Must be racial memory, then," he said, amused.

Who could tell if he was parodying himself, me, the remark, or all three? His books were full of comedy. At the same time, every moment was weighted with significance. The hero's glance took in the random world and transformed it into one where light, falling on a house, a wall, a hillside, spoke of cosmic matters. Material things and events could be more than one knew, Bellow's novels told us, and his heroes all searched for that "more." He had a mystic's awareness of hidden matters, and a skeptic's humor about his avidness for them.

Saul looked up from my folder.

"Something's wrong with your stories," he said. He recognized whose work I had been reading, and told me to lay off Henry James.

"The trouble is you're not writing in your true voice. Listen to yourself when you fight with your mother."

The trouble was that when I fought with my mother, *she* was the one who spoke in her true voice. I argued in fancy language designed to drive my mother mad. He leafed through my manuscript again while I brooded that probably *my mother* should have been the writer.

I instantly knew he must be right, though. When it came to voice, there was no mistaking Bellow's. Much was made of the "breakthrough" voice of the new book. As far as I was concerned, all his works were written in one voice that transcribed the world into Bellow-sensibility, as if it were a key in music.

I had submitted two stories for his criticism. The first was called "Love Trip." A man and woman travel together until the time comes to part. The woman, as I not very originally wrote, was shaken by sobs.

"Do you understand why she's crying?" Saul asked.

How could he not know? "Because it's *ending*," I assured him. "The love trip is over."

His next words stunned me. "No, it's because she doesn't love him enough."

The story I had submitted was more or less autobiographical, a piece ripped from my young twenties, fresh and bloody. And now Saul was telling me the female protagonist didn't *know* herself, didn't know that she was crying because she didn't love enough, and that was why the story, and the relationship in it, didn't work.

I had just completed my master's degree at Columbia University, then rife with "New Criticism" theory that warned against mixing biography or social context or literary history with readings of text. The writer's work must be kept free from all other considerations, a prohibition as dire as halachic interdiction against mixing meat and milk.

All the same, I mixed them. No words could have hit me harder than Bellow's. This was a charge to which not only my story but my life was vulnerable. I had been alternately accusing myself and my ex-husband of the failing of "not loving enough" that brought our marriage down. I could probably re-think the character I had created in the story, but how could I re-think myself?

Because I seemed so crushed, I suppose, Saul added briskly, "I wouldn't tell you this if I didn't think your writing was worth it." I took what comfort I could from those words.

The title of the second story is beyond recall, but I remember that the protagonist was a painter. She writes her lover a note, but for some now unremembered reason wants to prevent recognition of her handwriting. Finally she pastes together something like a kidnapper's ransom note. I confessed that I was dissatisfied, but unable to come up with anything better. At once, Saul suggested that she pick up a brush and paint the message. I felt something like awe. "My God," I blurted, "what a genius idea!"

"It's what occurs to you," he said calmly, "when you're writing deeply enough, and paying attention."

There was no question that Bellow was writing deeply enough, and because he was so calm, so sure about his judgment, I naturally assumed that in the realm of love, too, life held no mystery for him.

After that summer, and through the years that followed, I devoured the brilliant novels and stories Bellow published after *Augie March*: *Seize the Day*; *Henderson, the Rain King*; *Herzog*; *Mosby's Memoirs*; *Humboldt's Gift*, and many more. Each work was a lesson in writing deeply and paying attention.

Though Bellow's novels are mostly explorations of ideas about society and individual freedom, about the pressure of the general culture on the individual, about the nature of reality, about the old Greek idea that character is fate, and about Jews who struggle or do not struggle against debased contemporary morality, many of his protagonists, I saw, also feel balked, betrayed, and enraged by women.

One of them, Tommy Wilhelm, says to the wife he left in *Seize the Day*: "You've got to let me breathe." Even though he has lost his job, she is demanding that he pay the alimony she needs to support their sons.

He adds, "'If I should keel over, what then? And it's something I can never understand about you. How you can treat someone like this whom you lived with so long. Who gave you the best of himself. Who tried. Who loved you.' Merely to pronounce the word 'love' made him tremble."

Other protagonists proclaim, at various times, that the women they are with cause them to feel sensations of suffocation, choking, their hearts near to bursting.

Eight years after that Bread Loaf summer, I published my first novel, *Joy to Levine!* It was set in a sinking publishing company where Arnold Levine, who courts obscurity to foil his father's hopes for him, tries to convince the overweight secretary he loves to stay unchanged. Though he lectures her on the crassness of "getting ahead," she has her own ambitions, involving slenderness and glamour. I sent Saul a copy. The next time we met, he told me he liked it. I couldn't have felt happier.

The occasion of that meeting was a performance of his play, *The Last Analysis*. That evening he stood in back of the orchestra seats, gauging the temper of the audience.

"I save my weirdest jokes for the theater," he said during intermission, laughing. Though the critics had not been friendly, his assurance about writing was intact. And so, I learned from that theater performance, was his dissatisfaction with love.

In the play, a has-been comic called Bummidge, as mad for transcendence as any Bellow male, declares that nothing in his life has been satisfactory. When his mistress protests that they had their love, he replies, "Love, but not right. Love, sweet but grimy. . .like eating ice cream from a coal scuttle."

"Potato love" is what Bellow in his novels calls family love, a clutching that smothers the heart. On one hand "potato love," on the other "not right" love, love like "ice cream from a coal scuttle."

Bummidge ejects all the women—wife, sister, mistress—from the stage and from his life, and arranges for his own rebirth, wrapping himself in a womb-like blanket. "Oh, fallen man, as you lie suffering in the profane, longing for what is absolutely real," Bummidge cries broken-heartedly, getting back only laughs from the audience.

During the play's intermission Bellow kindly asked how my life was going. I told him I was married, had a wonderful new baby, but little time to write. He answered that he knew just the fellowship for me, and I could put him down for a recommender. In due time, a Rockefeller Foundation application arrived, but Saul wasn't at home to answer their request. Israel was again at war, and Saul went there to write about it. When he returned I sent him news of my rejection.

The letter he wrote back was astonishingly fierce. He told me not to be bitter. (I didn't know enough to be bitter: I felt embarrassed about failing to get the fellowship he'd wanted for me.) He said I had no idea how full of "garbage" the literary world was, how many enemies he had acquired who would block someone merely because his own name was attached. It is still startling to realize that despite indelible honors and a large and loving reading public, Bellow felt beset by those he thought wanted to bring him down. He was always there before them, though, picking up his brush and unforgettably inscribing the page.

Over the years, Bellow made his way through marriages and novels in which his heroes suffered betrayals by women. Despite the admiration of many women in and out of his novels, Bellow didn't seem to have a really good word to say for them. Until, that is, his young fifth wife, who appears largely undisguised in his last novel, *Ravelstein*. Pretty, intelligent, resourceful, Rosamund is showered with praise for battling to save the narrator's life after he eats a poisonous fish. She is admirable, but she doesn't sizzle or crackle, as Bellow's other female characters have done.

Bellow's heroes suffer at the hands of their lovers, but in none of the novels are they so sunk in misery that they forget to satirize their women. Lily, in *Henderson, the Rain King*, must exit the house frequently to have her portrait painted, leaving domestic chaos behind; Madeleine, in *Herzog*, jealously takes up Herzog's intellectual interests and then preens herself as his intellectual superior.

What, where, is enough love? Saul Bellow certainly made his female characters memorable, his Theas and Renatas and Madeleines, but to my mind, at least, never awarded them the affectionate depth of complexity of an Augie or a Herzog or a Henderson. Male protagonists burst out of themselves with longing for superior reality beyond "the veil of Maya" (a favorite Bellow locution for the world of shallow appearances). The women—beautiful, sexy, driven—go for achievements in the "Now," comic foil for Bellow's Mad Hatters of Transcendence. As Henderson, in *Henderson, the Rain King* famously puts it: "I want, I want, I want." For such a wanter, what woman can ever love enough?

Sometimes I think of that old protagonist of mine, and of Bellow's declaring she didn't love enough. I don't know where the story is anymore. I can't read it over to check out how I'd feel about it now. Anyhow, I have no wish to defend that long-ago "Love Trip." All I'd like to defend is the undoubted fact (I feel sure it's there) that the woman gave the man what most men, I have heard, consider a hard time—disagreeing, mentioning mistakes, pointing out wrong turns in the road. For a while, after that summer, I put every story I read or wrote to the question: "Does she/he love enough?" "Who loves *anybody* enough?" "What's enough?" I wondered if a woman's need to challenge a man might be part of some Darwinian strategy to ensure survival of the race, the way a picky female bower bird will in the end select the most artful and most patiently undiscouraged mate. (I certainly don't know the answer: I'm flying on one wing here.)

"For love has two faces," Virginia Woolf wrote, "one white, the other black; two bodies; one smooth, the other hairy. It has two hands, two feet, two tails, two, indeed, of every member and each one in the exact opposite of the other. Yet, so strictly are they joined together that you cannot separate them."

What Woolf wrote is poetically impressive, but how much did Virginia Woolf know about love? How much does anybody know? Splitting love off like that and then joining it together again does take into account the sometimes-I-love-you-sometimes-I-hate-you aspect of love. But that's ordinary love, and not, I think, what Bellow meant.

Despite Bellow's birth in French-speaking Lachine, Canada, every one of his male protagonists (with the exception of *Mr. Sammler*, too old for such pastimes) pursues love as passionately, mistakenly, and broken-heartedly as if he had never heard of *chagrin d'amour*.

Bellow's novels, taken collectively, sometimes seem to me to be one long lesson in the hero's education in love—a sort of *Education Sentimentale*, à la Flaubert. Or one long lesson in the quality of love that is "enigmatic," to borrow a word from the title of Sarah Blacher Cohen's fine study, *Saul Bellow's Enigmatic Laughter*.

Whole sections of Bellow's final novel, *Ravelstein*, depict the fierce focus of the young wife, Rosamund, on saving the life of her husband, Chick—just as happened in reality when Bellow ate a dish of poisoned red snapper.

If Bellow's depiction of Rosamund lacks the electricity of his other portraits of women, it is probably owing to the absence of irony or caricature. It conveys instead a loveliness of devotion and appreciation.

Does the opposite of "not right love," "not enough love" appear at last in Bellow's final novel? The narrator's wife, Rosamund, rescues him from near-fatal food poisoning. (I, too, tried to rescue my second and final husband from his illness. I loved him body and soul, but nothing I did could save him. And alas, Bellow's death from other causes came soon after he completed *Ravelstein*.)

For me there are hints, in that final Bellow novel, that he may at last have found love he could say was enough. In *Ravelstein*, Bellow writes this about Rosamund, the fictional characterization of the real-life young wife who was at his side during his time in the Intensive Care Unit of the hospital:

"Her alarm was set for seven, and she was at the hospital very early in the morning. She could name all the drugs prescribed for me, and the doctors found that she could tell them how I had reacted to each one, what I was allergic to, or what my blood-pressure readings had been the day before yesterday. There was an extended sorting apparatus in the pretty woman's head. She told me, confidently, that we would live to be very old. . . ."

Such complete and utter devotion-love, minus the medical details, brings up an echo. I can't know how Bellow thought of it, but there may be a chance that he heard it too, so little escaped his notice. The echo, of course, is from the Bible's *Song of Songs*: "Love is as strong as death."

For the space, at least, of Bellow's final novel, that appears to be what love is. And it may have been, at last, enough.

End

Norma Rosen, author of *Joy to Levine; At the Center; John and Anzia: An American Romance;* and *Touching Evil*

Diversity Is More than Skin Deep:

An Academic's African Memoir

Evelyn Avery

In a few moments my husband and I were to take off for an experience that would shape us for the rest of our lives. Surrounded by incredulous parents, grandparents, and a few friends at Idlewild Airport in 1961, we waited anxiously for the American government chartered propeller to fly us thousands of miles to East Africa. While our mothers wept, our grandparents prayed and blessed us. Off in a corner, our fathers, shaking their heads, stared ahead stone-faced, unable to comprehend what we were doing. Adopting a false bravado, so as not to increase their panic, I joked about our great adventure, although I, too, was a nervous wreck about teaching in East Africa for two years. Little did I realize then, forty-eight years ago, the impact those two years would have on my future educational choices, views towards multiculturalism and the world. How could I have even guessed at the challenges and rewards that awaited us, teaching in Uganda, traveling throughout East and South Africa, where the majority of people were Black but very different from each other, a concept not understood in America then and even less so today with all the contemporary rejection of racism? Actually one of our reasons for enrolling in Teachers for East Africa was our desire for change

Newly married, in our early twenties, neither of us had ever lived outside our enclaves in Brooklyn. I, in particular, was born and raised in Borough Park, an homogenous large Modern Orthodox Jewish community where I attended day school for several years, lived partially with my grandparents, and joyfully celebrated Jewish events. On May 7, 1948, for example, Borough Park streets were teeming with Jews, singing *Hatikvah*, the Israeli national anthem, and dancing in the streets that had been roped off by the police. We all joined in to recognize Israel's independence. Nothing in my life at that time could have foreshadowed my unusual future outside the Jewish community. In fact years later, attending Brooklyn College with a 98% Jewish population simply reinforced my background. However, I had not counted on extraordinary professors introducing me to communities beyond my own, and to meeting my future husband, Don Avery, a student of John Hope Franklin, with a passion for African American history. In 1960 we were Kennedy kids, motivated by our young idealistic president to improve the world. As a young woman, who had spent twenty years in Brooklyn, I was ready for something different and to make a difference.

After teaching in New York ghetto schools for one year, we were inspired to join Teachers for East Africa, sponsored by the United States and the United Kingdom, with existing native governments participating. Teachers College, Columbia University organized the program, recruited and trained 150 high school teachers for one month, followed by six weeks at Makerere University (later the University of East Africa) in Kampala, Uganda, before our two-year teaching assignments started. Our initiation began at Columbia University with four weeks of introductory lectures and study of East African geography, tribal and colonial history, and Swahili, the language used everywhere except ironically in Uganda, where we were to be posted. On our last evening in New York, the distinguished Julius Nyerere, future president of an independent Tanzania (then Tanganykia) moved us with tales of his country, the beauty and promise, the problems and conflicts, the need for our skills and passions. We could hardly wait to board the plane the next day.

Intent on our emotional airport goodbyes, I had momentarily forgotten that this was my first flight, and naively assumed that the U.S. government would provide us, its valuable charges, the best accommodations possible. Were we surprised when an aging propeller rolled in and we were told to prepare to board! Several of our group wondered how such a "puddle hopper" would make the several thousand mile journey across continents, but it was too late; we were being ushered on the plane where more surprises awaited. Directed to take our seats, we discovered that there were only 148 seats for 150 of us; we would have to rotate with two of us sitting on the floor for the whole flight. The surprise turned into shock as we ran out of drinking water over the Sahara, and one of our tires blew out, forcing a landing in Kano, Nigeria, where we slept on the floor in a tiny hotel. Since the nearest tire replacement was in Spain, our education continued in Nigeria, West Africa, where a local school bus drove us through the dusty roads of Kano, teaching us our first lessons about the diversity of African geography and economy. Poverty cast its shadow everywhere, from the brownish mud huts we passed, to the skinny but bloated–belly, ragged children who passed us, begging for money, shouting "dash." While some of our group threw coins out the window, Don and I were immobilized by the degrading scene, which would reappear later in Uganda.

Fortunately, however, within a day our "re-tired" plane landed smoothly at Entebbe Airport, near lovely Victoria Lake and the town, where in the early dawn, we could see lush greenery and tropical flowers as we were whisked to the elegant Victoria Hotel to rest. The cool air, the topography, the hotel, the service, the contrast, between Kano and Entebbe in 1961, was incredible, a memory that has never allowed me to generalize about the "third world."

Nor, given my Makerere University experience in the following six weeks, would I ever be able to generalize about Jews again. Separated from our spouses into single gender dorms, I was assigned to room with Ruth Davis, an African-American Orthodox Jew, who, since kosher meat was unavailable, became a committed vegetarian for two years. While I, who had already fled Borough Park, assimilated and enjoyed meat, Ruth maintained Jewish Law, even observing the Sabbath as well as *Kashrut* (kosher laws). Years later when I, a granddaughter of a rabbi, returned to my roots, I was to remember Ruth, granddaughter of a convert, who never left hers. Our friendship taught me that Jews come in all colors, that religion can, for some (such as the Ethiopian Jews that I was to meet in Israel) supersede race. Knowing Ruth has also provided a connection to the several Africans in our Baltimore Suburban Orthodox Synagogue.

Occasionally, however, even in our program, interaction with Ugandans could be negative, as in the case of Lee Jefferson, a black American, who on our third day warmly embraced market peddlers with a few words of Swahili and was laughed at. Since Lee assumed color was their common bond, he couldn't understand but quickly learned that they didn't consider Americans as tribal members, and that Swahili was the *lingua franca* of Kenya, not Uganda. Such offense might not have been intended, but it was never forgotten, since Lee continually griped about those "damn so-called African brothers." Twenty years later, teaching *Brown Girl, Brown Stones* at Towson University, I vividly recalled the incident, when my students, confused about the conflicts of American Bayans and Negroes (as named in the 1959 novel), required historical and sociological background to understand that diversity was more than skin shade, that even within an ethnic group, individuals had choices, a concept repeatedly illustrated by our African experience and ignored by American bureaucrats invested in superficial racial categories.

Overall our group encountered hardly any prejudice except for our singular experience with anti-Semitism. Before we could even pack our bags at Makerere University, we received a call from TEA announcing rather apologetically that the Anglican headmaster had refused to accept us, because we were Jewish. Although we were non-observant then, it didn't matter to him and his colleagues there. If we couldn't encourage the students to worship Christ, we would be presenting a negative role model to the students, "which just wouldn't do."

Ironically, it was the Ismaili Aga Khan Senior Secondary School that requested us. Headed by a defrocked Irish priest, husband of a native Kenyan woman and father of five children, the school was comprised of 79% Asians (descendants of Indians and Pakistanis), 20% tribal Ugandans, 1% British, Americans, and some Israelis. Initially disappointed not to be located in the "bush," we didn't realize our good fortune. Aga Khan was located in downtown Kampala, a stone's throw from the college and the actual political, cultural, and entertainment center of Uganda. We had superb opportunities to observe the interactions of Muslims and Christians, of Asians and Africans, and even Israelis, who were assisting with agriculture, fishing, construction, and technological projects.

Although we were clearly in the minority as Jews, we were welcomed by our students, headmaster, and most of our colleagues. The exception were a handful of British colonials who considered Americans automatically inferior and mocked our accents, less formal teaching styles, credentials, and even dress. While we wore light-weight cotton, they dressed in woolen suits and ties, and chortled at our dialect.

Linguistically, the reverse was true; the Brits could be unknowingly comical to their American colleagues. Thus, Louie Burke, our next door neighbor offered "to knock me up" (awaken me early) mornings and give me "lifts" to my early class. Louie, a red-faced Irish man, with a sense of humor, enjoyed the joke with Don over a beer. Not so with Miss Irene Nash, a tall, slightly stooped spinster in her late forties, who cautioned her students not to adopt the Americans' slang usage "okay," but to continue to use the proper British word, "right" or "righto." Actually, my multicultural education began before I even met my students, and one incident did remind us of Kano, Nigeria.

Although advised by our British colleagues to hire locals as houseboys, cooks, and gardeners, since they were so cheap and honest, we were appalled. The idea violated our morality, defeated our purpose of living in Africa.. Even the six-room, two-story suburban house with a beautifully sculpted front lawn and large back-yard made us uncomfortable. We had expected to live simply and make sacrifices. However, after one day in the house, we two Brooklyn apartment kids learned another lesson. No sooner did we open our door, than we were greeted by a long line of Bagandans pleading for work. "Memsahib, I cook so good curry, can make beef and chicken"; "I cook and clean for little, please memsahib, I have many children." Confronting us was a growing line of desperate men and women who had heard about us. Having hastily out maneuvered them, we reached school, where our headmaster suggested we hire two people or face the problem daily. Within an hour we hired Robin Tikuson and Jackson Mbale, part-time school workers, to help us clean house and plant a garden, a compromise that still irritated our British neighbors, who complained we were fraternizing with the help and paying more money for less work than they were. "Raise your employees' salaries, and reduce their workload," we replied. Lines had been crossed on both sides.

While some of the British regarded us as intruders, a few reached out to us, illustrating the differences within the Anglo community, too. Robert and Jocelyn Smith, in their forties, with children in London boarding schools, had been serving as colonial administrators in Uganda for years. Our one- time dinner experience with them was unfortunately unforgettable. After a lengthy, grand tour of their government-owned, eleven room house and perfectly tended flower garden, we repaired to the dining room, where Jocelyn proceeded to instruct me in how to partake of the first course, whole artichokes, which I had never seen before. Her supercilious tone, the dull conversation, and the tough roast beef guaranteed that there would not be any further socializing together. On the other hand, an evening with Michael and Maggie Adams, which could have been disastrous, resulted in a long-lasting friendship. As young artists in their twenties, Michael and Maggie desired an escape from staid Britain and an inspirational new landscape, both of which Uganda offered. Although we arrived promptly for a 6:30 dinner, three hours of conversation and laughter rushed by until Maggie slipped into the kitchen again and we heard, "just a few more minutes." At 10:00 p.m., when we had consumed all the peanuts and given up hope, the kitchen door swung open and Maggie emerged carrying a huge pot of cheese fondue, (another new dish for us); only this time the fondue was the appetizer, main course, and dessert. Although we had not eaten since lunch and the fondue was dried out, the evening conversation led to a two-year friendship.

Happily the cuisine improved when we dined with members of the Ismaili community—businessmen, educators, parents of students—who invited us home for exotic meals and desserts. Unlike many British who stereotyped us as Yankees, Indians repeatedly greeted us as Jews, showing us sections of their Korans that elevated the Israelites. Though uncomfortable, we understood their situation: they, too, were minorities, vulnerable; though middle class, they extended outreach to other outsiders. Furthermore, in the early 1960s, Jews and Israel were viewed as survivors, the latter strong enough to extend aid and build bridges to parts of Africa. What a difference four decades would make, when anti-Semitism would resurface globally, and Israel would become a pariah nation even on American campuses.

However for the most part, religion/ethnicity was not an issue for us. At the end of two years we were friends with tribal Ugandans, transplanted Indians and Pakistanis, fellow TEAers, and a Jewish couple with the American consulate.

The experience was one of the high points in our young lives. During quarterly school breaks, we traveled throughout East and South Africa, continually learning about differences among people. In one instance we bogged down in the muddy Nairobi Game Park with fellow American, Dwayne Shirk, who, ignoring warning signs, drove his little Volkswagen off the main road into the elephant grass to view zebra. After thirty minutes of steering and pushing a sinking, mud-covered car, we decided to walk out of the Park by following the lights of nearby Nairobi. Another surprise!! We had not counted on Dwayne, a fundamentalist, insisting that our end was in sight and we were fated to die. We jokingly conspired in whispers to send our friend to his fate should we be attacked by the moving forms padding alongside of us. An hour later, following the same circular park path, we finally stumbled on a wide, straight road with lights ahead, indicating a six foot gate, which Don pushed me over to avoid a nearby tree with a growling black panther. Dwayne was left with his prayers, which apparently were answered since we met him in downtown Nairobi the next day.

However, as memorable as the game park and Nairobi were, they could not compare with our month-long visit to the Millers, my husband's older cousins, who had escaped from Germany in the early 1930s and settled in Johannesburg. Three decades later, financially well established, with grown children, they, along with many other Jews, lived in luxurious gilded ghettoes. The society was highly stratified, where native Blacks occupied the lowest tier, Colored and Asians the next rung up, and Jews, though white, were never quite accepted socially by the British or certainly the Afrikaners, who disliked each other. Many Jews had money and good lives, but as a minority, little political power, as reflected by the lonely voice of progressive M. P. Helen Suzman. We were treated royally by the family that had several servants. However, we noticed a distinct difference between generations, a barely concealed tension. While the retired Millers and their friends were paternalistic toward their servants and inferiors, indifferent to the social and political problems percolating around them, their college-educated children, with whom we socialized, were sensitized and active politically, trying to improve conditions for non-whites. One, a lawyer, had become involved in an explosive national case defending a white artist who had painted a Black Christ. As the lawyer's friends, we were invited to the all-white trial and tasted South African justice, circa 1962. That evening we attended a gathering of lawyers, artists, intellectuals, Johannesburg bohemians, a mixture of Blacks, Whites, and Coloreds, who drank and chatted nervously while two people kept a lookout for a police raid. The lines were clearly drawn. Interracial socializing was not permitted! We may have well been in Mississippi or Georgia. I recall uncomfortably parking myself by the door for a quick getaway. If one came from a democratically open society, interracial tensions in South Africa were shocking. On another occasion we were invited for a week to the Durban home of the Graves, a gentile couple in their sixties. On the way we stopped for lunch in Ladysmith, a rural town of 200, in the middle of which stood a broken bench designated "whites only." In Durban, our hosts had purchased tickets for a Shaw play without realizing that it was open to "Coloreds and Asians" also. Once inside, Betty and Jack played musical chairs so that she would not be seated next to a non-White. Our Durban "vacation" exposed us to bigotry, contempt for Blacks, denigration of Coloreds, and superiority of Whites.

By the end of four weeks we could not wait to return to East Africa, specifically Uganda, where the British were trying to educate and train people, remove racial barriers, and prepare the colonies for independence. Still, when the latter arrived in 1962, there were fears among the Asians and Europeans of displacement, of property and business appropriation, and even of exile for those who had lived in Uganda for several generations. As the Irish headmaster of our Islamic school nervously informed us, we should be prepared to be stormed and barricade ourselves within the inner court. Thankfully little occurred at the time, although several Asian store windows were defaced with white markings: "go home; this country is for Blacks only." By the time we left in May 1963, Milton Obote, the new prime minister, and a representative parliament had been democratically elected, promising a decent future for Uganda, but tribal conflicts were bubbling beneath the surface, and border feuds were threatening to spill over. Still, compared to the rest of the continent, East Africa was relatively calm for some time, and we could retain our lovely memories until Idi Amin and his thugs took over. We had already had a taste of this mammoth bully on the basketball court when Don found himself on the opposite team attempting to block him. Amin definitively proved that decency and fairness were not intrinsic racial traits.

Although most Ugandan Blacks did not discriminate against each other on the basis of race, tribalism could often cause problems. Thus, to our surprise, the Black Kampalan Chief of Police, to whom we had reported missing money, immediately arrested Johnson, a temporary helper replacing Robin for three weeks. The evidence, we were told, was not only Johnson's ready accessibility to our cash, but his tribal Jaluo markings and visible resume as a thief, one missing hand. As trusting Americans, we could not accept the generalization until he confessed his crime. To underscore the difference between Ugandan legal justice and tribal law, the police chief offered us a choice: take our money back, drop the charges, and return him to the Jaluos or hold a trial that could sentence him to prison for five years or more. We dropped the charges; the chief looked disappointed; Johnson was smiling as we paid for his train ticket since the government would not.

We had a lot more to learn. Some of our best lessons came from our students, desperate for education, their only avenue to success for themselves, their families, and in the case of the natives, their tribes. In order to graduate from East African secondary schools, students needed to score well on the British O and A level exams, required for decent jobs and university entrance. In the two years we were at the Aga Khan, two failed and committed suicide, while several students became deeply depressed. Instructors were held accountable for their students' success or failure, and everyone knew it. Thus, when my literature students refused to enter Mr. Rajib's chemistry section, it was apparent they had initiated a boycott, humiliating him by silently standing outside his room. Although he struggled through the trimester, he was gone by December. My students and I also had to make mutual adjustments: they expected my lectures to be exam based; I encouraged critical thinking and discussion; eventually we compromised by combining both. Not only were East African students exposed to diverse educational styles, standards, and individuals, but as American educators, we were profoundly affected, too, and somewhat more prepared for the complicated world awaiting us.

Evelyn Avery, Towson University

The Old System

Adapted by Sarah Blacher Cohen

from the story by Saul Bellow
with permission by the author

"The Old System," adapted by Sarah Blacher Cohen, was first presented with "A Silver Dish," adapted by Joanne Koch, as *Saul Bellow's Stories on Stage* in 1992 as a staged reading featuring Byrne Piven, directed by Joyce Piven at the Chicago Writers' Bloc New Play Festival with support from the Dramatists Guild Fund, Inc.; then in 1993 at the Lewis A. Swyer Theatre, the Empire Center at the Egg, sponsored by the New York State Writers' Institute and the College of Humanities and Fine Arts, University at Albany; at the Barbra Streisand Festival in San Diego featuring Hal Gould in 1995; in 1996; as a staged reading at the Florida Atlantic University Library Series in 2000; at the Empire Center at the Egg in Albany, New York, in a memorial performance directed by Rebecca Kaplan and sponsored by SUNY Hillel in 2005; as a staged reading at the Spertus Institute in Chicago and at the Milwaukee Public Library in 2005, both presentations directed by Sandy Shinner.

THE OLD SYSTEM

Cast of Characters:

Samuel Braun—An inward, ruminating intellectual in his sixties whose family reminiscences interrupt his scientific detachment. Referred to in the script as Dr. Braun or Dr. Samuel Braun.

Ilkington— a seventy-year-old stuffy WASP gentleman with a streak of criminality.

Young Sammy Braun—an earnest young boy.

*Young Tina—an angry hulk of a girl on the verge of puberty who is seductive and menacing.

Aunt Rose—a hard-driving business woman with a slight Yiddish accent who has veto power over her family's choices.

Uncle Braun—the docile Yiddish-accented survivor of the Czar's army and his domineering wife.

Isaac—Born in Europe, coming to America as a boy. Initially an upright young man is his twenties who, in the course of the play, becomes a middle-aged man with old-world spiritual values and strong attachment to family.

*Adult Tina—an embittered middle-aged woman who feels mistreated by her family and patriarchal society.

Rebbe from Williamsburg—the religious equivalent of a perceptive psychiatrist who immediately discovers what's wrong and offers the right advice. He speaks with a slight accent from his Lubovitcher Hasidic ancestors.

Mutt Braun—a streetwise tough-guy who, beneath the outward bravado, is still a little boy taking orders from Tina.

*(If the right actress can be found, she can be both the younger Tina and the older Tina.)

THE OLD SYSTEM adapted by Sarah Blacher Cohen from the story by Saul Bellow.

Lights up on One Actor, who will play the part of the older Samuel Braun, scientist.

DR. BRAUN

Winter. Saturday. The short end of December. Alone in my apartment. Working with a thought... a feeling.

(Braun strides up and down, grappling with an idea, struggling to ascertain its meaning.)

They said that I, a scientist, a specialist in the chemistry of heredity, did not love anyone. Not true. I didn't love anyone *steadily*. But *unsteadily* I loved, at an average rate...

Especially my two cousins, in upstate New York... Isaac Braun and his sister Tina... from Albany and Schenectady. Isaac, a boy from Europe, grew up to be a man in the direct Old Testament sense, as that bird on the sycamore was born to fish in water. Isaac had the outlook of ancient generations on the New World.

Tents and kine and wives and maidservants and manservants. His old country Jewish dignity was very firm and strong... In childhood he showed me great kindness. He took me for rides in the wagon with the old sway-back horse. He used to call me Sammy, sometimes Sammele.

Actors playing ISAAC and SAMUEL BRAUN as a boy are lit sitting atop a cube, swaying as if in a horsedrawn buggy. OLDER DR. SAMUEL BRAUN glances lovingly upon them.

(A very soft musical three or four minute bridge of a Jewish-sounding Klezmer tune.)

ISAAC

You know, Sammy, you almost didn't get born. I helped bring you into the world.

SAMMY

How could you? Weren't you a boy then?

ISAAC

I was old enough. *Tante* Rose sent me to the saloon to get that *shicker*, Doctor Jones, when it was time. The only one who would treat us Jewish immigrants before we could educate our own doctors. He had so much *schnapps* in him I had to crank the Model T and help him drive. He barely had the strength to tie your mother's hands to the bedpost.

SAMMY

Was he afraid she'd run away?

ISAAC

No. He wanted to make sure you'd come out of hiding. You were born in a small wooden house where they washed you and covered you with mosquito netting and put you at the foot of the bed. And later *Tante* Rose held you at the *bris*. And nearsighted old Krieger, the chicken slaughterer, cut away the foreskin.

SAMMY

What is it with the foreskin? Why does everyone make such a fuss about it? Even cousin Tina wanted to have a look.

(Seductive yet bouncy Jewish music, like the strains of the "Greene Cousine," to underscore Braun's introduction of Tina.)

DR. BRAUN

An old mill. A pasture with clover flowers. What did I know? I was just a kid. I wanted to make a wreath for cousin Tina. To put on her thick savory head, her smoky black harsh hair. She was big then, very big.

("Greene Cousine" music ends.)

SAMMY

Tina, I think she likes me. There are some clover flowers by that rotten stump. I'll push it over and get some for her.

(*He pushes the stump over and imaginary hornets come flying out at him. He waves his hands wildly to chase them away.*)

Oh, oh, a hornet's nest under there. (Full of panic and flailing his arms.) Get away, you hornets, get away! They're landing all over me. Ouch! they're stinging me. Ouch! Look at all these red blotches on my arms and legs. Oh my god! (Starts to cry.) Help me! Someone help me!

YOUNG TINA

(TINA menacingly steals up behind him and puts her arms around him.) Don't be such a cry baby. (Seductively) I can take care of you. Come with me up to the attic. I have some lotion to rub anywhere you want.

SAMMY

(Clutching his arms and legs) Will it hurt?

YOUNG TINA

(Seductively) No, it will make you feel real good... all over. Come with me.

(TINA, a junior rotund Eve, takes SAMMY, a miniature junior Adam, to a pile of pillows on the stage to suggest an attic bed, along with a chair beside it.)

DR. BRAUN

Tina came huge into the attic to console me. An angry fat face, black eyes and the dilated nose breathing at her little Sammy.

SAMMY

These hornets' bites still feel like needles in my skin.

YOUNG TINA

This calamine lotion will get out the sting. Take off your shirt and trousers. I'll smooth it all over your arms and legs and . . . thighs.

SAMMY

(SAMMY takes off his trousers and shirt and TINA bends over and starts rubbing the inside of his thighs.)

No hornet stung me there.

YOUNG TINA (getting more and more sexually aroused)

Are you sure? It's better to be safe...than sorry. (She keeps rubbing.)

SAMMY (starting to enjoy her attention)

Maybe, maybe you're right.

YOUNG TINA

It looks like you're getting hot. I'm going to lift up my dress and petticoat to cool you.

(with her formidable derriere facing the audience, YOUNG TINA lifts up her skirt and puts it over his head.)

AUNT ROSE (Angrily shouting)

Tina! Tina! What are you always doing up in the attic?

YOUNG TINA

(Quickly puts her skirt down and shouts back)

Thinking.

AUNT ROSE

You can think another time. Come down and help me clean the house.

TINA

Why can't Isaac help you clean?

AUNT ROSE

Isaac's got to help with the business.

TINA

Why can't I help him with the business? He likes to have me along. I make up songs and tell him jokes.

AUNT ROSE

Business is not for girls. Neither is monkey business. Cooking and cleaning is for girls. Now come down right away.

TINA

In a coupla minutes. I got to *clean* up a few things *here* first.

AUNT ROSE

You're always cleaning, but, by you, it's still dirty. Hurry up and finish what you're doing.

TINA

(petulantly shouts back)

In a few minutes. Just hold your horses. (Turns back to Sammy) Now Sammy, (seductively) I want to hold *your horses* and finish what we started.

SAMMY

(In fear and ecstasy) Finish what we started?

YOUNG TINA

Yes. I'm going to sit on this chair so I can pay more attention to you. (As she sits down, the chair creaks from her weight.) But first I have to rest my legs on you cause I'm getting tired from being your nurse. (Seductive) Maybe you'll take care of me for awhile.

SAMMY (scared and suspicious)

What do you want me to do?

YOUNG TINA (panting)

Just press yourself against my thighs.

SAMMY

I... I can't. My, my stings are starting to itch.

YOUNG TINA

Forget about the itching. Just press your thigh against my thigh.

DR. BRAUN

With agonies of incapacity and pleasure, I did what she asked. Tina did not kiss, did not embrace. Her face was menacing. She was defying. She was drawing me—taking me somewhere with her...

YOUNG TINA

I'm not promising you anything or telling you anything about me. You were just lucky to be with me... And don't let anyone know what we did. It will be our secret.

SAMMY

Yes, our secret. (*End of strains of Greene Cousine.*)

DR. BRAUN

All was silent. Summer silence. The aroma of Tina lingered. She must have been a 250 pound girl, but the shape of her mouth was very sweet, womanly... She was more feminine in childhood than later.

(*Brief strains of Prokofiev's "Lieutenant Kiji Suite" to introduce Uncle Braun*)

What Tina did in childhood was never known to Uncle Braun who was too busy scratching out a living. Life was hard for him even in Russia. With his short, humiliated legs, his little beard and great eyes, Uncle Braun was ordered by irrational decree to leave wife and child to eat maggotty pork in the Czar's army.

UNCLE BRAUN

How I hated those goy wars—far away, on the lid of hell—conscription, mustering, marching, leaving the corpses everywhere, buried, unburied, army against army.

(*Male actor playing Uncle Braun pantomimes the actions which are described about him.*)

DR. BRAUN

And when the War was lost, he escaped from Sakhalin via Manchuria to become... monarch of used stoves and fumigated mattresses in the Mohawk Valley.

(*end Prokofiev music*)

UNCLE BRAUN

Now I lead a good Jewish life in upstate New York. I have a little money, a little learning. And they respect me in our *shul*. But such fights you wouldn't believe!

Even families stop talking! Everyone thinks he's better than the other one. They start out as peddlers but now they act like they're princes. And I'm no different. But my princes are my sons who I want to marry to Jewish girls good enough for them...

Sunday mornings I read aloud to them the Yiddish Matrimonial advertisements from the *Forwartz*: "Attractive widow, 35, dark-favored, owning her own dry goods business in Hudson, excellent cook, Orthodox, well-bred, refined. Plays the piano... Two intelligent, well-behaved children, eight and six." What do you think of her, Mutt?

MUTT

She's a little too fancy for me. You know, I'm like that song I sing:

"I stuck my nose up a nanny goat's ass/ And the smell was enough to blind me/ But just then gold fell from her *tush*/ And that was enough to bind me."

UNCLE BRAUN

Mutt, that's no way for a nice Jewish boy to talk about a nice Jewish girl. Isaac, how about this one? "Intelligent and studious, Winner of the Finkel Award for best Student in Teacher's College, Adventurous and Cosmopolitan, Travels in own car to Miami Beach regularly, Knows how to change a tire."

AUNT ROSE

Forget about changing a tire. What about her family?

ISAAC

Never mind her family. I found someone I like already.

AUNT ROSE

Who could that be?

ISAAC

You know, Clara Sternberg.

MUTT

What does her old man do?

ISAAC

He's a manufacturer.

AUNT ROSE

A manufacturer. Not true. I made a long trip to Teaneck, New Jersey, to make what they call a "genealogical investigation."

UNCLE BRAUN

And what did you find out?

AUNT ROSE

Some manufacturer. He started out as a cutter and then married a housemaid. Such connections I don't need.

MUTT

Maybe he loves her.

AUNT ROSE

Love can't pay the bills, but a rich father-in-law can.

UNCLE BRAUN

What about feelings?

AUNT ROSE

What good are feelings? You got so many of them they give you heartburn and make you take Bromo-Seltzer every five minutes.

Dr. BRAUN

Aunt Rose vetoed all the other young women Isaac preferred, her judgments severe without limit.

AUNT ROSE

"A false dog," "Candied poison," "An open ditch. A sewer. A born whore!"

ISAAC

Why do you disapprove of all of my choices? You don't seem to be that particular who Tina goes with.

MUTT

Tina is smart. She don't bring her boyfriend to Albany for her old lady's inspection.

AUNT ROSE

Tina can't be that particular. She got to take who she can get. But still... I wanted to find out more about him. He shouldn't bring germs to infect everyone. So I went to his house in Coney Island to see for myself. What a family! The father sells pretzels and chestnuts from a cart; the mother cooks for banquets. And the groom himself—so thick, so bald, his hands so common, his chest like fur. He's a beast. He could be a hired killer, a second Lepke of Murder Incorporated.

DR. BRAUN

Upstate, the old woman read the melodramas of the Yiddish Press, which she embroidered with her own ideas of wickedness.

ISAAC

You always imagine the worst about people. I gave up Clara Sternberg cause you said she lied, like her father. But I won't give up Sylvia. She never lies and I'm going to marry her.

AUNT ROSE

You just met her. You hardly know her.

ISAAC

I know enough about her. She's pleasant, mild... respectable, even though she's a farmer's daughter.

AUNT ROSE

He's an ignorant, common man.

ISAAC

He's honest, a hard worker on the land. He recites the Psalms even when he's driving. Keeps them under the wagon seat.

AUNT ROSE

I don't believe it. A son of Ham like that. A cattle dealer. He stinks of manure.

UNCLE BRAUN

Rose, is that a way to talk about a fellow Jew?

AUNT ROSE

Jew or no Jew. If he stinks, he stinks. Tell your bride to wash her father before bringing him to the synagogue. Get a bucket of scalding water and 20 Mule Team

Borax and ammonia, and a horse brush. The *schmutz* is *deep*. Be sure to scrub his hands.

UNCLE BRAUN

Are you that clean to call other people dirty? Maybe his skin is dark from the sun.

AUNT ROSE

I know dirt when I see dirt. I don't want it touching me. If you like it so much, go out and sleep in it... with the animals.

DR. BRAUN

Uncle Braun died angry with Aunt Rose. He turned his face to the wall with his last breath to rebuke her hardness. His sons burst out weeping. The tears of the women were different. Their passion took other forms. Aunt Rose bargained for more property. She defied Uncle Braun's will and collected rents in the slums of Albany and Schenectady from properties he left to his sons.

AUNT ROSE

(painfully walks back and forth across the stage shouting at her "tenants.")

Mr. Schneider, Mr. Schuster, where is your rent? What do you mean you don't have it? You got to pay up or get out. Your child is sick, you don't have enough customers, your husband left you, your wife is fooling around. Is that my fault? No more extensions. You got to pay up or get out. You say you only want to pay your rent to Isaac Braun. Well I'm his mother and I have his buildings. You can give me your money. (Laughs) It will be in safe hands for a long time... cause I'm strong like an ox... except I got a little trouble with my bladder and arteries. But I don't take no pills for it. A curse on those fancy medicines! If you want to know something, I blame my husband's death on Bromo-Seltzer. It enlarged his heart.

DR. BRAUN

Aunt Rose was the primal hard mother. She was building a kingdom with the labor of Uncle Braun and the strength of her obedient sons. And when Aunt Rose lay dead, Tina, who had been excluded from the kingdom, tried to usurp her power. She took from her mother's hand the ring Isaac had given her years ago.

ISAAC

Tina, give that ring to me. Give it here.

TINA

No. It was hers. Now it's mine.

ISAAC

It was not Mama's. You know that. Give it back.

TINA

I'm the daughter. The daughter gets the mother's jewelry.

ISAAC

I gave Mama that ring. Got it from an immigrant who owed me money. And now I want it for Sylvia.

TINA

That farmer's daughter. What'll she do with a ring?

ISAAC

You sound like Mama... Come on now, Tina, Hand over the ring. Give it to me.

TINA

Give, give. Mama and Pappa were always giving things to you, not me. I was just their fat daughter. You remember what Mama called me when I wasn't the good little girl— the *shtick flaish with tzway aygen*, the hunk of flesh with two eyes. But you were the handsome son, a boy who could carry on the family name, a boy who could say *kaddish* for them when they died. But you're not going to be the favorite *boychik* anymore. You won't get what you want this time.

ISAAC

Tina, it's not right to argue like this... at Mama's deathbed. We'll talk about the ring later.

TINA

There'll be no later. I'm keeping the ring!

DR. BRAUN

Though Isaac did not get the ring, he became a millionaire. The others simply hoarded, immigrant style... Isaac's orthodoxy increased with his wealth. He kept a copy of the Psalms in the glove compartment of his Cadillac which caused Tina to remark:

TINA

He reads the Psalms aloud in his air-conditioned caddy when there's a long freight train at the crossing. That crook. He'd pick God's pocket. He may recite

"Answer me when I call, O God of my righteousness," but what do you think? Does he remember his brothers when there's a deal going? Does he give his only sister a chance to come in? Did he carry the family into real estate where the tax advantages were greatest? Did he care that we had our money in savings accounts at a disgraceful two and a half per cent?

DR. BRAUN

Isaac had tried, in fact, to include the Brauns when he built the shopping center at Robbstown.

(TINA, MUTT and ISAAC meet in a family huddle.)

ISAAC

To buy the Robbstown Country Club for the Shopping Center, we each need to put up $25,000 and pay the entire amount... under the table... to Ilkington, the Director, so he can persuade the board members to sell it to us.

MUTT

Yah, I know that old WASP, Ilkington. I used to caddy for him at Robbstown in the early twenties. Not big on the tips. Always stiff and proper.

TINA

Yeah, if he's so proper, why does the old WASP want the hundred thousand off the record?

ISAAC

Internal revenue. Ilkington's now seventy and wants to retire to the British West Indies.

TINA

On my money he wants to skip town and have a good time.

ISAAC

You'll make a lot more money than he will. The shopping center will be worth a half a million a piece to each of us. I have a friend on the zoning board who will clear everything for five grand. I'll take care of all the contracting.

TINA

Enough of this, "you'll take care." We have to form a separate corporation to make sure the building profits are equally shared.

ISAAC

That's fine with me.

TINA

To set up the books we'll hire a *trained* accountant, not a *self-taught* contractor.

DR. BRAUN

All the difficult problems were examined. Players, specialists in the harsh music of money, studying a score. In the end, they agreed to perform.

DR. BRAUN

But when the time came, it was a different story.

ISAAC

Well, Mutt, I have my $25,000.

MUTT

How do you know Ilkington can be trusted?

ISAAC

I think he can.

MUTT

You think. He could take the money and say he never heard of you in all his life.

ISAAC

Yes, he might. But we talked that over. We have to gamble.

MUTT

I ain't slept.

ISAAC

Where's the money?

MUTT

I don't have that kind of cash.

ISAAC

No? And what about Tina?

MUTT

I don't know.

ISAAC

She must have talked you out of it, didn't she? I have to meet Ilkington at noon.
Sharp. Why didn't you tell me sooner? I have an hour to raise this money.

MUTT

Tina says that in our bracket the twenty-five would cost us more than fifty.

ISAAC

You could have told me this yesterday.

MUTT

You'll turn over a hundred thousand to a man you don't know? Without a
receipt? Blind? Don't do it, Isaac.

DR. BRAUN

But Isaac decided to do it. He put his stake together penny by penny, old style
and then borrowed $75,000 from the bank at full interest. Without security he
gave it to Ilkington in Ilkington's parlor. (Begin the strains of elegant refined
Mozart or Baroque violin music to suggest refined WASP elegance.)

ILKINGTON

Come right in Mr. Braun.

(Isaac uneasily enters, clutching to his side the satchel containing the $100,000.)

ISAAC

This is a very nice place you have.

ILKINGTON

Thank you. We have been very comfortable here. But I'm afraid we've become
too attached to our possessions.

DR. BRAUN

Furnished in old WASP taste and disseminating an old WASP odor of tiresome, respectable things... decorated with the pork-pale colors of gentility.

ISAAC

I know what you mean. You get used to a place. (Looks around) Oh, I see you like old furniture.

ILLKINGTON

We prefer to call them antiques. To be more precise, English antiques. I'm afraid we've collected so many of them that our home looks a bit like a museum. (Smiles) But as long as it's not a mausoleum, we're still alright... May I get you a martini?

ISAAC

(Hesitating) Why... yes... sure.

ILKINGTON

(Brings back a shaker of martinis, hands a glass to Isaac and proceeds to drink one glass after another himself.)

When you reach my age, no matter how attached you are to a given locale, you become eager for a change.

ISAAC

I'm just the opposite. I like things to stay just the same.

ILKINGTON

But you're a young man. At 70, you get cold. You look forward to the warmth of exotic yet... civilized places... like the British West Indies. My friends from Cornell days, Class of 1910, have invited us to join them there . . . Oh, I see you finished your drink. Let me pour you another. But first let me take that satchel from you.

(Isaac clasps the satchel tightly and Ilkington has to wrench it from his hands. Isaac looks pained as Ilkington triumphantly seizes it and smugly puts the satchel at his side.)

ILKINGTON

Mind you, however, I can't promise that the Board of Directors will approve of the sale. After all, you haven't exactly been a member of the club. Now what is it Groucho Marx used to say? He was one of your people, wasn't he? He said, "I

wouldn't join a club that would have me as a member." (Laughs at his own joke)
But Mr. Braun, you understand what I mean.

ISAAC

Yes, I understand.

ILKINGTON

But don't worry. I'll try my best. Just relax. I'll get us some more drinks.

ISAAC

Yes, relax. (Whispers to himself) But it's daytime. Does one have more than one
drink in the daytime?

DR. BRAUN

Isaac sat there sturdily, but felt lost, lost to his people, his family, lost to God, lost
in the void of America.

ISAAC

It's getting very late. I really have to go.

ILKINGTON

If you must, you must... (Ilkington shakes Isaac's hand) Thank you for coming.
And remember... no written instrument can replace trust and decency between
gentlemen.

ISAAC

(With nervous uncertainty) Yes, trust and decency.

ILKINGTON

Good day Mr. Braun.

ISAAC

Good day, Mr. Ilkington.

DR. BRAUN

Isaac drove home and sat in the den of his bungalow. Two whole days. Then on
Monday, Ilkington gave Isaac his answer.

ILKINGTON

Mr. Braun, I'm happy to report that the Robbstown directors have decided to accept your offer for the property. I trust you and your people will make good use of it. I shall think of you when I'm in the British West Indies. *Bonne chance*!

ISAAC

This news calls for a *schnapps*, even in the daytime!

DR. BRAUN

Isaac took possession of the country club and filled it with a shopping center. The green acres reserved for idleness were now paralyzed by parking for five hundred cars. He filled the Mohawk Valley with housing developments and spoke of "my people," meaning... those who lived in his buildings. Yet Isaac himself grew more old-fashioned and... tight-fisted.

ISAAC

Sylvia doesn't need a mink. Her Hudson seal coat is good enough. My old Studebaker is good enough too. It'll last for ten more years. Why do I have to join the men's club, the country club, the Fort Orange club? I don't play cards. I don't drink. I don't golf. I'm satisfied to stay at home. I don't care to go to Florida, to Europe. Even the State of Israel I can wait to see.

DR. BRAUN

What Isaac had plenty of time for was reminiscences. He tried to distance himself from Tina's accusations:

TINA

When the big deal comes along, he shakes off his family. He refuses to cut us in.

MUTT

Listen. We deserted him. We didn't bring the cash we promised.

TINA

He's still a crook. Mama lent him money; he wouldn't repay; that was why she collected those rents.

MUTT

I'm not so sure about that.

TINA

Well I am sure. Besides Isaac's a whoremaster.

MUTT

Oh, no. Not in years and years.

TINA

Come, Mutt, I know his shenanigans. I keep an eye on the Orthodox. Believe me, I do . . . . Governor Rockefeller, his buddy, has put him on a commission. Which is it?

MUTT

Pollution.

TINA

The right one for him.

MUTT

You shouldn't say such things. He's our brother.

TINA

He feels for *you*.

MUTT

Yes he does.

TINA

A multimillionaire— lets you go on drudging in a little business. He's heartless. Thinks only of himself.

MUTT

Not true.

TINA

Listen. He never had a tear in his eye unless the wind was blowing. Now that he's got what he wants, he can paint the past with his sentimental colors.

(Brief strains of the music without words of "A Bicycle Built for Two")

ISAAC

I remember... in 1920 Mama wanted fresh milk, and we kept a cow in the pasture by the river. And how delicious it was to crank the Model T and drive at dusk to milk the cow beside the green water. We sang songs. "Daisy, daisy, give me your answer too, I'm half crazy over the love of you." Tina was ten years old. She must have weighed two hundred pounds then.

AUNT ROSE

Tina, don't sit down on that chair. There's a kitten there. *Oy vey*. Too late.

YOUNG TINA (holding the dead kitty)

Oh, I didn't mean to crush the kitty. I just plopped down and forgot she was there.

AUNT ROSE

You *shtick flaish*! You animal!

TINA

(Sobbing)

I'm not an animal! I'm your little girl... your daughter. Why are you always saying mean things to me?

AUNT ROSE

Cause you're clumsy. You're careless. You don't look what you're doing.

ISAAC

Mama, don't talk like that to my little sister... (Turns to Tina) Tina, you're not clumsy. You're a big help to me. You do a lotta things right... How about teaching me that new song you learned? You know the one about the mares and oats. I can sing it to my horse.

TINA

(Brightening up) Oh you mean "Mairzy dotes." Okay. (Does a soft shoe shuffle or tap dances and sings) "Mairzy doats and dozy doats / And liddle lamzy divey / A kiddley divey too, wouldn't you?" (She curtsies and bows).

ISAAC

(Claps his hands effusively and shouts) Wonderful! Wonderful! You are talented, Tina. You are! Now let me see if I can sing it with you. (Isaac sings somewhat haltingly with Tina) "Mares e dotes and does eat oats and liddle lambs eat ivy. A kiddle eat ivy too, wouldn't you?"

DR. BRAUN

But Tina grew into a gloomy, obese woman. Absorbed in the dictatorship of her huge person. In a white dress, and with the ring on her finger she had seized from her dead mother. By a war maneuver in the bedroom. At other times, the thoughts of Isaac, the builder, were caught up with elevations, drainages, mortgages, with piety superadded. With Psalm-saying at construction sites:

ISAAC

"When I consider the heavens, the work of Thy fingers...What is Man that Thou art mindful of him?" God of Mercy. *El Malei Rachamim Schochen Bam'romim.*"

(The Strains of Bruch's "Kol Nidre" *softly* underscores the ensuing paragraph)

At the cemetery before the Day of Atonement, I visit my dead parents, stifled in clay. There they are in those two crates, side by side. Mama and Pappa, I'm worried about you, down there. The wet, the cold and those worms. There's going to be a frost tonight. But thank God, you're buried below the frost line. But you're still so unsheltered.

DR. BRAUN

And then the annual trip to Tina's to forgive and seek forgiveness from the living before the Day of Atonement (Strains of *Kol Nidre* music fades out)

TINA

What do you want?

ISAAC

Tina, for God's sake, I've come to make peace.

TINA

What peace! You swindled us out of a fortune.

ISAAC

The others don't agree. Now Tina, we are brother and sister. Remember Mama and Pappa. Remember...

TINA

You son of a bitch. I do remember. I remember how they never came to visit us in Schenectady. Like it was a foreign country. Too far away. Too dangerous.

I remember how everyone always spent the holidays at your house... eating Sylvia's sponge cake and chopped liver. My place wasn't kosher enough, wasn't comfortable enough. Mama probably thought we had too many germs.

ISAAC

No, that wasn't it at all. They knew you worked hard at your store all week and they didn't want to burden you with entertaining. They had your best interests at heart.

TINA

Bullshit. The only times Mama had any use for me was when I went away to college, lost weight and married a guy who took me out of the house. So much for everyone's best interests. Now get the hell out of here. You're not going to practice your goddam religion on me. I can take you straight. In a deal. Or a swindle. But I can't stand your fake holiness.

DR. BRAUN

Isaac walked later to the synagogue with an injured heart. Striking breast with fist in old-fashioned penitence... The modern rabbis did not go for this operatic fist-clenching. Theirs was the way of understatement. Anglo-Saxon restraint. But Isaac Braun, covered by his father's prayer shawl, wept near the ark.

(Strains of some heart-rending cantorial piece by Yossele Rosenblatt or Richard Tucker or Jan Peerce or some violin strains of their cantorial pieces with ISAAC praying, weeping and beating his chest.)

ISAAC

Tina, Tina, *Al Chet, Shechatanu,* For the sin which I have committed, forgive me, pardon me.

DR. BRAUN

These annual visits to Tina continued until she became sick. When she went into the hospital, Isaac came to me to find out how things really stood.

ISAAC

Tell me, Sammy, you're a doctor. What's wrong with Tina?

DR. SAMUEL BRAUN

But I'm not a medical doctor.

ISAAC

You're a scientist. You understand it better.

DR. SAMUEL BRAUN

The tests are not conclusive but it appears that Tina is dying of cancer of the liver.

ISAAC

Oh my God. Cancer of the liver.

DR. SAMUEL BRAUN

They tried cobalt radiation. Chemotherapy. They both made her very sick. There is no hope.

ISAAC

No hope? Oh my God... (Sighs heavily) I must see my sister. Mutt is the only one who can get her to see me.

DR. BRAUN

And gentle, dog-eyed Mutt softly urged Tina to see her big brother.

MUTT

Tina it'll mean an awful lot to Isaac to see you.

TINA

That I don't believe.

MUTT

You should see him, Tina.

TINA

No. Why should I? A Jewish death-bed scene, that's what he wants. No.

MUTT

Come on now Tina.

TINA

No! (said with greater vehemence) I hate him... (in a softer, rueful voice) I can't help him.

MUTT

You ought to let him come.

TINA

Because I'm dying.

MUTT

People recover.

TINA

Not this time.

MUTT

He calls every day.

TINA

Then give Isaac my message, Mutt. I'll see him, yes, but it'll cost him money.

MUTT

Money?

TINA

If he pays me twenty thousand dollars.

MUTT

Tina, that's not right.

TINA

Why not? For my daughter. She'll need it.

MUTT

No, she doesn't need that kind of dough. Mama left for all of us. There's plenty and you know it.

TINA

If he's got to come, that's the price of admission. Only a fraction of what he did us out of.

MUTT

He never did me out of anything. But I'll give him your message. "For twenty grand cash Tina says yes, otherwise no."

DR. SAMUEL BRAUN

Tina had discovered that one need not be bound by the old rules. She had seized upon the force of death to create a situation of opera. Which at the same time was a situation of parody.

ISAAC

Mutt, What does Tina say?

MUTT

She says you did us all dirt.

ISAAC

I? She got scared and backed out. I had to do it alone. You've got to explain it to her. She doesn't know what's right.

MUTT

She says you shook us off. You wanted it all for yourself.

ISAAC

She begrudges me my wealth. She won't let me enjoy it.

MUTT

You may be right, but these are her terms: For twenty grand cash, Tina says she'll see you. Otherwise no.

ISAAC

(Incredulous) Are you serious? A sister asks money from a brother to visit her at her deathbed? (Getting progressively more angry) Twenty thousand dollars to talk to her? Twenty thousand dollars to get close to her? What is she a prostitute?

MUTT

Calm down Isaac, calm down. What can I say? (Sighs)

ISAAC

Robbery, theft, blackmail! And against her own brother!

DR. BRAUN

Isaac was beside himself... He came to me for advice.

ISAAC

Sammy, you're the expert. You've been written up in *Time*, in all the papers for your research. What should I do about Tina? It's eating me up alive.

DR. BRAUN

I don't know, Isaac. Scientists can't put the vast world in rational order. So how can I help you with your little sister, Tina?

ISAAC

(Scornful) Intellectuals. The more people have in their heads, the less they know how to explain it. (Brief strains of the Hasidic song "Dudele") Better I should see Rabbi Belsky in Williamsburg... such a wise man, . . . He doesn't know all the new things in the computer, but he knows the old things in the human heart.

DR. BRAUN

Isaac took the Twentieth Century when it left Albany just before daybreak. With just enough light through the dripping gray to see the river. He felt like one of the forty million foreigners coming to America.

(End of "Dudele.")

ISAAC

Rabbi Belsky, I had this opportunity to buy a piece of land— a country club— for building a shopping center. I invited my family to invest with me. But my sister, Tina, told the rest not to give me their money. So when I went to this Mr. Illkington, the president of the country club board, I felt... (groping for words)

RABBI

Abandoned? Like Joseph by his brothers?

ISAAC

Yes, Rabbi, abandoned. They deserted me.

RABBI

They turned their faces from you. But did that mean you didn't have to share?

ISAAC

Yes.

RABBI

They turned their faces from you, but that made you rich.

ISAAC

Yes. I became a wealthy man from this deal and many others. But my sister is jealous of my good fortune. Accuses me of cheating her.

RABBI

Your sister, poor thing, is very harsh. She is wrong. She has no ground for complaint against you.

ISAAC

I'm glad to hear that.

RABBI

She's not a poor woman, your sister?

ISAAC

No, she inherited property. And her husband does pretty well. But she still thinks she's a pauper.

RABBI

Maybe she suffers from an *impoverished* soul.

ISAAC

Maybe. But I suffered from an *injured* soul when I went to Tina before the High Holidays and she kicked me out.

RABBI

You were right to try to make peace before Yom Kippur.

ISAAC

But now she is on her deathbed and again I have asked to see her.

RABBI

Yes? Well?

ISAAC

She wants money for it.

RABBI

Ah. Does she? Money?

ISAAC

Twenty thousand dollars. So that I can be let into the room.

RABBI

She knows she is dying, I suppose.

ISAAC

Yes.

RABBI

(Snickers) Yes. Our Jews love deathbed jokes. People assume that God has a sense of humor. Such jokes made by the dying in anguish show a strong and brave character, but skeptical. What sort of woman is your sister?

ISAAC

As a child very big.

RABBI

I see. A fat child. Staring at the lucky ones. Like an animal in a cage. People sometimes behave as though they were alone when such a child is present. So their little monster souls have a strange fate... They see people as they are when no one is looking... You can afford the money. I don't ask you for the figure of your fortune. It is not my concern. But could you give her the twenty thousand?

ISAAC

(His anger increases in intensity)

If I had to. But I don't want to. Why should I have to pay for love from my own sister?

RABBI

Would it make any great difference in your fortune?

ISAAC

No.

RABBI

In that case why shouldn't you pay.

ISAAC

I don't want to reduce the feelings we once had for each other to a harsh business transaction.

RABBI

It's not for me to tell you to give away so much money. But you gave—you gambled—you trusted the man, a total stranger.

ISAAC

Ilkington? That was a business risk. But Tina? For years I have been hurt by her... She's driven me away every time I've tried to make peace with her...

RABBI

Maybe she's never been at peace with herself.

ISAAC

So you think I should risk getting hurt by Tina again?

RABBI

Yes. Take the risk. Judging the sister by the brother, there is no other way.

ISAAC

This is very hard for me to do, Rabbi. But, but, I'll... I'll follow your advice... (Resigned and relieved) I *will* pay her the money... Had she asked me for $50,000, maybe not. But $20,000, alright. Tina's figure was a shrewd choice.

DR. BRAUN

After Isaac gave in, he felt a kind of deadly recklessness. He took a plane home to Albany. He had never been in the air before. But perhaps it was high time to fly. When he saw the ground tilt backward, the plane rising from the runway, he said to himself in clear internal words,

ISAAC

"*Shma Yisrael!*" Hear, O Israel, God alone is God. Above the marvelous bridges, over clouds, sailing in the atmosphere, you know better than ever that you are no angel.

DR. BRAUN

Isaac went from the plane to the bank to the hospital outside his sister's deathbed.

ISAAC

How is she, Mutt?

MUTT

Very bad.

ISAAC

Well, I'm here. With the money.

MUTT

The money? I didn't want to make you do this.

ISAAC

That's all right, Mutt, if I have to pay. I'm ready. And on her terms.

MUTT

She may not even know.

ISAAC

Take it. Say I'm here. I want to see my sister, Mutt.

DR. BRAUN

Isaac was sixty years old. He knew the route he, too, must go, and soon. But only knew, did not yet feel. As for the payment, it was like things women imagined they wanted in pregnancy... hungry for peaches or beer, or eating plaster from the walls. But as soon as he handed over the money, he felt no more concern for it. Isaac went into her hospital room. He only wanted to see Tina.

DR. BRAUN

The glorious, fleshly Tina of my boyhood was no more. (Dr. Braun enters the hospital room section of the stage.) Now Tina's face was yellow and lined. Her belly was huge with the growth. Her legs, her ankles were swollen. Tubes extended from all parts of her body.

ISAAC

Tina.

TINA

I wondered.

ISAAC

(He hands her the briefcase.) Here's the briefcase. The money's all there.

TINA

(Knocks the briefcase over and says in a choked voice) No, I don't want it. Take it back.

ISAAC

I brought the $20,000. Just like you said.

TINA

I only wanted to see you.

ISAAC

(Overcome with emotion) Tina, Tina, let me hold you. (He tries to embrace her and she lifts her free hand and tries to hold his hand.)

TINA

(Uttered in a feeble, slurred speech that is still audible)

Isaac, Isaac... Mamma loved you more than me. But you... you tried to stand up for me.

ISAAC

I did, Tina. I tried.

TINA

Remember that poor kitty I sat on? (She feebly laughs.)

ISAAC

(Isaac laughs.) Yes, I can still see the look on Mama's face: "Oy Vey. Too late."

TINA

I swear I didn't see it there... Maybe I'll see that kitty in the next life. (Tina coughs and coughs and is ravaged by pain.)

ISAAC

(CRYING) Tina, my little sister. Don't leave me.

DR. BRAUN

The ring Tina had taken from Aunt Rose was tied to her wasted finger with dental floss. She weakly extended her hand with the ring hanging from it.

TINA

Isaac, my big brother... please cut the thread. (Isaac cuts the ring with a scissors) Not the money. I don't want it. You take Mama's ring.

ISAAC

(Looks at his mother's ring in his hands)

(Now with controlled weeping) Mama's ring. Without you, Tina, what do I need Mama's ring for?

(Isaac puts his arm around Tina and she lays her head on his shoulder, locked in each other's embrace.)

DR. SAMUEL BRAUN

(Stands behind them with tears in his eyes) Oh, these Jews—these Jews! Their feelings, their hearts. Why can't we stop all this? For what comes of it? One after another you give over your dying. One by one they go. You go. Childhood, family, friendship, love, all are stifled in the grave. And these tears! When you weep them from the heart, you feel you justify something, understand something. But it is only an intimation of understanding. A promise that mankind may, through a possible divine gift, comprehend why it lives. Why life? Why death? Why these particular forms—these Isaacs and these Tinas?

(*The poignant strains of Bloch's* Nigun *underscores the above speech*)

(With his eyes closed, Dr. Braun sobs audibly and then tries to pull himself together as the controlled yet awed scientist.)

I see red, I see black, something like molecular processes. That's the only true heraldry of being. (Looks upward out of an imaginary window.) Look at those stars, those things cast outward by a great begetting spasm billions of years ago.

A Silver Dish

by Joanne Koch

Adapted with the author's permission from the short story.

Presented with "The Old System," adapted by Sarah Blacher Cohen, as "Saul Bellow's Stories on Stage" as a staged reading directed by Byrne Piven at the Chicago Writers' Bloc New Play Festival with support from the Dramatists Guild Fund, Inc. in 1996; at the New York State Writer's Institute, University at Albany, 1994; at the Barbara Streisand Festival in San Diego in 1995; as a staged reading at the Florida Atlantic University Library Series in 2000; at The Egg Center For the Performing Arts in Albany, New York, in a memorial performance directed by Rebecca Kaplan and sponsored by SUNY Hillel in 2005; as a staged reading at the Spertus Institute in Chicago and at the Milwaukee Public Library in 2005, both presentations directed by Sandy Shinner.

CAST OF CHARACTERS

WOODY SELBST....................................expansive, likeable man of sixty

YOUNG WOODY...................................teenager shuttling between sex and the seminary

MRS. SKOGLUND...............................wealthy, Swedish widow, once a cook

WOODY'S MOTHER...................................English woman with Victorian airs (doubles as NURSING MOTHER at the fair)

POP...loveable con man, zesty, crude, unpretentious

REVEREND DOCTOR KOVNER.............a Polish Pat Robertson (doubles as FARMER)

WOODY'S AUNT REBECCA.................suspicious, smart wife of Rev. Kovner (doubles as OLD PROSTITUTE, MAID HJORDIS)

TIME: 1980 & 1932

PLACE: Chicago

Note on accents: Woody's mother and Aunt Rebecca were born and raised in England. Woody's father was born and raised in Russia, spent his adolescence in Liverpool and has since hung out in pool halls and betting parlors in Chicago. Reverend Kovner has Polish accent, suggested by the "v" for "w." Mrs. Skoglund came from Sweden as a young girl and retains her accent. Suggestions of these rhythms, rather than any attempt to simulate thick accents works best.

WOODY SELBST, a man of about sixty, a warm teddy bear of a guy, paces in a hospital waiting room, pauses to look out a window, listening to the distant sound of church bells.

WOODY

(to audience) I can't go back to Pop's room just yet. For weeks now, every time I see him, I think, this could be the last time. What can I do?

SOUND OF CHURCH BELLS RINGING

What do you do about death? Be realistic. There's not much you can do.

We're not much better at dealing with it than, well, water buffaloes, like the ones I watched in Africa.

I'm a tile contractor with plenty of responsibility, believe me—a wife here, a mistress there, a mother, two sisters that don't exactly play with a full deck. . . and a father who may not last out the day. *(He casts a somber glance back to the window.)*

But once a year, I get away. I go far—Japan, Mexico, Africa. It was on a launch near the Murchison Falls in Uganda, I saw a buffalo calf seized by a crocodile from the bank of the White Nile. *(He gets into the telling of the story, moving downstage.)*

There were giraffes along the river, and hippopotamuses, and baboons and flamingos and other brilliant birds crossing the bright air in the heat of the morning, when the calf, stepping into the river to drink, was grabbed by the hoof and dragged down. The parent buffaloes couldn't figure it out. Under the water the calf still thrashed, fought, churned the mud. It looked to me as if the parents were asking each other dumbly what had happened. They were just animals, but I believe they felt grief.

SOUND OF CHURCH BELLS RINGING

WOODY

(listening for a moment) Sunday. . . Bells. I have plenty of connections with bells and churches.

Technically, I was born a Jew, but when I was still a kid our whole family—except for Pop—was converted by my uncle, the Reverend Doctor Kovner. Kovner had gone to the Hebrew Union College in Cincinnati, but then, I guess he got another calling and became a minister.

He established a mission in Chicago, with the help of Mrs. Skoglund.

ORGAN MUSIC

REVEREND KOVNER lit with MRS. SKOGLUND

KOVNER

Dear Lady, you will be blessed for this contribution. The Kovner Mission, thanks to your generosity, will be a beacon of light to the misled. With your help, I will begin the conversion of the Jews, the prelude to the Second Coming. Will you pray with me for their conversion?

MRS. SKOGLUND kneels with REV. KOVNER.

KOVNER

The Skoglund name will of course be featured prominently on a plaque on the front of the mission. *(in a reverential voice)* And we pray, in the name of the Lord. . .

KOVNER & MRS. SKOGLUND

"In the name of our Lord. . ."

WOODY

This was in the thirties, religion was about the only business worth having then. The Jews came—why not. They got coffee, canned pineapple, day old bread, dairy products, bacon. The Jews had to listen to the sermons to get the food. This was the Depression and you couldn't be too particular—but they sold the bacon.

Reverend Kovner got the dairy products from Mrs. Skoglund. She had come to this country a cook for an Evanston family that owned a dairy, married one of the sons and inherited a large dairy business.

KOVNER

I believe, Mrs. Skoglund, your arrival is part of a divine plan. You came to this country a humble cook, but you were destined to marry Gunnar Skoglund, destined to be his bride, and his widow, destined to inherit the Skoglund Dairies. And why? Why Mrs. Skoglund? So you, you personally would speed the Second Coming.

How, Mrs. Skoglund? First, by establishing the Kovner Mission, but even more importantly, Mrs. Skoglund, by putting my nephew, young Voodrow, through seminary school.

We must claim Voodrow for Christ before the forces of evil claim him, before he succumbs to the dark temptation to follow his father's path of gambling, womanizing, atheism. Voodrow must be saved.

For Voodrow must lead the next generation of conversions. The Gospels say it plainly: repeat with me Mrs. Skoglund:

KOVNER & MRS. SKOGLUND

"Salvation is from the Jews."

LIGHTS DOWN ON KOVNER & MRS. SKOGLUND

I was 14, ya see. I needed Mrs. Skoglund's special protection—I needed to be protected from the greatest force of evil on the planet, or at least in Chicago—Pop!

POP comes out followed by YOUNG WOODY and MOTHER

POP

What kinda seminary? What does he need that for? What he needs is to learn to wash under his arms and dry between his toes. What he needs is to keep his crotch clean. And it wouldn't hurt if he learned to pick the right horse in the fifth at Arlington.

MOTHER

(to YOUNG WOODY) Your father acts just like he did when he slept next to the coal bin in Liverpool. Then, at least, he was no threat to us.

POP

Woody is old enough to be out working. I was only 12 when I got left behind in Liverpool.

YOUNG WOODY

Why'd they leave you, Pop?

POP

They saw I had an eye infection that wasn't getting any better. They didn't want to get to America and then get sent back to Russia from Ellis Island. They had to leave me there.

MOTHER

If your family had an ounce of civilization, they wouldn't have abandoned a boy in a big city without a farthing. But of course, they didn't have an ounce of breeding. *(to YOUNG WOODY)*

If my family hadn't taken him in, he would have starved.

POP

I would never have starved. And mind you, I earned my keep. Your family was so bloody civilized they kept me working like their personal slave and sleeping by the coal bin.

MOTHER

My family doesn't deserve to be mentioned in the same breath with yours. *(to YOUNG WOODY)* He was too common to sleep in our quarters.

POP

Not too common to pat your ass and have you love it.

MOTHER

He took advantage of my naiveté. I was only 16.

POP

It wasn't your naiveté I took advantage of. And no one forced you to follow me.

MOTHER

By that time I felt obligated.

POP

I was the one with the obligations. I scabbed during a seamen's strike, shoveled my way across the Atlantic, jumped ship in Brooklyn.

MOTHER

(to YOUNG WOODY) He made me think he was a citizen.

POP

I became an American. It's just that America never knew it.

MOTHER

He votes without papers, drives without a license. It's a wonder he hasn't been arrested.

LIGHTS DOWN on them.

WOODY

Pop did not pay taxes either. He cut every corner. Horses, cards, billiards and women were his lifelong interests, in that order. Finally, one Spring day, he decided to make his move, with a little help from me.

YOUNG WOODY now practices his golf swing.

YOUNG WOODY

(casually, to AUDIENCE) I borrowed these from the Sunset Ridge Golf Club, way out in Winnetka. I worked there last summer as a caddy. Don't worry. I'm going to return them, eventually. Dandelions are great to practice with.

YOUNG WOODY takes another swing.

WOODY

Pop came into the yard in his good suit, and when he took off his fedora the skin of his head was marked with a deep ring and the sweat was sprinkled over his scalp—more drops than hairs.

POP

(addressing YOUNG WOODY, who lines up another dandelion) I'm going to move out. It's no use. I can't live a life like this.

WOODY

I should have known. Pop in the billiard parlor, Pop under the El tracks in a crap game, or playing poker at Brown and Koppel's upstairs. Pop had to be free. I should have seen it coming. But I didn't. I just kept swinging.

YOUNG WOODY, oblivious, whacks another dandelion.

POP

You're going to be the man of the house. It's okay. I put you all on welfare. I just got back from Wabansia Avenue, the relief station.

YOUNG WOODY

I was wondering about the suit.

POP

They're sending out a caseworker. You got to lend me money to buy gasoline—the caddie money you saved.

YOUNG WOODY

Pop! That's all I earned the whole summer. Do you know how big that golf course is at Sunset Ridge? How heavy those clubs are? And the Winnetka guys, they're rich, but they don't always give big tips. I'm telling you Pop.

POP

Does your mother want me?

YOUNG WOODY

Well, not the way you are now, but if you would change. . .

POP

And your aunt Rebecca? And her husband the Reverend Doctor. They don't want me the way I am. And that's how it is. I come as I am.

YOUNG WOODY

But if you would only—

POP

Halina likes me the way I am. This is one thing I've learned. A woman's gotta like the way you are. If a woman only likes what you could be after she does the fixing—Run! Run as fast as you can. So, I'm running. How about that loan?

WOODY

He stood there with his bent nose and his ruddy face. He was Dick Tracy, then, and I did what he said.

YOUNG WOODY digs in his pocket and hands POP a roll of bills.

But what I did was, I bankrolled by own desertion. Ha.

POP pockets the money.

POP

You did the right thing, kid. Better to lay odds on me than on someone droppin' outa the sky to save the Jews, believe me.

POP walks away.

He left to move in with Halina. Mom and my sisters never saw him again.

YOUNG WOODY looks after POP. KOVNER comes in, puts an unctuous hand around his shoulders.

KOVNER

Your father is a dangerous person. Of course, you love him. You should love him and forgive him, Voodrow, but you are old enough to understand he is leading a life of vice.

MRS. SKOGLUND enters, prompting KOVNER to straighten his tie, quickly comb his hair.

Ah, Mrs. Skoglund, what a pleasure to see you. Go Voodrow. Go and count the cans of pineapple. We want to be sure the janitor's not stealing.

YOUNG WOODY

But it's my day to be the janitor, sir.

KOVNER

Go count, Voodrow. *(turning to MRS. SKOGLUND)* "And a little child shall lead them." Yes, Voodrow will soon be ready to lead them back to Christ. Pray with me. Mrs. Skoglund, together, on our knees, with your whole heart.

MRS. SKOGLUND

In the name of Jesus-uh-Christ-uh, help this child. . .

KOVNER

Give yourself over to it, Mrs. Skoglund. Eyes closed, hands clasped over your bosom, together. . .

KOVNER & MRS. SKOGLUND

"In the name of Jesus-uh. . .

YOUNG WOODY sneaks around in back of them, hiding several cans in his pants. He hands POP a can of pineapple, puts the other can in his pants.

YOUNG WOODY

(whispering) This time it's pineapple, Pop.

POP

But Halina likes peaches.

YOUNG WOODY

Maybe next time.

POP

(on his way out, glancing at KOVNER) Kovner works up all those broads. He doesn't even know it himself. I swear he doesn't know how he gets them. *(POP leaves.)*

WOODY

Pop especially hated Reverend Kovner.

WOODY'S MOTHER joins MRS. SKOGLUND and KOVNER, kneeling in prayer.

Pop was always for real life and free instincts, against religion and hypocrisy.

YOUNG WOODY joins his MOTHER, kneeling in prayer.

MOTHER

I hope you put that brute in your prayers. Look what he has done to us. The girls are instructed never to admit him. Remember, only pray for him. Don't see him.

LIGHTS DOWN on the praying group. YOUNG WOODY grabs canned goods from a shelf, warily puts it in a bag, shaves bacon and, gobble a piece for himself.

YOUNG WOODY

But I see him all the time. I lead a double life, sacred and profane. I accept Jesus Christ as my personal redeemer. But I also pick the lock of the storeroom. I take canned pineapple and cut bacon from the flitch with my pocketknife. I can't help it. I'm hungry all the time.

YOUNG WOODY puts bacon in the bag, checks to see if anyone is watching, then slips the bag to POP.

YOUNG WOODY

I have to show them, Mom and Aunt Rebecca, that I haven't deserted Pop.

But I have to do what Mom and Aunt Rebecca say. I have to testify. I get fifty cents a shot.

YOUNG WOODY kneels.

"I accept Him, yes, I was just a Jew, but now I accept him. I lift up my eyes and I see the higher life."

(to audience) But it's always that mixture, sacred on Sunday. . .

MUSIC of a carousel, mixed with MUSIC for Sally Rand's fan dance.

YOUNG WOODY puts on his rickshaw boy's hat.

Profane the other days.

I got this job as a rickshaw boy at the Century of Progress World's Fair. I'm supposed to look like a coolie. *(YOUNG WOODY runs in place with a rickshaw or facsimile.)*

I have different passengers, sometimes people who, well, who work at the fair. . .

OLD PROSTITUTE

(climbs into the rickshaw) Woody. That's cute.

YOUNG WOODY

It's short for Woodrow.

OLD PROSTITUTE

I was thinking more of Woodpecker, or peckerwood. Peckers are my business, honey. You get any customer needs theirs taken care of, you send 'em right to me. There'll be a nice tip in it for you. I'm set up behind Sally Rand. She gets 'em all worked up with her fans and we deliver the goods.

OLD PROSTITUTE gets out of rickshaw. YOUNG WOODY runs in place for a moment.

SALLY RAND'S FAN DANCE MUSIC heard. FARMER gets in rickshaw.

FARMER

(drinking from a bottle, speaking in Southern Illinois accent) Boy, I ain't never seen anything loike that. Course, I'm not sure exactly what I did see with her movin' those big feather fans. But I thought I saw one helluva lot more than you'd get to see in Cairo *[kay-ro].*

(drinks) You wanna swig, son?

YOUNG WOODY

No thanks. Can't drink on the job.

FARMER

Ya know what poontang is, don't ya, son?

(YOUNG WOODY nods.)

Well, maybe you know where a person could get some poontang 'round here.

(YOUNG WOODY stops rickshaw, points the way.)

YOUNG WOODY

Right behind the Sally Rand pavilion, where you saw the fan dance. Tell her Woody send you.

FARMER

Much obliged, *(winking as he slips him a tip)* Woody.

YOUNG WOODY

(to AUDIENCE) Well okay, I'm a freshman at the seminary now, but I see nothing wrong with it, when girls ask me to steer a little business their way. I make dates and I get tips from both sides. Why not?

YOUNG WOODY resumes running with his rickshaw.

Course, sometimes I get great passengers. *(stops to let NURSING MOTHER step in, runs in place again)* She smells of milk. Mmm. I like milk.

NURSING MOTHER

You sure give a nice, smooth ride. Must make you tired, though, luggin' all these people around. I only have to carry Billy and he's just 9 months old. Weighs thirty-five pounds already. Yes he does. I should wean him, but when he gets to suckin' he has the sweetest, most contented look on his little face. Oooo. Look at that. My blouse is wet. Just talkin' about him makes the milk come in. Mmmm. Do they ever let you take a break?

YOUNG WOODY

I'm due for one, right now.

NURSING MOTHER

You could just set this cart down and come beside me.

YOUNG WOODY sets down rickshaw, climbs in beside her.

I ain't had no one but little Billy tendin' to me for a long time.

THEY kiss. NURSING MOTHER guides YOUNG WOODY's hand to her breast.

When you press 'em, milk comes spoutin' out, just like a fountain, like your own special fountain... *YOUNG WOODY kneels beside her as she unbuttons her blouse. He embraces her, buries his face in her bosom for a moment.*

NURSING MOTHER leaves.

YOUNG WOODY

Next morning I did my testifying in New Testament Greek: "The light shineth in darkness—*to fos en te skotia fainei*—and the darkness comprehended it not." *(looking up from his prayer)*

What do I really believe? I believe, well, something. God's idea was that this world should be a love world, that it should eventually recover and be entirely a world of love...

But I also know Aunt Rebecca is right when she leans close to my ear and says, "You're a little crook, like your father."

SOUND OF BELLS CROSSFADE from YOUNG WOODY to WOODY

WOODY gets up, goes to the window, takes a deep breath as BELLS stop.

WOODY

Such a day, a velvet autumn day, the grass finest and thickest, silky green before the first frost, and the chill sticking it to you in every breath... Pop, will you ever feel this blissful sting again?

It started out this kind of day when we took that trolley ride.

SOUND OF TROLLEY CAR. YOUNG WOODY followed by POP gets on "the trolley."

YOUNG WOODY

C'mon Pop. *(They sit as if on the trolley.)*

WOODY

The old Western Avenue line—cars the color of a stockyard steer—clumsy, big-bellied, with tough rattan seats and brass grips for the standing passengers. Used to make four stops to the mile. They ran with a wallowing motion.

YOUNG WOODY

Look at it come down.

WOODY

When the doors opened the snow blew in from the rear platform and clumped in the cleats of the floor. There wasn't warmth enough inside to melt it.

YOUNG WOODY

Ya know, Pop, I read the Western Avenue line is the longest trolley car line in the whole world. Twenty-three miles long. Starts on the south side in the prairies, ends in Evanston. I've never been in Evanston, never seen Mrs. Skoglund's house. We should have at least called. We don't even know if she'll be home.

POP

Where else would she be on a day like this? She'll be there.

WOODY

We rode and I watched out the window—factories, storage buildings, machine shops, used car lots, trolley barns, gas stations, funeral parlors, six flats, utility buildings and junkyards, on and on, wallowing toward Evanston.

YOUNG WOODY

Do we have to go? Mom and aunt Rebecca will be furious.

POP

Son, I'm in trouble. Halina took money from her husband for me and she's got to put it back before old Bujak misses it. He could kill her.

YOUNG WOODY

What did she do it for?

POP

Son, you know how the bookies collect? They send a goon. They'd break my head open.

YOUNG WOODY

Pop! . . . Why does it have to be Mrs. Skoglund? She pays for my seminary tuition. She buys dresses for Paula and Johanna. The Skoglund Dairies practically support the Kovner Mission. Why her?

POP

Why not? You're my kid, aren't you? The old broad wants to adopt you, doesn't she? Shouldn't I get something out of it for my trouble? What am I—outside? And what about Halina? She puts her life on the line, but my own kid says no?

YOUNG WOODY

Oh, Bujak wouldn't hurt her.

POP

Woody, he'd beat her to death.

YOUNG WOODY

(turned away, as if thinking these thoughts, sharing them only with the AUDIENCE) Maybe, maybe Halina's husband Bujak would draw the line at stealing. But maybe Pop is inventing the bookie, the goon, the theft—the whole thing. He's capable of that and you'd be a fool not to suspect him.

(speaking to POP) Mrs. Skoglund might not let us in. Mom and Aunt Rebecca have told her.

POP

What could they tell her? I'm your father, ain't I?

YOUNG WOODY

They've told her how, well, wicked you are. They painted you for her, like one of those monster movie posters: purple for vice, black for your soul, red for Hell flames.

POP

(Unfazed) It's okay.

YOUNG WOODY

They've told her you're a gambler, smoker, drinker, deserter, screwer of women, atheist—

POP

Don't worry. Christers like sinners.

YOUNG WOODY

What will you tell Mrs. Skoglund?

POP

The old broad? Don't worry, there's plenty to tell her, and it's all true. Ain't I trying to save my little laundry-and-cleaning shop? Isn't the bailiff coming for the fixtures next week?

YOUNG WOODY

(staring out the window, hoping the weather will offer an excuse) Wow, it looks like five feet out there. They've got those green platform cars out, Pop, with the big brushes. They're sweeping the tracks.

POP

Got to save the business is all. She'll understand that.

YOUNG WOODY

Hey, Riverview! *(as if wiping the vapor from the glass)* Nothing's moving. It's boarded up.

WOODY

The trolley was almost empty. People weren't leaving the house. This was a day to sit legs stuck out beside the stove, wrapped in blankets like a mummy. Only a fellow with an angle, like Pop, would go and buck such weather. But fifty dollars—fifty soldiers! Real money in 1933.

POP

That woman is crazy for you.

YOUNG WOODY

Mrs. Skoglund? She's just a good woman, sweet to all of us.

POP

Who knows what she's got in mind. You're a husky kid. Not such a kid any more, either.

YOUNG WOODY

She's a religious woman. She really has religion.

POP

Well your mother isn't your only parent. She and Rebecca and Kovner—they aren't going to fill you up with their ideas. I know your mother wants to wipe me out of your life. Unless I take a hand, you won't even understand what life is. Because they don't know—those silly Christers.

The girls I can't help. They're too young. I'm sorry about them, but I can't do anything. With you, it's different.

WOODY

He wanted me like himself, an American.

POP and YOUNG WOODY lurch forward and back, as if the car has come to a sudden stop.

WOODY

We were stalled in the storm, while the cattle colored car waited to have the trolley reset in the crazy wind, which boomed, tingled, blasted.

YOUNG WOODY

(to POP) At Howard Street we'll have to walk straight into it, due north, Pop. We might not even be able to walk in these drifts. They're high as mountains.

POP

You'll do the talking at first.

WOODY

Pop was like the man in the song: he wanted what he wanted when he wanted it.

YOUNG WOODY

I'll do my best by you, but you have to promise Pop, not to get me in Dutch with Mrs. Skoglund.

POP

You worried because I speak bad English? Embarrassed I have a mockie accent?

YOUNG WOODY

It's not that. Kovner has a heavy accent, and she doesn't mind.

POP

Who the hell are those freaks to look down on me. You're practically a man and your dad has a right to expect help from you. He's in a fix. And you bring him to her house because she's bighearted, and you haven't got anybody else to go to.

YOUNG WOODY

I got you, Pop.

WOODY

It was after four when we reached the end of the line, and somewhere between gray and black, with snow spouting and whirling under the street lamps.

YOUNG WOODY

This is as far as she goes.

YOUNG WOODY leads POP out of the trolley car into the blizzard.

All those cars. They must be stuck. We'll never make it on the sidewalks. Come on. Nothin's moving except us. We can use the middle of the street. *(walking forward with difficulty)*

WOODY

For blocks and blocks we bucked the wind. Finally, we broke through the drifts to the snowbound mansion.

(YOUNG WOODY and POP stop, gasp at the mansion.

YOUNG WOODY

Look at the size of it. Here, help me with this gate. *(as they push open the gate)* Must be fifteen, twenty rooms in there.

POP

Who's she got with her?

YOUNG WOODY

No one. Her husband died. He's the one who owned the dairies. So it's just her and Hjordis. *[yor-diss].*

POP

Hjordis? What's that?

YOUNG WOODY

Her maid, kind of a watchdog woman. She's come to the mission, never smiles.

(uses the large brass knocker)

HJORDIS

(peaking out at them suspiciously from inside the house) Who is it and what do you want?

WOODY

We stood there brushing the slush from our sheepskin collars. Pop wiped his big eyebrows with the ends of his scarf, sweating and freezing. Hjordis uncovered the air holes of the glass storm door by turning a wooden bar. She was monk-faced, no female touch on her, just plain as God made her.

YOUNG WOODY

It's Woodrow Selbst. Hjordis? It's Woody.

HJORDIS

You're not expected.

YOUNG WOODY

No, but we're here.

HJORDIS

What do you want?

YOUNG WOODY

We came to see Mrs. Skoglund.

HJORDIS

What for do you want to see her?

YOUNG WOODY

Just tell her we're here.

HJORDIS

I have to tell her what you came for, without calling up first.

YOUNG WOODY

Why don't you say it's Woody with his father, and we wouldn't come in a snowstorm like this if it wasn't important.

WOODY

Back then it was High Episcopal Christian Science Women's Temperance Evanston. No tradespeople rang at the front door. Only invited guests. And here, after a ten-mile grind through the blizzard, came two tramps from the West Side. Right to their mansion, right to the Swedish immigrant lady, herself once a cook but now a philanthropic widow, right where she dreamed, snowbound, while frozen lilac twigs clapped at her storm windows, of a new Jerusalem and a Second Coming and a Resurrection and a Last Judgment.

(getting closer to the huddled outsiders)

Sure they let us in.

POP and YOUNG WOODY come in, cheeks frozen, exhausted, itching, trickling melting snow. HJORDIS, keys jangling from her belt, goes to get Mrs. Skoglund.

POP

(looking around) Not bad. Stained glass window. Like they say, a church away from church.

YOUNG WOODY

Smells kinda vinegary, sort of . . . Gentile. I don't think a Jew has ever been inside this place.

WOODY

Maybe when I was with Pop, I made more Jewish observations. Although Pop's most Jewish characteristic was that Yiddish was the only language he could read a paper in. Pop was with Polish Haline, and mother was with Jesus Christ, and I ate uncooked bacon from the flitch. Still, now and then, I had a Jewish impression.

HJORDIS comes in first with a mop, hastily wiping up the drippings. MRS. SKOGLUND follows.

HJORDIS

We can have them wait outside. I didn't come over in steerage and work forty years to have two shifty-eyed West Siders come in, messing up the floors, wanting who knows what. . .

MRS. SKOGLUND

That's enough Hjordis. I wouldn't think of making them stand in the cold. (warmly) Hello Woodrow, what a dreadful day to be out.

YOUNG WOODY

Mrs. Skoglund, I brought my dad to you.

POP

Nice place ya got here.

POP removes his coat, as HJORDIS eyes him with distrust.

HJORDIS

You're dripping. I'll take that. *(She takes his jacket, holds it at arm's length, mops after him.)*

WOODY

Pop's darting looks made him seem crooked. Hardest thing for Pop, with his bent nose and face was to look honest.

MRS. SKOGLUND

We'll go into the parlor where it's warmer.

YOUNG WOODY, POP, MRS. SKOGLUND walk to another area, YOUNG WOODY looking up and around at the magnificent room, POP eyeing the objects in the cabinet.

WOODY

Mrs. Skoglund led us into the front room, the biggest room in the house, fifteen foot ceilings and high windows, three quarters paneled in wood. In the corner was a kind of Chinese étagère—a cabinet, lined with mirrors and containing, trophies won by Skoglund cows, cut glass pitchers, goblets, silver platters and a silver dish.

YOUNG WOODY

I don't think you ever met my dad, Mrs. Skoglund.

POP

Yes, Missus, that's me, Morris Selbst *(sticking his chest out)*.

WOODY

Nobody intimidated Pop. He never presented himself as a beggar. There wasn't a cringe in him anywhere.

POP

I asked my son to bring me because I know you do the kid a lot of good. It's natural you should know both of his parents.

MRS. SKOGLUND

I have heard about you, quite a lot.

YOUNG WOODY

Mrs. Skoglund, my dad is in a tight corner and I don't know anybody else to ask for help.

POP

(moving YOUNG WOODY aside) Now Mrs. Skoglund, I can see you're a decent woman. And I'm sure you remember, way back, before you married into all this. You were cooking for this family, so you remember hard work, right? (moving a little closer)

Me, that's all I ever had. And I don't mind that. I like it. But what I mind is when the bailiff tells me all my hard work ain't gonna keep the courts from evicting me from my little laundry and cleaning business which I built from nothing. (a step closer)

What I mind is when two guys with wrists like thighs come and beat my brains in, crippling me for life, or maybe killing me altogether, so Woodrow here is left without a Pop. That's what I mind.

MRS. SKOGLUND

But. . . but I. . . I understand you don't support your children.

HJORDIS

That's right.

POP

I haven't got it. If I had it, wouldn't I give it? There's bread lines and soup lines all over town. Is it just me? What I have I divvy with. I give the kids. A bad father? You think my son would bring me if I was a bad father into your house.

(patting YOUNG WOODY's head) He loves his dad. He trusts his dad. He knows his dad is a good dad. Every time I start a little business going I get wiped out. This one is a good little business, if I could hold on to that little business. Three people work for me. I meet a payroll, and three people will be on the street, too, if I close down. Missus, I can sign a note and pay you in two months.

(giving it all he's got) I'm a common man, but I'm a hard worker and a fellow you can trust.

YOUNG WOODY coughs. HJORDIS jangles her keys and glowers.

WOODY

I was startled when Pop used the word trust. It was as if from all four corners a Sousa band blew a blast to warn the entire world: "Crook! This is a crook!" But Mrs. Skoglund heard nothing. Mrs. Skoglund, with all her money, was unworldly—two thirds out of this world.

POP

Give me a chance to show what's in me and you'll see what I do for my kid.

MRS. SKOGLUND

(hesitates, then picks up one of several bibles) I have to go upstairs. I have to go to my room and pray on this and ask for guidance. Would you sit down and wait. Come Hjordis. We'll pray on this together. *(They exit.)*

POP

(jumping up) What's this with the praying? She has to ask God to lend me fifty bucks?

YOUNG WOODY

It's not you, Pop, it's the way these religious people do.

POP

No. She'll come back and say that God wouldn't let her.

YOUNG WOODY

No, she's sincere, Pop. Try to understand, she's emotional, nervous, and sincere. She tries to do right by everybody.

POP

That servant will talk her out of it. She's a toughie. It's all over her face that we're a couple of chiselers.

YOUNG WOODY

What's the use of us arguing. *(He pulls up a chair, warms himself by the stove, while POP cases the cabinet.)*

WOODY

My shoes were wet through and would never dry. I watched the blue flames through the isinglass window, fluttering like a school of fishes in the coal fire. But Pop went over to the Chinese-style cabinet and tried the handle.

POP pries open the cabinet.

Then he opened the blade of his penknife and in a second forced the lock of the curved glass door. He took out a silver dish.

YOUNG WOODY

(as POP examines the silver dish) Pop, what is this?

WOODY

Pop, cool and level, he knew exactly what this was. He relocked the cabinet, crossed the carpet, listened. He stuffed the dish under his belt and pushed it down into his trousers. He put the side of his short, thick finger to his mouth. *(as YOUNG WOODY paces)* I was all shook up.

YOUNG WOODY confronts POP.

I looked into Pop's face. I felt my eyes grow smaller and smaller, as if something were contracting all the skin on my head. Everything felt tight and light and closer and dizzy. I was hardly breathing.

YOUNG WOODY

Put it back, Pop. Understand me? Put it back!

POP

It's solid silver. It's worth dough.

YOUNG WOODY

Pop, you said you wouldn't get me in Dutch.

POP

It's only insurance in case she comes back from praying and tells me no. If she says yes, I'll put it back.

YOUNG WOODY

How?

POP

I'll get it back. If I don't put it back, you will.

YOUNG WOODY

I couldn't. I don't know how. You picked the lock.

POP

There's nothing to it.

YOUNG WOODY

We're going to put it back now. Give it here.

POP

Woody, it's under my fly, inside my underpants. Don't make such a noise about nothing.

YOUNG WOODY

Pop, I can't believe this.

POP

For cry ninety-nine, shut your mouth. If I didn't trust you, I wouldn't have let you watch me do it. You don't understand a thing. What's with you?

YOUNG WOODY

Before they come down, Pop, will you dig that dish out of your long johns.

WOODY

Pop turned stiff on me. He became absolutely military.

POP

Look, I order you!

YOUNG WOODY tries to wrestle the dish out of POP

WOODY

Before I knew it, I had jumped my father. I began to wrestle with him. It was outrageous to clutch your own father, to put a heel behind him, to force him to the wall. Pop was taken by surprise.

POP

You want Halina killed? Kill her! Go on, you be responsible.

WOODY

Pop was resisting like mad. We turned about, him on top, then me on top, then him on top, when I remembered a trick I had seen in a Western movie. I tripped him and we fell to the ground. I already outweighed him by twenty pounds.

POP and YOUNG WOODY continue to struggle.

I was on top, pressing Pop's hard belly. But I realized it was impossible to thrust my hand under Pop's belt to get that silver dish. And then Pop turned furious. He freed his one hand and hit me in the face. He hit me three or four times. Then I dug my head into his shoulder and held tight only to keep from being struck and I said in his ear.

YOUNG WOODY

Jesus, Pop, for Christ sake remember where you are. Those women will be back!

WOODY

But Pop wouldn't give in. He brought up his short knee and fought and butted me with his chin and rattled my teeth. I thought he was about to bite me. I thought—I was a seminarian then, don't forget. . .

YOUNG WOODY

(whispering and holding POP tight) Like an unclean spirit.

WOODY

Gradually Pop stopped thrashing and struggling. His eyes stuck out and his mouth was open, sullen. Like a stout fish. I released him and gave him a hand up.

YOUNG WOODY helps POP up, just as MRS. SKOGLUND re-enters with HJORDIS.

MRS. SKOGLUND

Did I imagine, or did something shake the house?

HJORDIS scowls.

YOUNG WOODY

I was lifting the scuttle to put coal on the fire and it fell out of my hand. I'm sorry I was so clumsy.

HJORDIS harrumphs. *POP is still catching his breath.*

WOODY

Pop was too huffy to speak. With his eyes big and sore and the thin hair down over his forehead, you could see by the tightness of his belly how angrily he was fetching his breath, though his mouth was shut.

MRS. SKOGLUND

I prayed.

YOUNG WOODY

I hope it came out well.

MRS. SKOGLUND

Well, I don't know yet. I wish I had Reverend Kovner here to advise me. The gospels say, "It is easier for a camel to go through the eye of a needle than for a rich man to enter into the kingdom of God." So it's best not to be rich, and it also says, "God helps those who help themselves." Best for me not to give you a check. Yet the gospels also say, "His eye is on the sparrow." So perhaps my eye should be on you. Yet I'm not sure you're a sparrow, Mr. Selbst.

HJORDIS

More like a vulture if you ask me.

YOUNG WOODY looks down with guilt.

MRS. SKOGLUND

Hjordis, you bring the gentlemen some coffee. Go on now. *(HJORDIS relunctantly obeys.)*

Coming in such a storm. *(still undecided)* I'll just pray a bit longer. *(She goes off again.)*

POP

A check? Hell with a check. Get me the greenbacks.

YOUNG WOODY

(in a loud angry whisper) They don't keep money in the house. You can cash it in her bank tomorrow. But if they miss that dish, Pop, they might—

POP reaches below his belt. At that moment HJORDIS enters with a tray, concentrating on carefully setting it down.

HJORDIS

I suppose you'll want cream and sugar with your... *(noticing POP)* ... Is this a place to adjust clothing, Mister? A men's washroom?

POP

Well... which way is the toilet, then?

WOODY

Hjordis led Pop down the corridor, standing guard at the bathroom door so that he shouldn't wander about the house.

MRS. SKOGLUND

(looking in on YOUNG WOODY) Woodrow, come, you must pray with me for your... for Mr. Selbst.

YOUNG WOODY follows MRS. SKOGLUND to another area where she is lit, kneeling.

WOODY

I followed Mrs. Skoglund to her office, unable to resist a backward glance at the etagere and the spot where the fluted silver dish had been. *(YOUNG WOODY kneels beside MRS. SKOGLUND.)* Then once more I was on my knees, afraid that even my testifying face couldn't mask the heist. But Mrs. Skoglund's eyes were pressed together fervently in prayer. In her Scandinavian accent—and emotional contralto—she was raising her voice.

MRS. SKOGLUND

In the name of Jesus-uh-Christ-uh... *(MRS. SKOGLUND continues praying, mouthing the words.)* Send light uh, give guidance-uh, put a new heart-uh in the bosom of this poor sinner.

YOUNG WOODY

Yes, Lord, put a new heart-uh in the bosom of that poor sinner. *(looking up and whispering)* And please, please make Pop put the dish back. (praying in full voice again) He needs guidance, Lord. He needs light. He—

MRS. SKOGLUND

Are you finished, Woodrow? My knees aren't what they used to be.

YOUNG WOODY

Yes, sure. Amen. Here, let me help you. *(He helps her up.)*

MRS. SKOGLUND

(with great deliberation, handing him a check) You give this to your father.

YOUNG WOODY

Thank you. Thank you so much, Mrs. Skoglund.

MRS. SKOGLUND

You needn't thank me, Woodrow. You just keep thanking the Lord.

YOUNG WOODY

Yes, Ma'am. Mrs. Skoglund, your Christian generosity has been so beautiful, but there's just one more small thing.

MRS. SKOGLUND

Speak, Woodrow.

YOUNG WOODY

I know that Hjordis has a cousin who works at the Evanston YMCA. Could she please phone him and try to get us a room tonight so that we don't have to fight the blizzard all the way back? We're almost as close to the Y as to the car line. Maybe the cars have even stopped running.

MRS. SKOGLUND

Hjordis, come here a moment, please.

HJORDIS leads POP back into the room, going back to wipe the doorknob he's touched with alcohol.

WOODY

Suspicious Hjordis, coming when Mrs. Skoglund called to her, was burning now.

HJORDIS

(under her breath) First they barge in, make themselves at home, ask for money, have to have coffee, probably left gonorrhea on the toilet seat.

WOODY

Hjordis, against her better judgment, telephoned the Y and got us a room with two cots for six bits.

HJORDIS phones. MRS. SKOGLUND says good-by. YOUNG WOODY hands POP the check. POP says thank you. YOUNG WOODY says thank you. They leave.

Figuring Pop had been able to re-open the étagère, as soon as the two of us were outside, in midstreet again up to our knees in snow, I said.

YOUNG WOODY

(As if trekking through the snow) Well, I covered for you. Is that thing back?

POP

(trekking on) Of course it is. *(They exit.)*

WOODY

All that week, I flew along, level and smooth. Then on Friday, they were all waiting in Kovner's office at the settlement house—the Reverend Doctor Kovner, my Aunt Rebecca, Mother . . .

> *YOUNG WOODY enters to find the group lined up, though he doesn't see MRS. SKOGLUND turned away, kneeling in the corner in prayer.*

REV. KOVNER

Voodrow, vould you like to tell us something?

YOUNG WOODY

No. I mean. . . what's there to tell? Everything's fine.

REV. KOVNER

Vouldn't you like to tell us something about your visit to Mrs. Skoglund.

AUNT REBECCA

He's a little crook, just like his father.

REV. KOVNER

But he can be saved.

YOUNG WOODY

I'm innocent. We never touched Mrs. Skoglund's property.

MRS. SKOGLUND rises with a groan, revealing herself.

Mrs. Skoglund. I'm, I'm sure the missing object—whatever it is –has been misplaced, and, and you'll be very sorry when it turns up.

REV. KOVNER

(shaking his head sadly) Voodrow, Voodrow. Until you are able to tell the truth, you will be suspended from the seminary.

AUNT REBECCA

(taking YOUNG WOODY aside) You are a little crook, like your father. The door is closed to you here.

MOTHER

Why Woodrow, why?

MOTHER, REBECCA, KOVNER walk out.

MRS. SKOGLUND

(shaking her head) "Suffer you innocent children unto God."

YOUNG WOODY, looking miserable, skulks away.

WOODY

I was overcome with many bad feelings, the kind Pop never suffered. Never, never.

POP appears now with a pool cue, jauntily setting up a shot.

Pop never had these groveling emotions. Pop had no such feelings. He was like a horseman from Central Asia, a bandit from China. It was Mother, from Liverpool, who had the refinement, the English manners. It was the preaching Reverend Doctor in his black suit. You have refinements, and all they do is oppress you? The hell with that.

YOUNG WOODY walks over to POP.

YOUNG WOODY

She said I was a little crook like my father.

POP

(continuing to focus on the balls) So what, kid?

YOUNG WOODY

You shouldn't have done it.

POP

(*Making his way around the pool table*) No? Well, I don't give a care, if you want to know. You can have the dish if you want to go back and square yourself with all those hypocrites.

YOUNG WOODY

I didn't like looking Mrs. Skoglund in the eye. She was so kind to us.

POP

Kind?

YOUNG WOODY

Kind.

POP

Kind has a price tag.

YOUNG WOODY

But Pop. I've been expelled from the seminary, banished from the settlement house!

POP pulls out a ticket from his sweater, gives it to YOUNG WOODY.

POP

You want in again? Here's the ticket. I hocked the thing. It wasn't so valuable as I thought.

YOUNG WOODY

What did they give?

POP

Twelve-fifty was all I could get. But if you want it, you'll have to raise the dough yourself, because I haven't got it anymore.

YOUNG WOODY

Why did you do it, Pop? For the money? What did you do with the fifty bucks?

POP

I settled with the book, and the rest I put in the business.

YOUNG WOODY

You tried a few more horses.

POP

I maybe did. But it was a double, Woody. I didn't hurt myself and at the same time did you a favor.

YOUNG WOODY

It was for me?

POP

It was too strange of a life. That life wasn't *you*, Woody. All those women. . . Kovner was no man. He was an in-between. Suppose they made you a minister? Some Christian minister. First of all, you wouldn't have been able to stand it, and second, they would throw you out sooner or later. *(positioning his pool cue)* Now watch me sink both balls.

YOUNG WOODY goes off as WOODY takes his place next to POP as he gets ready to hit another imagined billiard ball.

WOODY

There was no winning such arguments with Pop. But we debated it in various moods and from various elevations and perspectives for forty years and more.

WOODY

(now taking his turn at the pool table) Maybe I wasn't meant for the seminary.

POP

And you wouldn't have converted the Jews, which was the main thing they wanted.

WOODY

And what a time to bother the Jews. At least I didn't bug them. *(taking a shot)*

POP

(standing back and surveying the pool table) You might say that's an impossible shot, a three-cushion combination. Willie Hope saw me make it in '42. What do ya say—five to one if I make it again?

WOODY

Sure Pop. . . . sure. . . you're on. . . *(POP sinks the shot, exits triumphantly.*

LIGHTS down on POP.

Pop had carried me back to his side of the line, blood of his blood, the same thick body walls, the same coarse grain. Not cut out for a spiritual life. Simply not up to it. Pop was no worse than me, and I was no better than Pop.

Pop spent most of life removing stains from people's clothing. He and Halina in the last years ran a Clean-o-mat in West Rogers Park—a so-so business like a Laundromat which gave Pop time for billiards, the horses, rummy, pinochle. If they needed help with the rent, sure, I gave it.

Mother and my sisters, well, they became dependent. I kept up their bungalow— the roofing, pointing, wiring, insulation, air conditioning—I paid for heat, light, food, dressed them all out of Sears, Roebuck and Wieboldt's, brought them a TV which they gradually began to watch more devoutly than they prayed.

After the new Disneyworld opened in Florida, I sent them all down—in separate batches of course.

I travel, too, once a year at least. Istanbul, Jerusalem, Delphi, Egypt. On the Nile, below Murchison Falls, I saw that buffalo calf disappear, snatched by the crocodile.

Mother has become lightheaded. She speaks of me, when I'm with her, as if I were a boy—

MOTHER

What do you think of my Sonny?

WOODY

—As if I were 10 years old. She's become silly with me.

MOTHER

We'll have high tea, and my sonny will have two biscuits.

WOODY

She always enjoyed acting the queen. She has those plump wrists and that faded Queen Victoria face.

MOTHER

My boy has excellent manners—nothing like his father. Eat your biscuits, dear.

WOODY

So said The Empress of India.

MOTHER

He's precious, isn't he? *(pinching his cheek)* My sonny is at the top of his class in the seminary.

WOODY

She just doesn't seem to know the facts.

For a moment, MOTHER is joined by KOVNER and AUNT REBECCA, who line up behind her.

And behind her all the others, like kids at the playground, waiting their turn to go down the slide: one on each step, and moving toward the top. *(Lights go down on them.)*

SOUND OF ONE CHURCH BELL.

WOODY checks his watch.

Time to check on Pop.

POP is now revealed lying in a hospital bed.

In the hospital room, Pop, with the sides of his bed raised, like a crib. . . Pop, so very feeble, and writing, and toothless, like a baby, and the dirt already cast into his face, into the wrinkles.

POP tries to pull an I-V out of his hand.

POP

(in a faint, wheezing voice) Damned if I'm gonna be their pincushion.

WOODY

No, Pop, you need that. That's what's feeding you. Leave it, Pop. . .

WOODY takes off his shoes, climbs into bed with POP. POP makes a weak death noise, an intermittent wheeze.

Now, Pop, Pop.

WOODY strokes him. POP struggles but weakly. YOUNG WOODY comes into the area and goes to the other side of POP.

Then it's like the wrestle in Mrs. Skoglund's parlor when Pop turned angry like an unclean spirit and I tried to warn him.

YOUNG WOODY

Mrs. Skoglund will be back, Pop!

WOODY

And he hit me in the teeth with his head and then became sullen, like a stout fish. *(POP flutters.)*

But this struggle in the hospital is weak—so weak! I hold him, fluttering and shivering.

POP

From those people, you'll never find out what life is, because they don't know what it is.

WOODY

Yes, Pop—what is it? What is it, Pop? *(YOUNG WOODY now touches POP tenderly.)*

Pop, who had dug in for 83 years and had done all he could to stay, now wanted nothing but to free himself. How can I allow him to pull the intravenous needles out? Pop—he wanted what he wanted when he wanted it. But what he wants at the very last I failed to follow. It was such a switch. After a time, Pop stops resisting. He subsides and subsides. He rests against me, his small body curled there.

WOODY and YOUNG WOODY hold POP.

I thought I had stilled Pop, but he had only found a better way to get around me. Heat was the way he did it. His heat was leaving him. Like with a small animal, while you hold it in your hand. I felt him cooling. Then, just as I was doing my best to keep him and thought I was succeeding, Pop divided himself. And when he was separated from his warmth, he slipped into death.

And here I am, still holding and pressing him, when there is nothing anymore to press.

WOODY gradually releases his father, climbs out of the bed, leaving YOUNG WOODY to hold POP. Lights go down on that area.

You could never pin down that self-willed man. When he was ready to make his move, he made it—always on his own terms. And always, always, something up his sleeve. That was how he was.

Letter to Sarah

Cynthia Ozick

From: Cynthia Ozick
To: Dr. Sarah Blacher Cohen

March 30, 2000

Dear Sarah,

Let us begin with a riddle: how many persons can you count among the following? A professor of English literature. An editor and publisher. A literary critic. A specialist in Jewish-American writing. A playwright and producer. A humorist. A historian of the Yiddish musical theater. If you counted nine, you would be altogether mistaken. The answer is one, and her name is Sarah Blacher Cohen. Sarah Cohen is all these things: a teacher, an essayist, an editor, an expert in the field of Jewish-American letters, a writer on comedy, a writer of comedy, a dramatist and a producer, an aficionado of the popular stars of the Yiddish stage. And, most recently, the theatrical biographer of a humanitarian heroine, Henrietta Szold.

One astonishing woman, nine demanding vocations! There was a time when ordinary Sarah Cohen was equivalent to merely three or four souls: a professor of English and the author of several critical volumes, and for most human beings, this would have been enough for a lifetime. But Sarah is an intrepid visionary, and she heard the siren's call: for years she longed to write for the stage—this was, for her, the road not taken—and when finally she dared to attempt it, play after play came flying from her pen, saturated in wit, pathos, passion, and laughter: and then, with her collaborators, the delights of song, sometimes sentimental, sometimes bawdy, but always spilling over with electric joy and dramatic force.

What can we next expect? Another play, certainly; an opera perhaps. And all the while Sarah inspires students, delivers papers at scholarly conferences, organizes anthologies, rescues a Russian violinist, arranges benefits for the disabled, travels west, north, south, casts the company, resolves backstage conflicts, and inconceivably more. She is writer and impresario; serious academic and entertainer: dreamer and achiever.

Most of us, contemplating roads not taken, muse and moon and mull and wish and wonder and yearn. But Sarah *invents* the road, brings it into concrete being, and marches gloriously along it to the destination that began as a small discerning seed in her imagination. She finds in herself the power to Make Things Happen—and when you are in her presence you can feel the wind of her will, and you can almost hear the sirens calling, Sarah! Sarah! You can, you will! And she will astound you yet again.

Cynthia Ozick, author of *Trust, The Cannibal Galaxy; The Messiah of Stockholm; The Puttermesser Papers;* and *Heir to the Glimmering World*

For Sarah

Miriyam Glazer

Sarah, we're needing a good laugh these days,
we're needing eyes that refuse to flinch
at the absurdities. We're needing
clarity eccentric enough to name
what really is instead of what everyone else
is saying is. Sarah, we're needing you.

It's a wild world out here, Sarah.
Contradictions go unnamed, injustice reigns.
Haredim in Holy Jerusalem deluge the cops
with dirty diapers to protest a parking lot;
the Feds here arrested a Brooklyn rabbi
for laundering dirty money. His friend,
another rabbi, admitted he bought
kidneys low to sell high.

I hear you say, "Some living."

In the U.S. Congress, no one questions if
human health should be a for-profit business.
In the great state of California
they solved their budget crisis today by cutting
funds for public education,
aid and services to the poor, the elderly,
the handicapped,
because they won't raise taxes on yachts.
Unemployment is soaring but bailed out
Goldman Sachs is making more money than ever.

Sarah, since you left, the worst became even fuller
of passionate intensity and the best?
The best twitter.

Sarah! surely a new musical comedy should be at hand
surely if you were here you would be immersed
in writing the libretto. I can see it now—
as organs play "My Yiddishe Mama," the stage fills up
with black-coated, white-bearded rabbis drawing
clothes pins from golden sacks as they
hang each other out to dry while
Sophie bedecks herself, Wall Street lucre, Molly prances,
and Fanny belts out one of your songs.
Julie—just married, you should know—applauds.

Together they overwhelm us all
with wry, pointed, outrageous jokes, making
us all laugh, laugh, laugh away
the exorbitant pain around us,
in us,
just as, for most of the years of your life, you knew
so remarkably how to do.

Miriyam Glazer, American Jewish University

Breathing

For Sarah

Myra Sklarew

If lightning strikes this house
or even a nearby oak,
you'd hear the ticking
of the respirator suddenly
stop; you'd hear the dance
of the machine stutter,
her breathing null
and void, the dime-sized hole
in her neck for naught, her words
pouring out through the opening.
You'd see the way they'd float up
into the universe, igniting
the air. What can we say
to her, the one who saved us
whom we do not save?
The one tethered here
who transformed disaster
into a comic art?

Myra Sklarew, American University

Sarah Rising

Myra Sklarew

While the miracle of Sarah's
resurrection is underway,
leaf blowers have already begun
driving their noxious fumes
under my doorsills, around
the frames of windows.
Sarah is strong and well
as she has never been in life.
In a hospital room, platefuls
of nourishing food wait
for her: heaps of scrambled
eggs, delicate croissants, tea.
And she moves, her crabbed hands
and feet entirely erased.
In their place, fingers dance
and toes unfurl. She rises, walks
while the leaf blowers pull me
away from my last
moments with the risen Sarah
into their world of doing
and getting done. A sluice
of sound comes down
between my dreaming
of her strong sacred new life
and this cold December morning.

Myra Sklarew, American University

Sarah and the Samovar

Myra Sklarew

When I left the house that day Sarah was sitting in a box
on the porch. I nearly passed by her without noticing, but I tripped and turned to
catch my balance and there she was, like the genie in the brass lamp, like poppy
seeds in hamantashen, like knaydls in chicken soup. Only this time it was a Russian
samovar, enormous and shimmering in the heat of summer.

Sarah called out: You've got three wishes! No problem, I said. The first: that you
would climb out of that samovar so we could have a real conversation. The second:
that you would finish your memoir, *The Junkdealer's Daughter*! The third: that the
Meshiach would give up this waiting game and make an appearance.

Don't be a *mazik*. Gather me up, Sarah said imperiously.
Carry me into your house. I am sweltering, shvitzing in this boiling tub! I lifted the
samovar out of its huge container, struggled under its immense weight, and gave
Sarah and her samovar the place of honor in my living room.

As for my three wishes, Sarah never did climb out of the samovar. Even so, we talk.
Sarah is making good progress on *The Junkdealer's Daughter*. But you, dear reader,
will have to invent the ending. That is the eleventh commandment, according to
Sarah. And about the Messiah, we think we saw her speeding away on horseback.

Myra Sklarew, American University

Hesped for Sarah Blacher Cohen, z"l

Friday, November 14, 2008

Julie Pelc Adler

My Aunt Sarah was feisty, rebellious, outrageous, brilliant, and creative. She excelled in intellectual and literary circles decades before women were ever encouraged or accepted as academics; her stubbornness and her desire to live on despite seemingly insurmountable illnesses, disabilities, and losses compelled her to press forward when most anyone else would have called it quits. This is the Sarah I respected: the one who taught me to persevere, to challenge norms, to redefine what it means to be a "survivor."

But this is not the Sarah Blacher Cohen I wish to share with you today. In quiet moments, another (entirely different) Sarah emerged. This is the Sarah I loved. This Sarah was desperately afraid of dying, afraid her life had been meaningless and wasteful, afraid she hadn't made an impact on anyone or anything. She looked at herself and saw imperfection. In these last months of her life, those who knew and loved her kept half-waiting for her to spring back, just as she had done so many times before. We joked about co-writing a play with her about the comic-tragedy of her illness. We waited to see how she would pull together the unseen strength she kept hidden in the recesses of her heart for just these moments of seeming hopelessness.

But, in many ways, dying was the bravest thing Sarah has ever done. It was the one thing she fought against harder and longer than anything else in her life. We read in the final book of the Torah, "*U'bakharta b'chayyim*—Choose life!" Upon hearing that she had died, I told a friend, "my Aunt Sarah didn't just choose life, she took a lasso and wrung it around Life and dragged Life toward her." Dying seemed antithetical to everything Sarah had been, everything she seemed to desire.

In her death, Sarah remains my greatest teacher about life. Sarah Blacher Cohen, the playwright, the scholar, the professor, the historian, the trailblazer did not die this week. What died this week is the fear, pain, and suffering she lived with silently for decades. The imperfect, mortal body died this week. My Aunt Sarah lives on.

Underneath her iron will, Sarah was soft, playful, loving, devoted, and giving. She loved listening to classical music, eating See's lollipops, speaking in Yiddish, singing old folk tunes, and spending time with Gary. Gary was the cherished love of her life. She loved her brothers and sisters, her nieces and nephews, her students, her colleagues, and her friends. She loved her work. She loved her life.

There is a Jewish tradition that says we help elevate the soul of the deceased when we do acts of goodness in their memory. I ask that we remember the whole Sarah—the Sarah she often did not allow us to see—the Sarah who was at once strong and fearful; determined and pessimistic; playful and professional.

Sarah was my great aunt, my grandmother's youngest sister. Maybe because my grandma helped to raise Sarah as a little girl—or maybe because Sarah and I shared more in common than anyone else in our family—our relationship was profound and sacred in a way that is impossible to quantify. A few years ago, she wrote me a letter, telling me that I was like the daughter she never had. And, in many ways, I am her progeny. She gave me a love of learning and a love of living.

I recently came upon a poem that I believe Sarah would have loved. It is called, "The Converse of Making Light":

You ask: "What goes faster than light?"
I know, sure as day follows night.
It's the inverse of spark,
that old demon Dark,
It always gets there first, alright?

May her memory be for a blessing. *Ken Yehi Ratzon.* May it be so.

Julie Pelc Adler, Rabbi and Director of Jewish Student Life at Santa Monica College Hillel

Contributors

Editors

Ann Shapiro is Distinguished Teaching Professor at Farmingdale State College, SUNY. Her books include *Unlikely Heroines: Nineteenth-Century American Women Writers and the Woman Question* and *Jewish American Women Writers: a Bio-Bibliographical and Critical Sourcebook*, winner of the Association of Jewish Libraries Bibliography Award.

Carole Kessner is Professor Emerita of Comparative Studies at SUNY Stony Brook. Her books include *The "Other" New York Jewish Intellectuals* and *Marie Syrkin: Values Beyond the Self*, winner of the 2008 National Jewish Book Award for Biography, Autobiography, and Memoir.

Contributors

Victoria Aarons is Professor of English and chair of the department at Trinity University. Her books include *Measure of Memory* and *What Happened to Abraham?*, both of which received the CHOICE award for outstanding academic book. She is currently writing about second-generation Holocaust writers.

Julie Pelc Adler is Rabbi and Director of Jewish Student Life at Santa Monica College Hillel. She also serves as the Director of the Berit Mila Program of Reform Judaism and the Executive Director of the National Organization of American Mohalim. She is co-editor of *Joining the Sisterhood: Young Jewish Women Write Their Lives*.

Joyce Antler is the Samuel Lane Professor of American Jewish History at Brandeis University. She is the author or editor of nine books, including *The Journey Home: How Jewish Women Shaped Modern America*; *Talking Back: Images of Jewish Women in Popular Culture*; *You Never Call! You Never Write!: A History of the Jewish Mother*.

Evelyn Avery is Professor of English and Director of Jewish Studies at Towson University, Maryland. Her books include *Rebels and Victims: The Fiction of Richard Wright and Bernard Malamud; Modern Jewish Women Writers in America;* and *The Magic Worlds of Bernard Malamud.* She is on the editorial boards of *Studies in American Jewish Literature* and *Modern Jewish Studies,* and she is coordinator of the Bernard Malamud Society.

Alan Berger is the Raddock Family Eminent Scholar Chair of Holocaust Studies and Director of the Center for the Study of Values and Violence after Auschwitz at Florida Atlantic University. He co-authored *Jewish-Christian Dialogue: Drawing Honey from the Rock* and co-edited *Encyclopedia of Jewish American Literature.*

Janet Burstein is Professor Emerita at Drew University. Her books include *Writing Mothers, Writing Daughters: Tracing the Maternal in Stories by American Jewish Women* and *Telling the Little Secrets: American Jewish Writing Since the 1980s.* She is currently teaching and writing about Israeli cinema.

Lewis Fried is Professor of English at Kent State University. His books include the *Handbook of American-Jewish Literature* and *Gliebreie la Grande Emigrazione,* an anthology of American Jewish literature for Italian readers. He is also the editor of the United States literature section of the *Encyclopedia Judaica.*

Miriyam Glazer is a rabbi and chair of the Literature, Communication and Media Department of American Jewish University. Her most recent book is *Psalms of the Jewish Liturgy: A guide to their Beauty, Power and Meaning.* She is also the author of *Dreaming the Actual: Contemporary Fiction and Poetry by Israeli Women Writers* and co-author of *The Essential Book of Jewish Festival Cooking.*

Sara Horowitz is Professor of Comparative Literature at York University, Toronto. Her books include *Voicing the Void: Muteness and Memory in Holocaust Fiction* and *Encounter with Aharon Appelfeld.*

Joanne B. Koch is Professor of English and director of the graduate writing program at National-Louis University in Chicago. She is the author of ten nonfiction books, numerous films and teleplays, including an Emmy-winning television series, and the creator of sixteen plays produced around the country, six of them collaborations with the late Sarah Blacher Cohen. She is co-editor with Sarah Cohen of the anthology *Shared Stages: Ten American Dramas of Blacks and Jews* and Artistic Director of the Chicago Writers' Bloc.

Sanford Marovitz is Professor Emeritus at Kent State University, where he achieved the Distinguished Teaching Award and President's Medal. He also received both

Woodrow Wilson and Fulbright fellowships. His books include *Abraham Cahan* and *Melville "Among the Nations."*

Cynthia Ozick is the author of several novels, including *Trust, The Cannibal Galaxy, The Messiah of Stockholm, The Puttermesser Papers,* and *Heir to the Glimmering World.* In addition, she has written many acclaimed volumes of short stories and essays. She is the winner of the PEN/Malamud Award for Short fiction, the Rea Award for the Short Story, and three first prizes in the O. Henry competition. She was also on the shortlist for the Man Booker International Prize and was nominated for the National Book Award and the Pen/Faulkner Award.

Norma Rosen is the author of five novels as well as many short stories and essays. Her novels include *Joy to Levine; At the Center; John and Anzia: An American Romance;* and *Touching Evil.* In addition to many short stories and essays in a variety of journals and magazines, she published a short story collection *Green: Eight Stories and a Novel;* an essay collection *Accidents of Influence: Writing as a Woman and a Jew in America;* and a volume of new midrash, *Biblical Women Unbound.*

Elaine Safer is Professor of English at the University of Delaware, Newark. Her books include *Mocking the Age: The Later Novels of Philip Roth; The Contemporary American Comic Epic: The Novels of Barth, Pynchon, Gaddis and Kesey;* and *John Milton: L'Allegro and Il Penseroso.* She is currently working on a book about the comic imagination in contemporary Jewish American fiction.

Ellen Schiff is Professor Emerita of French and Comparative Literature at Massachusetts College of Liberal Arts. Her books include *From Stereotype to Metaphor: The Jew in Contemporary Drama; Awake and Singing: Seven Classic Plays from the American Jewish Repertoire;* and *Fruitful and Multiplying: Nine Contemporary Plays from the American Jewish Repertoire.*

Myra Sklarew is Professor Emerita in the Department of Literature at American University. She is the author of three chapbooks and six collections of poetry including *Lithuania: New & Selected Poems*; a collection of short fiction, *Like a Field Riddled by Ants*; and essays, *Over the Rooftops of Time.* Forthcoming works include *Harmless* (poetry) and *Holocaust and the Construction of Memory.* A former president of Yaddo Artist Community, she has won the National Book Council Award in Poetry and PEN Syndicated Fiction Award.

Steve Stern is a writer-in-residence at Skidmore College. He is the author of several novels and short story collections, including *Lazar Malkin Enters Heaven,* winner of the Edward Lewis Wallant Award for Jewish American fiction, and *The Wedding Jester,* which won the National Jewish Book Award. Recent books include the novel

The Angel of Forgetfulness and the novella *The North of God.* His work has earned him Fulbright and Guggenheim fellowships.

Daniel Walden is Professor Emeritus of English at Penn State. He is the longtime editor of *Studies in American Jewish Literature.* His books include *American Jewish Writers from Cahan to Bellow* and *American Reform: The Ambiguous Legacy.*